# INTERIOR ALASKA

# INTERIOR ALASKA

## A Journey Through Time

Robert M. Thorson
Jean S. Aigner
R. Dale and Mary Lee Guthrie
William S. Schneider
Richard K. Nelson

The Alaska Geographic Society

Library of Congress Cataloging-in-Publication Data

Interior Alaska.

    Includes index.
    1. Natural history — Alaska.  2. Alaska — Description and travel.  3. Alaska — History.  I. Thorson, Robert M., 1951-  .  II. Nelson, Richard K.  III. Rennick, Penny.  IV. Doogan, Kathy.
QH105.A4158    1986        508.798       86-22363
ISBN 0-88240-318-4

Book design by TSI/Robert Chrestensen
Cover illustration by Catherine Giste


The Alaska Geographic Society
P.O. Box 93370, Anchorage, Alaska 99509

Printed in U.S.A.

# Dedication

This book is dedicated to Dr. William R. Wood, a man whose energy and imagination bring us more in touch with the spirit of Alaska. The idea of a book about interior Alaska was his own, a dream that he guided into reality, and we hope that it conveys something of his affinity for the land and the people who call this place home.

Dr. Wood has dedicated 25 years of his life to interior Alaska and his generous contributions have made it a better place to live. As president of the University of Alaska from 1960 to 1973, his wisdom shaped the direction of higher education throughout the state. As mayor of Fairbanks from 1978 to 1980, his leadership set the course for Alaska's second largest city. In late 1984, Dr. Wood received the first annual William A. Egan Outstanding Alaskan of the Year Award from the state Chamber of Commerce. And as executive director of Festival Fairbanks '84 for the past several years, his vision of commemorating Alaska's past has created lasting gifts for the present and future.

Dr. William R. Wood's example encourages all of us to take pride in our community and our state. His enthusiasm for life in the Far North inspires all of us to find ways to foster an appreciation of the Great Land.

# Contents

# Acknowledgements

Festival Fairbanks '84 acknowledges the timely and generous support of the following dedicated business and industrial firms of Alaska, who made possible the commissioning of the original manuscript of this book:

Alascom, Inc.
Alaska Airlines
Alaska International Contractors
Alaska National Bank of the North
Exxon Corporation
Fairbanks *Daily News-Miner*
NERCO Minerals Corporation
North Pole Refining

Planning for the historical and educational work was accomplished through a revenue sharing grant from the Fairbanks North Star Borough.

The ready understanding and early acceptance of the basic concept for the undertaking was most heartening. Each of the several individuals involved in the initial discussions added to the enthusiasm for accomplishing a genuinely significant lasting contribution to understanding the history of interior Alaska and its people. There could be no tribute more fitting to their recognition of Alaska's silver anniversary of statehood.

On behalf of Alaskans everywhere, the board, staff and volunteers of Festival Fairbanks '84 are proud and appreciative.

—William R. Wood

\* \* \* \* \*

The authors are deeply grateful to Dr. William R. Wood, who conceived of the idea for this book, worked tirelessly to assure it would be undertaken and carefully shepherded it toward completion.

We also wish to thank the staff and board of Festival Fairbanks '84, as well as the financial contributors to this project, for honoring Alaska's silver anniversary with a gift of knowledge. Special thanks to Mrs. Kathleen Berry of Festival Fairbanks '84 for her devotion and perseverance on behalf of this project.

We are sincerely grateful to those colleagues and friends who have read draft versions of chapters and helped so much to improve the quality of this work. We also thank the many people who have given so generously of their teachings and traditions, which we have incorporated into this writing. Among those who have been especially helpful to us are: Joan Antonson, Katherine Arndt, Sue Beck, Doug Best, Lydia Black, David Case, Peter Coates, Moses Cruikshank, Maureen Freeley, William Hanable, Terry Haynes, Dianne Gudgel-Holmes, Debbie Miller, Louis Renner, Louis Schnaper, Anne Will, Jane Williams, and the people of Beaver, Chalkyitsik, Hughes, and Huslia.

In addition, we acknowledge our debt to the many scholars, colleagues, and elders who have brought us whatever understanding we may have reached of interior Alaska's environment and people. While we have drawn heavily from the words and writings of others, we have formally cited only a few of our sources to avoid interrupting the flow of the text. Finally, our thanks to Pat Walsh for her fine graphics and to David Libby for searching out the photographs.

We sincerely hope that our writings will prove worthy of the efforts others have made on our behalf and that future generations will be somehow enriched by what is recorded here.

# Introduction

*By Richard K. Nelson*

Alaska is a broad peninsula of land pinched out from the northwestern tip of our continent, ending within a few miles of Asia. Physically separated from the country to which it belongs and set apart by a way of life all its own, Alaska is like a nation unto itself. It is a huge place: one-fifth the size of the United States mainland, stretched across some 25 degrees of latitude, encompassing a great range of physical and environmental settings. In fact, Alaska is so vast and diversified that we can scarcely comprehend it as a whole; and so the people who live here identify themselves with its different regions, areas of similar climate, geography, culture, history and patterns of living.

This book is about the environment and people of Alaska's great inland region, called the Interior. Probably no other area has so influenced the popular conception of Alaska — here are the lofty snow-covered mountain ranges, sprawling expanses of boreal forest, fabled northern rivers, overpowering cold, remote traplines, lone prospectors and log cabin villages. It is the epitome of North Country, the world of Jack London and Robert Service; and the reality of it comes remarkably close to our image of how it should be.

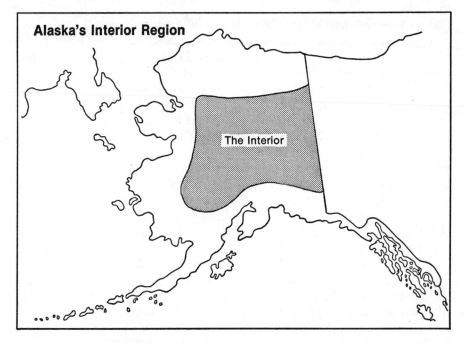

**Alaska's Interior Region**

The Interior

*Much of Alaska's heartland lies in the Interior, some 170,000 square miles of rolling terrain and braided rivers lying between the Brooks and Alaska ranges.*

The Interior is bounded by two great mountain walls, the Brooks Range to the north and the Alaska Range to the south. The Canadian border straight-lines the Interior's eastern limit, and its western margin is marked by a gradual transition to the Bering Sea coast. Interior Alaska includes an area of some 170,000 square miles, equal to the combined size of New York, Pennsylvania, Ohio and Indiana. But size is only one of its many extraordinary qualities.

First, there is the land itself. Aside from being huge it is truly spectacular. Dominating all of the southern Interior is the Alaska Range, with 20,320-foot Mount McKinley and the surrounding high peaks making up its core. Even in summer the range gleams white with perpetual snow and massive tongues of glaciers that curve down from the heights. Elsewhere, the Interior's mountains are less imposing, but they loom against the near horizon and march away in tiers that finally vanish in the clear distance. Maps show hundreds of nameless peaks, identified only by numbered elevations; even their Athabaskan names are lost or known only to nearby villagers.

Lying between the ranges are sharply carved valleys and wide flats, signatures left by rivers, glaciers, faults and unbroken sheets of continental rocks. Some flats are 50 to 100 miles across, even more, flecked with myriad lakes and ponds. Indeed, the Interior contains a goodly portion of Alaska's three million lakes more than 20 acres in size. Winding through the valleys and across the flats is a great system of coalescing rivers: the Kantishna, Toklat, Salcha, Nowitna, Hogatza, Kanuti, Alatna, Chandalar, Sheenjek, Fortymile, Kandik, Kateel, Nabesna and many more. Eventually these smaller rivers flow into the Copper, Kuskokwim, Kobuk, Koyukuk, Porcupine, Tanana, Nenana . . . and of course the Yukon.

It is a powerful, almost overwhelming piece of the earth's surface, made even more so by the force of a subarctic continental climate. Situated between 62 and 66 degrees North, the land mass of interior Alaska has extremes of weather equaled by few other places. Beneath the clear summer skies, temperatures routinely climb into the 80s and occasionally reach 100 degrees. On the other hand, midwinter cold spells often range to minus 50 degrees or lower, and the record stands near minus 80. At Allakaket, on the Koyukuk River near the Arctic Circle, the mean temperature is below freezing for seven months of the year.

Despite the abundance of lakes and streams, interior Alaska's climate is actually quite dry. Precipitation ranges from 6 to 12 inches per year, but evaporation is low and drainage is poor on the perpetually frozen ground. Winter thaws are rare, so the occasional snowfalls accumulate to waist-deep powder and moose vie with trappers for use of packed trails. Although winter skies are usually clear they are also oppressively dark. At the latitude of Fairbanks, the sun creeps above the horizon for about four hours each day around Christmas time, casting long shadows on the snow at noon. In midsummer, on the other hand, the sun is up for nearly 21 hours and there is no real darkness. Around the solstices, the period of sunlight grows or shortens by six or seven minutes per day. Interestingly, the total amount of light each year at interior Alaska's latitude is near the highest in the world, because the sun's low angle makes for long twilights.

A rich community of northern plants and animals has adapted to the demands

*Interior Alaska's terrain varies from the wetlands and streams of the Yukon Flats (above) to the spectacular ruggedness of the Alaska Range near 12,339-foot Mount Deborah (below). (Both courtesy of Richard Nelson)*

of this environment. More than 100 million acres of the Interior are covered in boreal forest, a mixture of tall spruce timber, thickets of smaller deciduous trees, and semi-open muskegs. In the uplands, tundra vegetation forms a low-growing carpet of plants designed for the more extreme cold and shorter growing seasons of higher elevations. Whatever else may be said of it, the boreal forest is the essence of beauty born from wildness and tranquility. Other environments are more lavish and diverse, to be sure, but the north woods have a special and undefinable quality that has taken the hearts of many who have lived or traveled here.

Animal inhabitants of the interior forest are widely known. The most common species include moose, caribou, Dall sheep, black bear, brown bear, wolf, wolverine, lynx, beaver, porcupine, snowshoe hare and an assortment of other small mammals. In summer the wetlands are alive with waterfowl and the forests well populated with other migratory birds, along with steadfast year-round residents. Rivers and lakes contain salmon, whitefish, pike, grayling and other northern fish species. But the richness we perceive here is more apparent than real; places farther south had far greater abundance of wildlife before most species were reduced or eliminated by wholesale changes in their environments. During these modern times, however, places like interior Alaska remain to show us how bountiful North America's endowment of wildlife was before the coming of European man.

Of course, people first arrived here thousands of years ago, but they were of a different sort. Filtering across from northern Asia, nomadic hunter-gatherers established themselves here and lived by harvesting resources of the tundra and forest. Their descendants still live throughout the Interior, pursuing a modern version of that ancestral lifeway, inhabiting villages of log houses scattered widely along the rivers. The persistence of Athabaskan people who still follow customary patterns of subsisting on wild game and fish is a remarkable phenomenon in the latter 20th century. They are among the last hunter-gatherers on earth, carrying on ancient traditions that have vanished almost everywhere else.

## About the Book

In this book we explore the natural environment of interior Alaska and the evolution of its human lifeways. Our perspective is that of contemporary science and history, and our goal is to bring knowledge of this place to anyone with a serious interest in learning about it. The authors are professionals taking a general look at their special fields. Each chapter is a summary of the scientific and historic information that has been gathered so far, discussed in non-technical ways and put into an everyday perspective.

Although we hope our professional colleagues will find much of value in this book, we are writing with another audience in mind. It is intended for people who visit Alaska and want to add depth to their experience, people who live here and want to understand more about their surroundings, and people who may never come to Alaska but want to explore it from afar. We have tried to fill this book with information of special interest to those who thrive on learning about the natural and human worlds. And perhaps most of all, we have written this book for all who are somehow captivated by the special fascination of Alaska and the North.

All of the book's authors have spent major parts of their professional careers in Alaska and have called the Interior home. When this book was written each of us was affiliated with the Fairbanks campus of the University of Alaska, perhaps the world center for studies of northern environments. We hope these personal connections with our subject give us a greater sense of responsibility toward it and toward our readers, because interior Alaska is much more than simply an academic interest for us. We are describing elemental parts of our own lives, the landscapes that have nurtured and intrigued us, the history that has breathed in our own communities, and the people whose customs we have observed or shared.

The book begins with a look at the land itself: the piecing together of Alaska's terrain, the processes of building and erosion that have shaped it to present form, and the ways that geological phenomena have influenced human life here. It describes the forces that have affected this northern terrain, giving a sense of the power of ice and water at work on the raw material of rocks for incomprehensibly long periods of time. This chapter shows us that even the most "permanent" parts of our world — the rocks and mountains underfoot — are always changing, not just throughout millions of years but even during our own lifetimes.

The second chapter traces the evolution of plant and animal communities on this landscape, especially during the last million or so years. During this time the climate has gone through dramatic changes and the living world of the modern boreal forest has come into existence. Paleontologists have shown that creatures as exotic as mammoths, camels, sloths and lions stalked the grasslands of interior Alaska only a few thousand years before our time. Still today, they discover new fragments of bone, even fleshy carcasses, washing from the frozen muck. This chapter shows how the evidence from long-vanished times can be pieced together and how it helps us to understand the origins of our modern surroundings. Then it delves into the intricate design of relationships among creatures in the boreal forest today and reveals some marvelous secrets of life near the northern limits of its existence.

Chapter three unravels a great human mystery: the origins of Alaska's native people. The stage is set as dry land emerges between Alaska and Asia, and migratory bands cross into the New World, establishing a tradition that has lasted 15,000 to 25,000 years. Examining fractured bits of stone tools and remnants of camps buried deep in layered soil, archaeologists reconstruct those past ways of life and try to reveal the connections between modern people and their earliest ancestors. Perhaps the most fascinating question here is whether Athabaskan people can be traced back to a very early migration from Asia, binding them to the Alaskan Interior for as long as 14,000 years. Readers can sift through the evidence and come to their own conclusions.

Chapter four takes us on to recent history, the major episodes and minor daily occurrences that have created the Interior we know today. It moves through the "back sloughs" of old time Alaska, looking especially at the meeting grounds between Athabaskan people and newcomers from Europe and America. The turning of human events comes alive in the written words of explorers and travelers, and in the recollections of old folks speaking today. The frontier is much closer in Alaska than it is elsewhere in the United States, so we can still talk with pioneers who forged their way into unmapped country, and we can listen to Athabaskan elders who watched sternwheelers steam upriver past their camps. This chapter describes the course and process of change in Alaska's history, and it places the modern Interior in perspective for the future.

Chapter five focuses on the present, describing life in modern Athabaskan villages during this time of great and accelerated change. In these isolated communities a rich native tradition is perpetuated, blending with newer ways and creating a pattern of life unique to the North Country. By visiting people's homes, watching their daily activities, and listening to the lessons they have to teach, we can reach at least part-way across the distance between our different cultures and appreciate what village life means to modern native people of the Interior. Most of all, we can develop some understanding of the challenges that face villagers, who search for a promising course into the future but hope to retain precious elements of their heritage.

Each chapter in this book is meant not only to stand on its own, but also to fit into a sequence that begins with the building of interior Alaska's landscape and ends with a description of modern life on the terrain that has resulted. Readers will find some unavoidable repetitions of material, especially in neighboring chapters, but this is necessary so that each can be read separately. As much as possible, we have tried to follow the same style and approach to our material without sacrificing our own perspectives or personalities. We hope the differences in our writing will create refreshing variety and not detract from the story we have tried to tell.

Finally, we hope that readers will find some of the same rewards that we have in exploring the richness and beauty of interior Alaska. And we write in the faith that understanding our natural and human surroundings adds immeasurably to the quality and meaning of our lives.

# The Ceaseless Contest

## Landscapes in the Making

### By Robert M. Thorson

*Editor's note: Geologist Robert M. Thorson worked and studied in the Interior prior to leaving Alaska to join the faculty of the University of Connecticut's Department of Geology and Geophysics.*

## Introduction

As you sit on a craggy summit viewing the vastness of interior Alaska, you are seeing a landscape that is vibrant with change. A rockfall echoes in a nearby canyon. The dried silt from last season's flood swirls in gusts of wind. The rushing streams — a dilute soup of water and dissolved mountains — tumble rocks along their beds. The hillsides move imperceptibly downslope as they shed their outer skins. On a grander scale, the entire landscape is floating like a large ship adrift on the earth's plastic interior, moving slowly across the globe. You ride as a passenger on the top deck.

Landscapes seem permanent in the scale of human time, but from a geological perspective each vista is fleeting, and each bears the mark of catastrophic and gradual changes. Learning to interpret and understand the forces and processes responsible for sculpting scenery increases your appreciation of what is already beautiful, and instills within you an awe of nature that is undescribable in human terms. Articulating this intuitive feeling in thoughts and images lies at the heart of geology — the science of the earth.

A landscape is like a theater. New productions begin and end as the episodes of geologic time, and each production is divided into scenes which open and close during shorter periods of time. We are there for but a single performance. Volcanoes, streams, wind and glaciers are characters played by fire, water, air and ice. The script is the climatic setting, operating within the immutable physical constraints of our solar system. The director, though never seen, ensures a continuity, balance and symmetry to the show. The changing seasons provide for lighting and mood, which control the intensity of processes. Occasionally the theater burns down and is rebuilt in a different style, just as Alaska has been torn down and rebuilt many times. As passive observers in the audience we can do little to influence the outcome of the play, but we can certainly enjoy the performance.

In this chapter I hope to convey something of the magic I sense when studying Alaskan landscapes, and to explain what little is known about the geologic history of the Interior. I will start by discussing the duality of landscape origins, the constant battle between forces that resist change and those that cause them. I will then explore the scope and patterns of geologic time, the origin and destruction of rocks and the processes of landscape sculpture. Once readers are fortified with an understanding of the processes, rates and causes of change (and with a knowledge of how geologists think), I will reconstruct the geologic history through which the present magnificent scenery of interior Alaska was created.

The science of geology is a human endeavor, rich in history, fraught with mistakes and illuminated by successes. Much of Alaska's early mapping and surveying was done near the beginning of this century by geologists who were plagued by pesky mosquitoes, recalcitrant guides and curious bears, just as we are today. But through many decades of persistent exploration and careful analysis of their findings, geologists have developed a picture of interior Alaska's past, an understanding of its present dynamic landscape and an outlook on its future.

Is Alaska really a giant jigsaw puzzle of crustal blocks welded together? Why is gold so common in the Interior? Why did we have broad seas of drifting dunes in areas now mired in bogs? Did glaciers ever cover Fairbanks? Is permafrost really permanent? When is Los Angeles scheduled to dock at Yakutat? You don't have to be a geologist to understand the answers to these questions, as the following pages will show.

## The Science of Landscape Origins

*The Ceaseless Contest.* The two elements of landscape genesis cannot be precisely defined, but they are best understood as a ceaseless contest between internal building forces and external destructive forces. A landscape is not like a car, which is manufactured once, wears out gradually, is occasionally repaired and is ultimately destroyed. It resembles more closely a child's sandbox which is reshaped from time to time and in different places, but always remains a box filled with sand. Consider the Interior as your sandbox. Pile up the Alaska Range by gouging sand from the north. Now watch it crumble into the depression during the next thunderstorm. So it is with landscapes.

Internal forces, fueled by the earth's heat and by density differences within its crust, thrust our mountains and plateaus upward to high elevations. Destructive forces, such as gravity, sunlight and the unwinding of chemical bonds, fuel the engines of weathering and erosion. Massive, lofty mountain ranges and plateaus testify that in some areas the building forces are victorious, at least temporarily. However, the steady grinding of glaciers and running water gives ruggedness to the mountains, indicating that such victory is not permanent or without cost. Vast lowland areas, such as the Tanana-Kuskokwim Basin, are beveled deep into the roots of old summits and represent a local, brief victory for the other contestant.

I use the terms local and temporary as a geologist would, because the world of the geologist is global in scale, and his clock measures time in eons and epochs instead of minutes and hours. Every part of the earth's surface and every process operating on it interact throughout long and short time scales within one grand interconnected system. Local, in this sense, can refer to vast individual mountain ranges or lowland provinces, or to only parts of them. The entire region between the Tanana and Porcupine rivers is but a single spot in a geologist's global view. The word *temporary* refers to short intervals of geologic time spanning tens of thousands to perhaps several millions of years. After all, the earth is more than 4.6 billion years old. In this sense, it has been just a brief

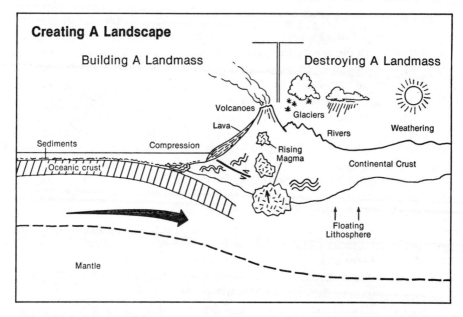

*The landscape we see is the balance between forces that create land and those that destroy it. Continents are higher than ocean basins because their lighter rocks float higher above the earth's mantle. When an oceanic plate smashes into a continental one, sediments are folded and faulted as they are scraped off by the continental edge, or they melt and rise to the surface as volcanoes and igneous intrusions. Once raised above sea level and exposed to the atmosphere, the rocks are weathered to soil and carried to the sea by glaciers, rivers and gravity. Our landscapes result from this ceaseless contest.*

moment since the Tanana River flowed to the south, instead of to the northwest as it does today.

Seemingly quiet, stable summits and hillsides are being gradually lowered by erosion, a few inches or several feet every thousand years or so. At these rates, Alaska could easily be transformed into a broad, irregular lowland in perhaps as little as 30 million years if mountain-building forces were stopped. To have the scenery we enjoy so much, we must accept violent earthquakes and fiery eruptions, for these apparently destructive events are the only ways that landscapes are raised for the carving.

You might ask yourself, why don't we have mountains hundreds of miles high in Alaska, or even five miles high for that matter? Or why are there so many lowland areas lying within a few hundred feet of sea level? The answer is found in the rules of the contest between destructive and constructive forces. Mountains can get only so high because they are parts of relatively light continents floating on a heavier, hot, plasticlike layer called the earth's mantle. Adding more height to a mountain would be like adding weight to a raft floating on the Chena River. The more weight (height) we pile on, the deeper the raft sinks, even though our load extends higher and higher. Unlike the raft, however, a mountain root cannot sink and rest on the bottom because the earth's heat melts the root. This causes the raft to sink farther until some balance, called isostatic equilibrium, is established.

Besides this internal limitation of floating equilibrium, the rate of destruction (erosion) becomes greater with increasing altitude; the higher and steeper a mountain gets, the more rapidly it is torn away. Conversely, the rate of erosion is greatly diminished on broad plains near sea level because erosion cannot act as effectively on such low slopes. This general phenomenon of rapid and slow erosion at high and low altitudes ensures that mountains are eroded more quickly than lowland areas. Removing mass from the land by erosion is like removing weight from our raft — both rise slowly until a new equilibrium is reached.

Another dual element in Alaska's landscape origins is the battle between resisting forces and driving forces. The driving forces are sunlight and gravity on the earth's exterior, and slow radioactive decay within the bowels of the earth. Resisting forces — which include the strength, structure and mineral composition (lithology) of surface rocks — control the land's susceptibility to weathering and remelting or recrystallization by internal forces. Grab a hammer and try to smash some rocks from the top of Ester Dome near Fairbanks. They will be harder to break than the relatively weaker rocks on nearby Birch Hill. This simple experiment should help you understand why Ester Dome is higher.

Another aspect of the duality is the difference between erosional and depositional landforms. Erosional landforms such as peaks, valleys or rock plateaus are usually carved from ancient rock exposed at the surface. In contrast, floodplains, deltas and coastal plains are built up by sediments broken away from upland areas. If we took all the gravel in the Tanana Flats and piled it back up on the Alaska Range where it came from, Mount McKinley would be rather small compared to the mountains we created.

Regardless of whether erosion or deposition is occurring locally, the net result is a smoothing of the landscape. High areas are steadily eroded downward, while low areas are steadily filled upward by sediments carried to valley floors and basins. Viewed this way, a landscape is nothing more than the combination of erosional scars carved in the tops of rocky continents and the collections of material redeposited by that erosion.

## A Geologist's View

Geology is an attempt to reconstruct and date events in earth history. The knowledge it offers is essential in the search for valuable resources such as oil, gas, coal and a wide variety of minerals. Geology also provides a basis for predicting or controlling geological hazards such as earthquakes and flooding. Also, as human beings we cannot help but be curious about the planet we live on. In this section we will learn how geologists reconstruct past events, how they arrange them in sequence and how they date these happenings with respect to the earth's calendar.

*Basic Principles.* How do geologists learn about earth history? Do they just stare at rocks until they are inspired, or is there a method to their madness? The most common and best way to interpret past events is to look at natural rock outcroppings in the field. By studying such exposures along valley walls, coastal cliffs, ridge tops and road cuts, geologists can interpret the sequence of events that formed and modified visible rocks. Sediment cores produced by

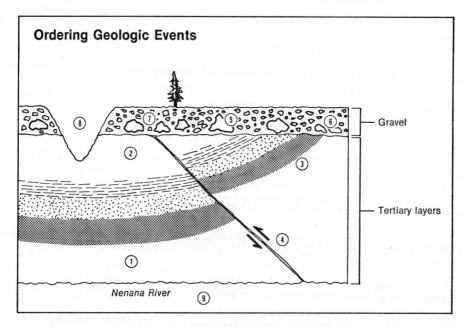

**Ordering Geologic Events**

Gravel

Tertiary layers

Nenana River

*This diagram of the east side of the Nenana River Valley shows how geologists reconstruct past events. The highest Tertiary sediment layers (2) must be older than lower ones (1) because all rock layers grow from the bottom up. Folding (3) and faulting (4) of the layers by compression (thrust fault) must have occurred next. Glaciation (5) brought boulders to the area and erosion (6) destroyed the glacial deposits, leaving only the boulders behind. This happened after the faulting because the fault is cut by the erosional surface. Glacial gravels were first deposited (7), then eroded by gullies (8). The flat-topped terrace was formed last when the Nenana River cut down to its present level (9).*

drilling oil and water wells give geologists a view of subsurface rocks. Correlating and comparing different rock exposures or well cores allow researchers to develop a regional picture. Geologists also attempt to recreate earth processes in scale model experiments to learn how rocks were crystallized, deformed and uplifted.

A key concept in geology is the principle of uniformitarianism, which states that the present is the key to the past. Modern processes that we can see today — such as flooding of the Chena River or sedimentation in Lake Minchumina, both in Alaska's Interior — produce certain kinds of sediments and landforms. If similar features can be recognized in ancient rocks, they must have been formed by the same processes. For example, sediments beneath the surface near Fort Yukon are similar to those of Lake Minchumina, indicating that the Yukon Flats were once covered by a vast inland lake. Likewise, we find that most of the rocks lying just north of Fairbanks were formed in an environment somewhat similar to the muddy Bering Sea today. The principle of uniformitarianism is especially useful in allowing us to interpret various kinds of ancient sedimentary environments.

*Ordering Events.*Geologists obtain relative ages for geologic events by several laws that are marvels of simplicity and common sense. Relative age means simply which is older and which is younger. A rock or sediment layer that lies on top of another must be younger, just as a layer cake must be built from its base up. Thus, silt from the 1965 Chena River flood lies on top of other sediments that were deposited by floods in earlier times. It would be ridiculous to suggest that the lower flood sediments were deposited underground.

Any landform, fracture or rock layer that cuts through or across another must be younger than the rock it cuts, just as the knife slice must be younger than the cake. Goldstream Valley on the outskirts of Fairbanks must be younger than the rock it cuts into. A rock bench or terrace high on its valley wall must be older than a similar bench near the valley bottom, because Goldstream Creek could have cut to its present position only after the higher feature was formed. Such relationships allow geologists to reconstruct the relative ages of bedrock and landform events, but they do not tell us exactly how old the rocks are nor when a particular event took place.

*The Ages of Rocks.* The approximate age of rocks can be obtained by studying fossils that commonly occur in layered sedimentary formations. Through most of the earth's history, new life forms have continually appeared, others have changed with time and still others have become extinct. If we find sediment layers with imbedded dinosaur fossils or woolly mammoth remains, we know approximately how old those rocks or sediments are. There are myriad species of marine animals whose fossilized shells or other remains can be used to correlate the ages of rocks throughout the world. For example, large squidlike creatures called ammonites evolved rapidly into many species that were widespread across the globe hundreds of millions of years ago. The appearance of certain ammonites in rocks on the Alaska Peninsula and in other parts of the world indicate that all of these rocks were formed at roughly the same instant in geologic time.

Studying fossils and correlating rock formations, paleontologists have classified all earth history into a hierarchical framework of geologic time. The major units of time they have established are called eras, periods, epochs and ages — going from the largest divisions to the smallest. This framework is similar to our system of millennia, centuries, decades, years, months, days and minutes in human time scales.

But the story doesn't end here. After they had designated the subdivisions of geologic time and could correlate rocks of similar age, geologists still had no idea how old the rocks actually were. Although many ingenious schemes were devised to estimate the true length of geologic time, none of them worked well. Accurate dating of earth events in real time would have to wait until radiometric dating methods were developed.

Techniques for radiometric dating revolutionized our understanding of geologic time and allowed scientists to obtain ages for rocks that didn't have fossils. Most dating techniques rely on the known rates of disintegration for radioactive isotopes of uranium, potassium and carbon. The decay of an isotope into another form, or the progressive loss of an isotope, occurs at a known rate that never changes. If we know how much of an isotope was originally present and can measure the amount of it remaining, we can obtain a true, if sometimes only approximate, age for the rock. For example, a large isolated mountain called Jumbo Dome, visible from the Parks Highway east of Healy, contains crystals that cooled into a frozen state about 2.75 million years ago. This age-date was obtained by pulverizing the crystals under a vacuum and measuring the amount of trapped argon gas. Using such techniques, the familiar eras, periods and epochs of geologic time can be accurately dated.

*The Geologic Calendar.* The breadth of geologic time is difficult to visualize because earth history is more than 75 million times older than an average human life. Now try to imagine that all geologic time was compressed into a single year. The oldest Alaskan rocks, which are found near Dillingham, were not even created until mid-October; Alaska is a young upstart in more ways than one. The ancient rocks near Fairbanks were deeply buried and partly melted by hot fluids just two days before Christmas, about 90 million years ago. The Alaska Range emerged in its present form in the morning of December 30, a mere 10 million years ago. The last great Ice Age would have occurred at five seconds before midnight on December 31. And the European discovery of Alaska by Vitus Bering occurred at the final instant of the last day. If each year of earth history were represented by the length of a human stride, you would circle the earth hundreds of times before your journey was complete.

Our planet was born about 4.6 billion years ago as cold interstellar dust gravitated together. The material that now makes up Alaska was around then, but it has been rearranged many times since the earth began.

The Precambrian era, which began about 3.8 billion years ago, was dominated by simple unicellular life, best characterized as slime. Its atmosphere would have been poisonous to us and the world was devoid of land plants or any other familiar living thing. If you float down the Yukon River near the Canadian border, you can see crumpled flinty beds of red and brown rock. Some of these contain late Precambrian fossils and bear mute testimony to a flourishing murky ecosystem more than 500 million years old. Nearly 85 percent of all geologic time occurred within the Precambrian, but we don't know how these landscapes looked because rocks this old have usually been destroyed or changed by later events. Alaskans are lucky to have even patches of Precambrian rock scattered about, like gravestones of a primeval era.

The Paleozoic era was an age of monstrous bony primitive fishes, luxuriant terrestrial plants dominated by archaic fern trees and an astounding assortment of shelly marine life. It began with an incredible burst of new complex organisms about 570 million years ago and lasted for about 325 million years. The number of early Paleozoic marine animal species is astonishingly high compared to the number living today. Paleozoic rocks are common in Alaska, especially in the Brooks Range and in Southeast. Just hike on any of the platy greenish-gray rocks immediately north of Fairbanks and you are probably walking amidst remnants of this great leafy era.

Sharks, horseshoe crabs and scouring rushes are among the few living descendants of this era, from which more than 90 percent of all species have vanished. The fragile, jointed, scouring rushes *(Equisetum)* that grow abundantly in moist birch forests and along riverbanks have persisted virtually unchanged since mid-Paleozoic time — living fossils easily viewed by any resident of the Interior.

The Mesozoic era, from 245 to 65 million years ago, is commonly called the age of reptiles. This era saw the rise and abrupt fall of the dinosaurs, a great

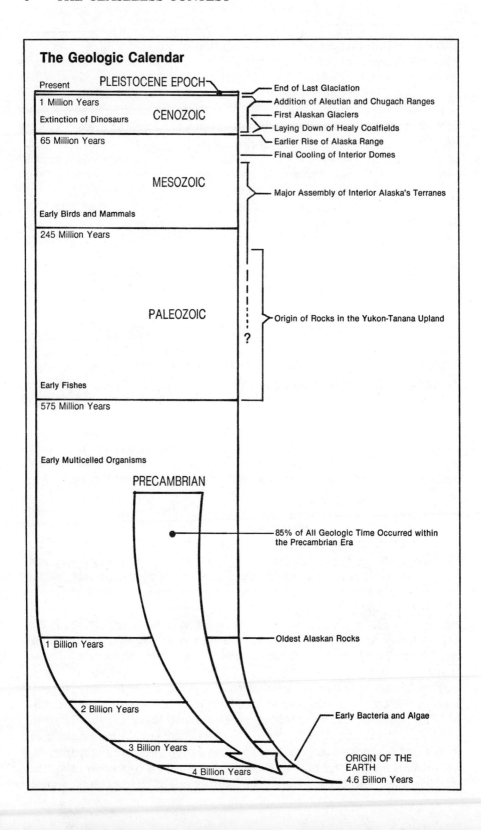

The Geologic Calendar

inundation of much of the earth by shallow seas, and the beginning of primitive mammals. Mesozoic rocks in Alaska are usually sandy and shaley and probably cover more of the state than those of any other era. Extinction of the dinosaurs at the close of the Mesozoic is one of the world's long-standing mysteries. Recent evidence suggests that a large asteroid impact blackened the atmosphere with dust, bringing about the demise of the dinosaurs and many other species and ushering the world into its current era.

The final chapter in earth history, the Cenozoic era, is still underway after more than 65 million years. This era saw the rise and diversification of mammals, a bloom of flowering plants, the beginning of humankind and periodic global ice ages. The Cenozoic era consists of two periods, the Tertiary, which ended a mere 2 million years ago and the Quaternary, in which we still live.

Cenozoic rocks are usually less consolidated and less deformed than older rocks. The tilted semi-soft rock layers of the Healy coalfields just north of the Alaska Range are the best local examples of Cenozoic strata. If you are reading this book in the Fairbanks area, your electricity was probably generated by burning Healy coal — the deposits of decomposed forests. If you can stretch your imagination, you are reading with trapped mid-Cenozoic sunlight.

The Quaternary, last period of the Cenozoic, is further subdivided into two epochs. First is the Pleistocene, when great ice sheets periodically covered much of North America, but paradoxically when less than half of Alaska was glaciated. At this time, sea level changes intermittently created a vast plain of dry land connecting Alaska with Asia, perhaps allowing the first native Americans to step into the New World. Second is the Holocene epoch, which includes the last 10,000 years of earth history — the final word of the last chapter in the book of geologic time.

*The Rocks.* As even the most casual observer can see, not all rocks are alike. In Alaska's Interior the common types include flinty hard, muddy black, crystalline white and limy fossil- bearing rock. There are three general rock types: igneous, which are crystallized from melted material such as volcanic lava; sedimentary, composed of fragmented material, like sand or silt, or material precipitated from saline water; and metamorphic, rocks that have been altered by heat and pressure without melting. If you drive to the top of Ester, Cleary or Murphy dome near Fairbanks, you will see chunks of a white speckled igneous rock called granite. Look closely at the many different crystals — light and dark, dull and shiny, platy and blocky — which can be seen with the naked eye. These coarse, grainy rocks cooled slowly far below the earth's surface, allowing the crystals to grow large enough to see. Now drive north to the Livengood area or west toward Nenana. Along road cuts here you will see black or dark brown sheets of rock, most of them tilted at various angles — these are ancient lava flows like the ones from Hawaiian volcanoes today. Examine a piece of the hard dense rock and you will probably see few, if any, crystals. This rock, called basalt, is also igneous but it cooled so quickly when erupted that large crystals could not grow.

An amazing variety of sedimentary rocks can be seen throughout the Interior. Most are slabs made up of sand, mud and gravel originally laid down in broad, flat sheets on ancient ocean bottoms. These rocks are usually folded and fractured by deep burial and earth upheaval, so don't expect them to be horizontal today. The Healy coalfield example was mentioned earlier. Sedimentary rocks form the core of the Alaska Range, and are widespread along the Elliott Highway near Livengood. Go to the Rainbow Mountain area along the Richardson Highway in the central Alaska Range and you will see thousands of layers of sand, mud and gravel standing on end. In Polychrome Pass along the Denali Park Highway, you will see dozens of layers of mud and sandstone interbedded with lava. These sedimentary sequences usually give rise to brilliantly colored mountains because the composition of each layer is different.

Another major type of sedimentary rock common in the Interior is limestone; for example, it forms the core of the White Mountains north of Fairbanks. Limestone can be precipitated directly from the saline water of ancient oceans, just as salt crystallizes in a pan left to dry in the sun. More commonly, marine organisms including algae, corals and mollusks use calcium carbonate for their shells and exoskeletons. Gradual buildups of shelly debris form massive reefs which are first buried and later uplifted into tan-colored mountain ranges. A careful traverse of the White Mountains near the Elliot Highway is certain to turn up the shelly fossils of ancient tropical reefs.

Fairbanks residents know that along nearly every local road the rocks are mostly brownish, slabby and fractured. Half of the fireplaces in town are made of it. This rock is often finely layered and has a delicate sheen, because light reflects from billions of tiny mica crystals aligned parallel to the surface, like a deck of cards spread out on the table. This is a good example of a metamorphic rock called schist. Other less common metamorphic rocks include the marble at the Fox Quarry and amphibolite at the tip of Chena Ridge, both near Fairbanks. The original character of all such rocks has been altered by heat and pressure, resulting in a different appearance. The schist near Fairbanks was originally mudstone and sandstone that was deeply buried and partially melted. More local metamorphism usually occurs when rocks are baked near igneous bodies that cool underground.

Rocks are almost always broken by fractures of various sizes. Just drive around Fairbanks and I doubt that you will find any rock larger than several feet that is not broken in at least one spot. These fractures, of whatever size, are called joints. They commonly form when subsurface rocks expand elastically like springs in response to erosion of overlying material. Joints are also formed by large stretching forces related to plate motion and by cooling of igneous masses after final crystallization.

Rock fractures caused by crustal blocks moving past one another are called faults. Small faults can be seen in most road cuts and can be identified by sharp breaks in the layering. Movement along faults can be vertical, as the blocks are pulled apart or squeezed together. The sliding of one block past another horizontally is called a strike slip fault; some of these are thousands of miles long. An example is the Denali Fault, which crosses both the Delta and Nenana valleys and can be identified by an abrupt break between schist to the north and sedimentary rocks to the south. Thrust faults occur when one block slides over another at a low angle during horizontal compression. Earthquakes are produced when large amounts of energy, stored by fault motion, are suddenly released, causing brittle fracture and violent shaking.

Rather than being fractured, rocks of all kinds can also be folded into many curves and shapes. This usually occurs some distance below the surface, where high pressure and hot temperatures allow rock layers to be deformed plastically. The gentle folding of the Healy coalfields or the tight convolutions of layered schist are good local examples. Various intervals of folding, faulting, melting and disordering of rocks can be reconstructed by careful examination of exposures by geologists. In this way geologic history can be unraveled.

## Piecing Alaska Together

*The Giant Parking Lot.* The rocks that underlie different regions of Alaska are surprisingly different from one another. When we study the landscape, we are able to identify a series of great, irregularly shaped crustal blocks called terranes. Each of these distinct blocks has a characteristic sequence of sedimentary, igneous and metamorphic rocks and a style of deformation and history significantly different from the adjacent blocks.

A good analogy is to visualize a parking lot full of automobiles — different ages, sizes and styles — all packed closely together. The interior decor, body shape and styling of each car is consistent with its overall design and age and the component parts blend nicely together. An adjacent car may also have its own overall design, but it is completely unlike its neighbor, no matter how close together they are parked. Although each car is made from the same materials as every other one, it also stands on its own as a discrete unit.

The same thing applies to adjacent terranes in Alaska — they are composed of the same minerals but are quite distinct from one another, with their own designs and arrangements. For example, the crustal block between the Porcupine and Yukon rivers contains rocks of similar character and age, yet they are totally unlike the adjacent terrane south of the Yukon River. They are as different from each other as a 1958 Oldsmobile and a 1983 Subaru. Boundaries between each terrane are normally large strike slip or thrust faults along which different terranes slid to their present juxtaposition.

The presence of an Oldsmobile or a Subaru in Alaska does not mean that either was made here. Nor were the tropical reef sediments in the White Mountains or equatorial magnetics in the Alaska Range necessarily formed where they are located today. Instead, the White Mountains and the Alaska Range could have been created at different times in different places and arrived independently of one another, just like two autos driven up the Alaska Highway.

This patchwork concept of continental growth, called microplate tectonics, is a relatively new development in earth sciences and a significant refinement of continental drift theories, which themselves were accepted only about 20 years ago. But what could cause terranes to move about as discrete units and to accumulate like different cars in a parking lot?

According to the theory of plate tectonics, the continents and the sea floor can be divided into large segments many miles thick that float passively on a soft underlying layer called the earth's mantle, moving like large flat ice floes carried by the tides in Cook Inlet. Because each plate moves independently over

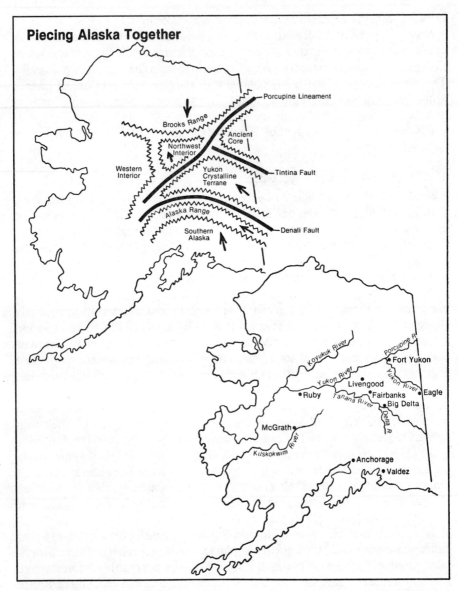

**Piecing Alaska Together**

*Interior Alaska was assembled like a jigsaw puzzle of different crustal blocks that moved together from all directions and accreted around an ancient core. Movement of crustal blocks happened along great faults such as the Denali Fault.*

the globe in a fixed direction and rate, motion along the edges of such plates is inevitable. It is along these plate boundaries that most mountains are made and perhaps where geology has its most exciting moment.

Alaska is now part of the North American Plate. The Pacific Plate, which extends far into the southern hemisphere, is sliding along North America near the southeastern Alaska coast, but is thrusting directly beneath it below the Aleutian Islands. When one plate, usually the oceanic one, is pushed beneath another, ocean sediments may be scraped off the diving plate and plastered up as coastal mountains like the Chugach Range. The oceanic plate may also be shoved down to great depths, where it remelts and rises to the surface as volcanoes, as in the Aleutians, or as large masses of granitic molten rock, as on the Alaska Peninsula. When one plate slides alongside another, larger strike slip faults like the Denali Fault are produced, where the blocks on opposite sides glide past each other like trains moving in opposite directions. When two continental plates collide directly, the great forces of compression build massive mountain ranges like the Himalayas.

*The Geological Log Jam.* Alaska has grown gradually, as a log jam grows, with different types of logs (terranes) floating in at different rates and from different places. The Pacific Plate, moving northward at rates of inches per year, flows continuously under and past the original core of North America like water moving along a permanent bend in a river. Discrete islandlike blocks of crust are carried as passengers on the plates until they are jammed into Alaska like logs into the stream bank. The terranes that are added to the log jam come from different places and could be different in age, just as an old birch log from the Old Crow Flats and a young spruce log from the Chandalar River could arrive at the same log jam near Fort Yukon. Occasionally, two or more blocks of crust may have joined together before their arrival, like a clump of floating logs reaching the jam.

Alaska is steadily growing toward the south as more and more terranes are added, just as a log jam grows in an upstream direction. As the jam accumulates, early-formed parts are compressed, thickened and sheared past one another; some blocks break under the tremendous force while others are shoved up, over and ahead. Alaska has developed in this fashion by the intermittent attachment of single and composite blocks from different regions and by the deformation of these blocks after arrival. The details of Alaska's growth are speculative and controversial at this stage in our understanding, but most geologists agree on the basic model.

This concept really forces us to rethink what Alaska is. Alaska is not a single permanent part of the continent as most of us usually think of it. Instead it is a jigsaw puzzle of fragments that came together from distant places in the Pacific Ocean and its bordering continents. The youngest arrivals lie on the southern coast, because that is where the Pacific plate slides against the North American continent. Assuming the present rates and styles of deformation, Los Angeles and all areas west of the gigantic San Andreas Fault will continue to slide northward, arriving at Alaska's south coast as a new terrane in a mere 20 million years.

## Pieces of the Interior

*The Ancient Core.* The beautiful suite of yellow, red and brown layered rocks between the Porcupine and Yukon rivers — limestone, chert and lavas of ancient seas — has remained attached to the rest of North America since at least Precambrian time. Although bent and compressed, these rocks retain their original character. Scratched and broken pebbles in unlayered mud within this deposit look suspiciously like modern glacial gravels, suggesting that this triangle of land was scoured by ice caps long before land plants were even present. Although we think this region has remained attached to our parent continent since eons ago, we are not quite sure where the continent was at that time.

*The Brooks Range.* North of the ancient core lies the Brooks Range, a massive and complex mountain chain that marks the Interior's northern boundary. The Brooks Range is remote and jagged, a tundra-carpeted world with peaks extending to more than 10,000 feet. Its broad, curved valleys were once the passageways for large glaciers that sliced the mountains like a serrated knife, laying open its heart for the geologist to examine.

If you travel along any south-flowing rivers here, you will see layer on layer of brilliantly colored Paleozoic rocks, most dipping southward. The layers are broken and shoved above one another like a giant tilted pile of plywood. Vast sequences of gray shale deposited in abyssal seas are thrust above river gravels and above shallow carbonate reefs suggestive of the Bahamas. Along the southern edge of the Brooks Range is a belt of late Paleozoic-early Mesozoic volcanic rocks, probably resulting from the collision of the Brooks Range and North America. This meeting of mountains melted an elongated band of sediments and welded them together as they remain today.

Rocks of the Brooks Range and the events that took place during its growth are somewhat understood. But nobody knows where the exotic terranes comprising the range came from. Some geologists argue that sediments of the Brooks Range were laid down near the Canadian Arctic Islands, perhaps as far east as Greenland. According to this view, the sediments were rifted from northern Canada as the Atlantic Ocean was born, then rotated through what is now the Arctic Ocean and crushed against the ancient core. No matter how preposterous this might sound, there is evidence to support it.

Other geologists postulate that Brooks Range rocks slid great distances northward along the west side of North America, rising during the deformation like an early version of the mountains bordering southern Alaska. Still others would say the marine sediments were laid down and deformed into lofty mountains near their present positions. And yet others see Asian origins. The Brooks Range controversy shows that all may agree on what they see, but they interpret it in different ways. The study of Alaskan geology is clearly as exciting as the knowledge and ideas it reveals.

*The Yukon Crystalline Terrane.* The region east of Fairbanks — between the Tintina and Denali faults — is known as the Yukon Crystalline Terrane. It extends from Nenana far eastward into Yukon Territory and south into eastern British Columbia. The most widespread rock type is schist, an ancient metamorphic rock of unknown beginnings, which survived many episodes of partial melting, plastic deformation and tremendous compression. Look at a road cut on Chena Ridge near Fairbanks to get a feeling for schist. Veins of light-colored quartz which form latticed patterns were squirted through these rocks when they partially melted. Look at the folds and convoluted bends which prove that this now-solid rock deformed like putty during multiple episodes of mountain-building deep within the earth's interior. Only a thin belt of rocks near the southern edge of the Yukon Crystalline Terrane is unmetamorphosed. Exposures

## Deformation of Rock Layers

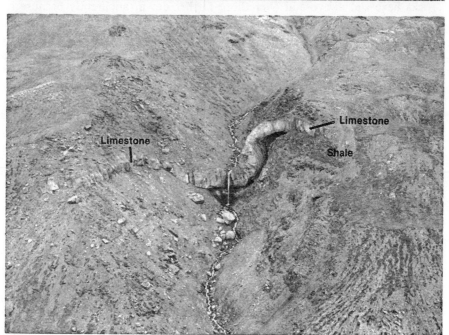

*Most mountains are made of piles of layered rocks that were folded and fractured by great forces during mountain building. The thin brittle layers of the top photo were once horizontal layers of oceanic mud. They were first converted to rock, then twisted plastically to their present shape during mountain building. A fault broke the folds after they formed. Cones of platy rock (talus) accumulate at the base of the cliff. A folded bed of limestone in a thick deposit of gray shale (bottom photo) forms a resistant ledge in the valley center, creating a waterfall 40 feet high. (Both courtesy of Robert Thorson)*

beside the Richardson Highway along the north flank of the Alaska Range reveal its shaley, muddy origin.

The regionally metamorphosed schist of the crystalline terrane is penetrated by many bulky granitic intrusions that cooled deep below the surface. The domes around Fairbanks — Ester, Murphy and Pedro — are plug-shaped bodies of granite that cooled in late Mesozoic time, when dinosaurs roamed the earth. They were formed by the melting of older primordial crust, miles below the surface during the final welding of this terrane to North America.

The Yukon Crystalline Terrane originated at more southerly latitudes, then slid hundreds of miles northward along the Tintina Fault, welded in place and cooled. Afterward, collisional forces tore the Interior into numerous faults that trend northeast to southwest, like the one near Badger Road in Fairbanks, which may still be active today. Occasional strong earthquakes in the Fairbanks region represent the progressive fragmentation of this terrane by such faults. The presence of late Tertiary volcanoes and warping of young river terraces indicate that this section of the earth's crust is still being broken up, almost certainly by compressional forces generated from the arrival of our southern mountains.

*The Northwest Interior.* The region north of Fairbanks between Livengood and Rampart consists of enigmatic terranes of widely different origins. Some lie as patches over younger and different strata; in other words, the surface rocks have slid above and over those farther down, apparently because of compression along low thrust faults. Others such as the White Mountains are sequences of limestone. Still other fragments of volcanic and metamorphic origin may have been dredged from deep beneath the sea floor near the earth's mantle. All of these large crustal blocks lie wedged together between the southcentral Brooks Range and the Yukon-Tanana Upland.

*The Alaska Range.* The rugged Alaska Range to the south is another Alaskan mystery. The Denali Fault system, a curved crustal break that can be traced almost continuously from the Bering Sea through western Canada, separates rocks of the Interior from those of southern Alaska and is largely responsible for uplift of the Alaska Range. Park your car at the snout of Castner Glacier, about 49 miles south of Delta Junction. Now look westward across the Delta Valley and the panorama beyond. On your right you will see the crystalline terrane — schist and highly deformed shales that crumble easily, creating lower mountains. To your left are higher mountains, composed of stronger, less deformed oceanic muds now compressed into firm bedrock. The Denali Fault, barely visible on the surface, separates these two rock types.

The Denali Fault's strike slip motion has slid the south side northwest at about an inch per year; thus in your lifetime, southern Alaska will have moved farther than you are tall. Although these forces act slowly in human terms, just imagine how powerful they must be to move every bit of southern Alaska. Yet even the creeping motion of southern Alaska is small, when compared to entire continents, which move over the globe like froth on a pond. Forces in this league would have no trouble elevating the Alaska Range, which is a mere wrinkle on the grand scale of plate tectonics.

The crystalline terrane north of the Denali Fault is juxtaposed against less deformed ocean sediments which have slid northward, perhaps as much as 300 miles. We can determine this by studying the magnetic signatures of crystals trapped in the rocks when they have cooled. When the sedimentary rocks to the left of Castner Glacier were finally compacted, tiny individual magnetic crystals aligned themselves in a way that modern rocks near Ketchikan would today. This indicated that the Black Rapids Glacier area may have been farther south than what is now Valdez and probably hundreds of miles to the east.

Now try to visualize yourself riding southward on the Alaska Railroad. In the narrow bronze-colored gorge between Healy and Denali Park you are traveling through the crystalline terrane, where the mountains are generally below 5,000 feet. The bronze color is caused by scattered reflections from billions of tiny mica flecks in the schist. At the entrance to Denali Park you cross the Denali Fault and before you are higher, rugged mountains. As you continue southward, tilted beds of sandstone and cemented gravel (conglomerate) called the Cantwell Formation lie above older shales and lavas of Mesozoic age along both walls of the canyon. These thick sequences of terrestrial sediments — debris from rapidly rising mountains — are a reminder of the cyclicity of earth processes.

Abundant granitic intrusive rocks and lava flows along the crest of the Alaska Range indicate that remelting of collided materials was common. Such remelting helped elevate the highest mountains of the Alaska Range: the McKinley-Foraker complex to the west and Hayes-Hess-Deborah to the east. These massifs are made of light granitic rocks that literally float higher than neighboring parts of the Alaska Range.

*The Western Terranes.* If you fly west from Fairbanks, you will see the remote rolling hills and low mountains of west-central Alaska. Upland tundra alternates with lowland forest in a seemingly endless series. The mountains are lower here because they do not lie along major fault breaks or at former plate boundaries and because they consist of monotonous sequences of gray Mesozoic sedimentary rocks that crumble easily. The northern Kuskokwim Mountains may represent a fragment of the North American continent that broke off and rotated to its present position amid a complex of smaller fragments. Most geologists agree that mountain blocks in the western Interior have not moved far from where they were created.

The locally ragged, circular Ray Mountains and Kokrine Hills are underlain by massive intrusions of granite surrounded by baked contact zones. The height of these local ranges, several thousand feet above lowland floors, is not due to original uplift, but rather to the strength of these rocks. Surrounding sediments, being less resistant to decay, have simply been removed more quickly and deeply by erosion.

*Summary.* We have reviewed the origin of rocks and the means by which they are broken. We then examined how the Interior is a jigsaw puzzle of terranes between the problematic Brooks Range and the great Denali Fault system. Attachment of sedimentary and metamorphic terranes was accompanied by the raising of mountains, by the melting and folding of attached blocks and finally by shearing of the terranes along great faults. Now that we understand the origin of the interior bedrock and the ancient images it conveys, we will turn our attention to the agents which sculpt scenery from this foundation.

## Dissolving the Landscape

On your next hike, pick up a piece of rock from a hill summit, hold it in your hand and look at it closely. Examine how it is made of different colored minerals, the ways it is fractured, and whether it is stained or lichen-covered. If rocks did not naturally break down, you couldn't find a piece to hold. Any rock you can hold was either pried from the mountain by mechanical processes, which break rocks apart, or released by chemical processes, which fragment rocks by dissolving them. Even the sediment that flows in stream waters is made of miniscule bits of broken rocks. If rocks did not break down, there would be no valleys and even soil could not exist; mountains would be permanent even over geological time scales.

All rocks will eventually dissolve in water, but the length of time required depends on their composition and on the fluids dissolving them. A grain of common table salt (the mineral halite) will dissolve almost instantly in distilled water, whereas a clear grain of sand (quartz) may not completely dissolve in your lifetime. An ironic fact of geology is that minerals formed at the highest temperatures and pressures deep within the earth decompose most readily at the surface. The minerals are accustomed to their formative environment and are out of place in a new one. Much of our sand is mainly composed of relatively stable quartz, which formed at low temperatures in molten rock. On the other hand, many of the dark minerals formed at higher temperatures and are rich in iron. These minerals dissolve rapidly, providing nutrients for plant growth and giving soils a rusty color.

Anybody trying to watch rocks dissolve in a stream could be considered a fool, but given enough time they will dissolve. The stream itself is a dilute soup of dissolving rock in water. Scale accumulations in your teapot or your house plumbing indicate that water contains an abundance of dissolved minerals.

Let's assume that you are walking above treeline in the hills north of Fairbanks or above Chena Hot Springs. Why are the rocks fractured and jointed nearly everywhere you look? As a landscape erodes, the weight of overlying rocks is removed from those underneath, releasing the great burden that formerly held them together. As the overburden pressure disappears, solid masses of rock expand elastically, breaking into a series of boxlike joints and fractures of all sizes. They virtually explode, sometimes with enough force to fly apart. Quarry operators and underground miners are familiar with rock bursts and their riflelike sounds, which sometimes occur as the overburden is artificially removed.

Mechanical disintegration also occurs when minerals dissolve at different rates, leaving voids or cracks, which are then exploited by water or ice. In any cold climate, ice is a major force in breaking rocks apart. Ice, frozen in fractures, pries rocks apart with the same pressure that bursts the pipes in an unheated house. The more resistant minerals will survive as broken fragments. This is common along the Richardson Highway opposite Harding Lake, where a rough angular sand called gruss is all that remains of a once solid mass of granite.

The combination of mechanical and chemical disintegration, called weathering, produces the familiar brown and black soils of your own back yard. When rainfall percolates through decaying vegetation on forest floors, it picks up organic acids that help dissolve subsurface material already broken mechanically. Weathering is essential for all plant growth because plants cannot obtain necessary nutrients unless they are first dissolved. Even your lunch must be dissolved before you can use its nutrients, because you can't nourish a brain cell with a solid sandwich. Plants not only grow as landscapes are broken down, but they speed up the process by adding acids to the developing soil.

Mechanical and chemical weathering act together in a simple but profound way. A handful of finely ground salt will dissolve much more quickly than a single chunk of equal weight or volume. In the same way, chemical weathering is most effective on small fragments because they have a high surface area in relation to volume. Thus, mechanical disintegration is vital to the weathering process because it produces smaller fragments. On the other hand, chemical weathering along weaknesses in rocks permits mechanical disintegration to occur more readily. Even the most solid rock is doomed to gradual destruction with time.

Now that we have broken up the rocks of our hills and mountains, the pieces can be carried away by erosion. All agents of erosion — such as glaciers, streams and wind — are ultimately controlled by gravity. Each process modifies the rock fragments in its own way. In the Tanana River particles are rounded and sorted into various sizes; below Black Rapids Glacier they are beveled, scratched and ground up into a paste. Weathering does not stop when the rock is first picked up, but continues through every step along the way.

A good way to see how rivers change would be to canoe down the Delta, Tanana and Yukon rivers to the Bering Sea. As you put your canoe in the Delta River along the Richardson Highway, you observe the turbid water rushing over bouldery gravel bars in a narrow channel. Where did all the gravel come from? Was it transported down-slope by gravity piece by piece or was it quarried by the river cutting its banks? The scene is different on the Yukon Delta, with a wide channel and much smaller sand and silt particles. The reduction in particle size confirms our expectation that particles are gradually broken down during transport and that lower river gradients cannot transport as much coarse material.

En route to the sea a particle may be trapped temporarily in a moraine, which is a pile of debris left by a glacier, or in a flood plain along a stream. These rest stops are brief by geological standards, for the fate of most particles is to be bathed in salt water before they are uplifted again above the sea. Without weathering, streams would have nothing to carry and could not effectively excavate their channels. Without streams, all mountains would become buried in their own rubble as smooth rolling hills. Clearly this combination causes the spectacular variation in scenery from jagged canyons to endless rolling hills.

# Ice in the Ground

*A Shattering Experience.* The climate of Alaska's Interior exerts a strong influence on the types and rates of weathering and erosion. Cool ground temperatures and long dry winters greatly reduce the rate of chemical weathering and increase the importance of mechanical disintegration. Thick, reddish, clayey

## Permafrost

*Permafrost has many different appearances. The top photo shows permanently frozen muck typical of many mining cuts throughout interior Alaska. The foul-smelling muck consists of organic-stained silt rich in plant fragments and the bones of extinct ice-age mammals. The muck is permanently frozen below the active layer, which freezes and thaws each year. Note the large ice wedge to the left, which formed gradually as the ground cracked and froze in the same area. The bottom photo shows a permanently frozen deposit of glacial lake silt and clay in the southern Brooks Range. Veins of clear ice formed between the silt layers. When this material thaws, it loses its strength and oozes downslope. (Both courtesy of Robert Thorson)*

soils, so common in warmer regions, cannot form because cold restricts chemical breakdown. Instead we have silty, brown-stained soil horizons on well drained uplands and boggy black soils in lowlands. Piles of fresh, angular rock fragments are abundant, indicating that chemical decomposition is slight and that shattering of rock by freezing of internal water is common. Rocks with water-filled cracks break when the water freezes, as it does each night during spring and fall. Anyone who stands below a steep rock valley wall in alpine areas and hears the repeated clink of falling particles knows that the mountain he stands by is being pried apart piecemeal.

*Nature's Deep Freeze.* Permafrost is any ground that has been frozen for several years or more. Some permafrost, especially in areas above the Arctic Circle, may have been frozen for hundreds of thousands or even millions of years. Permafrost forms whenever more cold is pumped into the ground in winter than can be pumped out of it during summer. If you take a driving tour of the Fairbanks area, you cannot escape the importance of permafrost. The north-facing slopes of Goldstream Valley are covered with muskeg and stunted black spruce because permafrost lies near the surface. On south-facing slopes, which receive more of the sun's warmth, aspen and birch predominate and permafrost is usually absent. Boggy valley bottoms are usually underlain by permafrost that can be as much as several hundred feet thick. If you have a chance to go berry picking along Chena Hot Springs Road east of Fairbanks, dig down a couple of feet with a shovel and you will find a frozen black goo.

I once watched some placer miners hose down a frozen bank near Chicken on the Taylor Highway. The black, foul-smelling muck contained bones and flesh from an extinct Pleistocene bison. It smelled because even the long-dead insects, plants and fragments of beasts had not yet completely rotted away. What struck me most about this scene was how much permafrost reduces the rate of weathering. This bank could not weather because it had been completely frozen for the last 30,000 years.

It is difficult to walk over the landscape of Alaska's Interior without seeing the pervasive influence of frost action, the myriad effects of freezing and thawing water on surface materials. Go to any summit, such as Wickersham Dome, and you will see piles of angular rubble produced by water freezing in rock pore spaces. Exposed rocks on all of the Interior's highlands are literally split apart by frost shattering. Anyone who has walked over a bare windswept exposure in the foothills of the Alaska Range and seen a veneer of angular rock fragments realizes how effective frost shattering is. Seasonal freezing also stirs the ground and hinders development of good soil. During spring snowmelt, water rushes off the saturated land without a chance to leach rock materials slowly.

Freezing and thawing also sort surface materials into polygons, stripes and circles of angular stones around cores of finer material. Go to Eagle Summit north of Fairbanks and see for yourself. This sorting occurs because surface soil is a hodgepodge of coarse and fine fragments that behave differently during freezing and thawing. Fragments of similar size are usually separated from one another, resulting in a honeycombed appearance on gentle slopes or stripes on steeper ones.

*The Swirling Soil.* When winter arrives, the ground begins to freeze down toward the underlying permafrost. Saturated soils are squeezed between the frozen ground above and the permafrost below. These masses of dirt (usually silt) ooze toward areas of lower pressure, forming cells of circulating gunk that commonly reach the surface as mud boils. These are best seen on gentle slopes well above treeline. Such constant mixing causes the soil to swirl into chaotic patterns that can be seen near the tops of many road cuts near Fairbanks.

Slab-shaped rocks and boulders that often jut through the vegetation mat in alpine areas have been literally jacked out of the ground with their points upward. Rocks conduct cold better than the surrounding fine soil, so lenses of ice form underneath and push them upward until they stab through the surface like knives. Every time the ground freezes, ice lenses expand upward as much as several inches because ice takes up more space than water of equal weight. These lenses may even push telephone poles and fence posts out of the ground. If you think about all of these frost action processes working together, you should be able to imagine surface soil layers being swirled, fractured, sorted and heaved continuously year after year. No wonder some of the experienced sourdoughs didn't want to be buried here. The ground you walk on is alive with motion caused by freezing.

*Explosive Cracking.* If you are lucky, you can see and hear one of the most dramatic frost action processes, ground cracking. A friend who lives on the North Slope told me that when the temperature falls rapidly to minus 30 degrees or more, the frozen ground under his house cracks in great resonating booms. When all is quiet, gaping jagged rifts up to a foot wide can be seen in the snow-covered tundra. The ground also cracks near Fairbanks, but less violently and with less regularity than farther north.

Frost cracking occurs only when frozen ground is quickly chilled, causing the ground to contract just like a bridge, gate, pipeline or any other substance. When enough contraction happens, tensile stresses within the ground exceed the strength of the permafrost, pulling it apart like a burst chain. On horizontal surfaces of uniform material, the cracks are spaced at regular intervals of five to 50 feet in a polygonal or rectangular pattern. Before the ground expands and heals itself, meltwater or material like windblown sand can fill each crack and create a well-defined vein. Once established, the veins are weak zones, where later cracking usually happens. Repeated cracking and addition of water causes the growth of large ice wedges up to 10 feet wide, in a regular geometric surface pattern. Growing wedges push nearby ground upward, leaving shallow polygon-shaped depressions whose centers often fill with water.

Most of the mining cuts near Fairbanks have exposed ice wedges that formed prior to the last glaciation, tens of thousands of years ago. The booms of cracking ground must have been quite noisy there in the distant past. Ice wedges are still forming near Ballaine Lake, just north of the University of Alaska's Fairbanks campus, but nobody that I know of has ever heard them explode. Spring water hazards on the Fairbanks golf course are depressions left by melting of ancient ice wedges.

*Buried Ice Cubes.* Permafrost throughout the Interior and northern Alaska is loaded with ice of many different varieties, especially in areas with silty sediments. Ice exposed in mining and road cuts can be clear or bubbly, black

## Frost Action

*Frost Heaving: The top photo shows a slabby boulder that is being pushed out of the soil by ice that freezes at its base. Building foundations and telephone poles commonly experience the same fate. Frost Cracking: The lower photo shows a weathered sandstone boulder that is being pried apart by the growth of ice crystals. Water seeps through the weathered exterior and freezes, forcing the outer layers to spall off. (Both courtesy of Robert Thorson)*

or white, clean or dirty, or layered sideways or upright. Blocky chunks of ice may be surrounded by the gooiest of clay, yet be clean enough to chill your favorite drink. Ice wedges look like giant icy carrots growing in the ground. Flatter, more irregular lenses common in silty sediments can reach thicknesses of 30 feet. They form when ice crystals attract unfrozen water like a magnet, and they can heave the ground upward as they grow. Ground ice can also exist as small veins and between fine particles of soil, locking the permafrost together like reinforced concrete. No wonder the gold miners melt it rather than blast it away. Any body of water, such as an old river channel or pond, can be frozen solid if it becomes buried, preserving a silent aquatic world below the surface.

A pingo is an isolated cone-shaped hill composed almost entirely of ice, but covered by a veneer of peaty soil. Pingos on the North Slope can be as high as several hundred feet and look like miniature mountains. But pingos are also common in the Interior. Five pingos at the junction of O'Connor and Goldstream creeks, near Fairbanks, are isolated mounds in the otherwise flat and featureless valley bottom. The largest is a forested bulge, 200 feet in diameter and 35 feet high. At the top, a large crater with bent and collapsed trees reveals just how ephemeral these features are, for the ice underneath is gradually melting as the crater expands. Pingos form in permafrost regions where gravity-fed pressurized water is forced to the surface and freezes.

When people buy property or houses in the Interior, they are wise to check for buried ice. Ice melted by artificial heating is responsible for many of the tipped, bent or jackknifed houses visible in the Fairbanks area. Clearing of vegetation by human activity, forest fires or climate change can also upset the delicate stability of permafrost, leaving mounds and ponds as irregular pocks on the surface. Such chaotic pitted and collapsed ground, visible on almost every cleared homestead, is called thermokarst. Of Alaska's 3 million lakes, most are shallow and result from the melting of ground ice; not surprisingly, they are known as thaw lakes.

## The Shedding Slopes

Let's assume that you have just driven northeast to Twelvemile Summit, well above treeline at Mile 86 on the Steese Highway. As you look across the broad mountain slopes, you may see small subtle steps that are a foot or so high near the bases of hills. In some places they overlap like shingles or siding on a house. What you see are slopes alive with motion, where the thin skin of surface debris is gliding down at a rate of inches per year. This happens because of two processes that are strongly influenced by our climate: solifluction (soil flow) and frost creep.

When you revisit a familiar hillside, the scene may look unchanged, but you might be surprised to learn that thousands of tons of material have moved down-slope since you last saw it. Your surprise results from a simple limitation of perspective, for if the whole surface is moving how can you see only part of it move? You may be moving along with it. Some forests glide down on top of the shedding skin while others, rooted deeper, remain in place while a stream of materials moves slowly by like people past a phone booth.

## Frost Action on Slopes

Solifluction Slopes

Smooth Slopes

Tors

Solifluction Lobes

Blockfield

Frost-Rived Blocks

Bedrock

*The top photo shows rock ridges midway between Fairbanks and Fort Yukon that are covered with a nearly continuous layer of cold, wet, fine-grained rock waste. The rock waste oozes downhill over the permafrost as a solifluction layer and glides past resistant rock spires called tors. The entire hillside has been lowered at least 30 feet, the height of most tors. The lower photo shows a hilltop along the northern edge of the Yukon Flats that is mantled with large blocks of rock. The bedrock is pried apart along fractures by ice, forming large blocks that creep downhill during freezing and thawing of the ground. (Both courtesy of Robert Thorson)*

One important factor in this process is frost creep, the progressive ratchetlike movement of particles downslope as the ground freezes and thaws. When it freezes, any grain of sand or rock is lifted slightly toward the cooling surface. But when it thaws, particles move downward under the influence of gravity. Thus, for any hillside there is a slight downslope movement for almost every particle during each freeze-thaw cycle.

The second cause of moving hillsides is solifluction, an extremely common phenomenon in cold climates. Wherever permafrost occurs, it forms an underground barrier through which water cannot percolate. As ground above the permafrost becomes saturated, it turns into a mush of rock waste and soil that slowly oozes downslope. Solifluction and frost creep occur on nearly every slope in the Interior and are the dominant means of shedding debris down into stream valleys. The effects are everywhere, but can best be seen near alpine summits, where forest does not obscure the results.

If solifluction and frost creep take place uniformly, they produce broad, smooth, unforested hillsides called solifluction sheets. Near a valley's floor, where the slopes become gentler, the rate of flow diminishes. This causes the sheet to pile up on itself, so it thickens and bulges upward, forming shinglelike terraces as it flows over immobile zones like the tracks of a tank. Solifluction lobes at Twelvemile Summit, recognized by their spatulate shapes, occur where saturated rock waste in one place moves more quickly than in the areas on either side. In some areas, lobes are so common that whole slopes of house-sized blocks testify to the strong but patient delivery of rock materials to streams by frost creep and solifluction working together.

Isolated pinnacles of rock standing tens of feet above ridge crests are called tors. Excellent examples can be seen on any flight from Fairbanks to Fort Yukon. The Granite Tors, a common hike destination near Mile 50 of Chena Hot Springs Road, are examples of this landform. Tors have not been shoved above the remainder of the slope, nor have they always been there. They are simply remnants of the original rock that have withstood the powers of erosion better than the rocks surrounding them. When you see a high tor, try to visualize the whole slope originally being that high; you can then appreciate how fast the landscape is changing.

We can often find places with even more dramatic evidence of downslope movement. One such movement is the rockfall, a violent avalanche from a fragmented cliff. Rockfalls are rarely seen in the Interior, but large blocky piles of rubble below cliffs afford evidence they do occur. Massive earth-flows are a more common form of dramatic slope movement. They are often many acres in size and glide slowly down weak valley walls like a sleigh, with forest and animals oblivious to the fact they are moving. Many good examples can be seen in the Dietrich Valley, along the Dalton Highway (North Slope Haul Road) through the southern Brooks Range. They look like unhealed scars with tipped trees.

A third and more common type of slope movement is called talus or scree. As you drive through any steep canyon, such as the Delta or Nenana canyons, you will see large cone-shaped piles of rock fragments on the slopes below cliff faces; each piece was rived from the cliff by frost and tumbled to the growing

## Rock Avalanche

*When valley walls in weak rock are too steep, large portions of the slope can fracture and tumble violently into the valley bottom as an avalanche of house-sized blocks. This avalanche deposit is in an unnamed glacial valley in the southern Brooks Range. (Courtesy of Robert Thorson)*

pile. Sometimes you can hear the clink and crash of continued talus growth. The looseness of rubble on such talus slopes indicates how fast it is accumulating, for stabilization has had no chance to occur.

Snowbanks exert their own special effects on the interior landscape. Shaded areas with late-lying snow have especially vigorous frost action, because the slush helps saturate the rock before freezing and aids in moving the debris as a slurry of rock mud. Because snowbanks create intensified erosion, they countersink themselves into hillsides, forming broad hollows which hold even more snow to keep the process going. A snowbank hollow cannot carve itself too deeply into a hillside, because it almost always needs some slope so the debris will move out rather than accumulate. Consequently, the hollow tends to broaden rather than deepen in the hill below a shaded notch. Prolonged expansion of a snowbank hollow forms a nearly flat, gently sloping surface called a cryoplanation terrace. Terraces visible at Wickersham Dome, 27 miles northwest of Fairbanks, look as if someone neatly carved the hillside into a series of giant steps.

# River Sculpture

*The Birth of Valleys.* When you watch the Tanana or the Yukon river, you cannot help but be impressed by their awesome power, but you might forget that each begins as a tiny rivulet on a hillside. A traveler is never more than

## An Evolving Valley

*This view of the outer canyon of the Teklanika River, flowing toward the reader, shows several stages in the evolution of this valley. The river must have been here before the hills were raised or the canyon would not have been able to cut through them. The broad, flat bench in the center is an ancient valley floor that the river carved slowly during a time of stability. The slopes of the hills adjusted themselves to this ancient river level. The final stage of valley evolution occurred when the river cut a deep inner canyon, leaving the old valley floor as a terrace, and causing the slopes to become unstable as seen by the fresh rubble on the slope to the left. (Courtesy of Robert Thorson)*

a mile or so from any stream, a single part of the delicate network of channels that extends over the entire land. The patterns of streams are delightfully symmetrical, arranged in such a way as to convey water off the landscape with maximum efficiency. Small gullies merge into tributaries of increasing size which finally join forces to form mighty rivers as the land sheds itself of falling rain and melting snow.

In areas where rocks are nearly the same, stream valleys form regular patterns of channel division like the veins of a leaf. In areas of sheared and tilted rocks, streams will exploit the weaker zones. As this occurs, they arrange themselves in a pattern controlled by the structure of the underlying bedrock. Goldstream and Chatanika valleys run in the same direction because they follow parallel breaks in the rocky crust.

Erosion of landscapes is a by-product of the perpetual hydrologic cycle, moving sediments out and giving them a free downhill ride to the sea. Once delivered to the stream channel by slope processes, rock particles are moved in different ways. Dissolved rock travels in solution as invisible molecules. Clay and silt travel as tiny grains held in suspension by the turbulence of even the smoothest flowing river. The Tanana and Yukon are painted with murky grays and browns by the particles suspended in their waters. Coarse fragments roll along the bottom in fits and starts between flood episodes and become rounded as they travel.

Streams change in predictable ways along their courses. The amount of water and its rate of flow increase with the merging of tributaries. A tumbling mountain stream does not carry water downhill as fast as the channel of a major river. It just looks that way because of the turbulence.

Small water courses in the Interior vary between two extremes. Frothy, turbulent, clear-water streams in steep-walled valleys are actively carving their channels. Rock debris from the slopes provides the tools for cutting, which deepens the channel, which increases the slope, which increases the rate of slope processes, and on and on. A V-shaped stream like upper Engineer Creek, northeast of Fairbanks, reflects a balance between movement of hillside debris and valley cutting, for if slope debris were shed too slowly the stream would cut itself a narrow notch like a box canyon.

At the other extreme, slope processes can overwhelm the water's ability to remove materials delivered to it. The results are broad, choked valleys like the upper Chatanika, which is mired in its own muck. The original V-shaped canyon can become covered in rubble, forming a wide, flaring, poorly drained valley in which the stream may be only several feet below the drainage divides. Changes in climate, capture of one tributary by another, or episodes of mountain building can cause streams to alternate from one type to the other, giving rise to our present diversity in stream-cut landscapes.

Why do canyons exist anyway? Let's imagine that a river like the Nenana is flowing over low country and the Alaska Range gradually rises across its path. If the river's cutting can keep pace with the rate of the land's rising, a canyon will be born. Some geologists think Nenana Canyon formed this way. Now let's visualize that the ancient Teklanika River is flowing northward over a broad gravelly plain that covers resistant rock at depth. If the gravel is slowly removed

## Contrasting Rivers

**Braided River — Upper Tanana**

Gravel Bar

Water Flow Path

Gravel Bar

**Meandering River — Lower Porcupine**

Point Bar

Oxbow Lake

Cut Bank

Point Bar

Cut Bank

Flood Channel

Frozen Floodplain

Slough

Channel Scars

*The upper Tanana (braided) and the lower Porcupine (meandering) are good examples of contrasting Alaskan rivers. Braided rivers have many temporary channels which merge and diverge over broad gravel floodplains. Meandering rivers have a single sinuous channel, which migrates back and forth across silty, sandy and commonly frozen floodplains. (Both courtesy of Robert Thorson)* and the river is let down to carve away the harder rocks, a different kind of canyon will be formed; the canyon may look the same, but its origin is different. On your next bus trip into Denali Park, look at the outer canyons of the Teklanika and Toklat rivers and try to imagine the river flowing thousands of feet higher, slowly descending through the present notches in the outer range.

A canyon such as that on the Porcupine River may have formed when vast amounts of water spilled over ridges that held in lakes. A canyon may also be formed by a drop in the level to which a stream flows. For example, if the Bering Sea suddenly dropped, the Yukon and Kuskokwim rivers would carve narrow notches below the continent's present edge; or if the Tanana River suddenly lowered, the same would happen to the Chena. Though most canyons formed quite rapidly, they remain for a long time as some of our most scenic landforms.

*Changing Patterns.* The channel patterns of large rivers also vary between two extremes. The meandering type consists of a sinuous channel that migrates, snakelike, over its floodplain. Steep banks, where the river is aggressively cutting its channel, stand opposite the broad sand or gravel bars where it is depositing debris or sediments. Take a riverboat downstream from Fairbanks along the meandering Tanana and you will notice high cut banks where trees are being tipped into the channel. But on the opposite side you will see gravel bars built from debris eroded from the last cut bank you passed upstream. Meandering rivers form where large amounts of fine sediment are being carried or where the banks are relatively stable.

Braided rivers usually occur where the channels have a steeper grade and where an abundance of pebble- and cobble-sized materials is available for transport. This causes the river to spread itself out into a lacelike sheet of interconnected shallow channels like braids in a girl's hair. The Delta River, viewed anywhere along its length, is an excellent example. Fairbanks is located where the Tanana River changes from a meandering to a braided river. The founder of Fairbanks, Capt. E.T. Barnette, could navigate his steamboat up the sinuous meandering channels of the Tanana as far as Fairbanks, but it became stuck in the shallow braided channels which begin at that point. Perhaps Fairbanks would be located near Manley Hot Springs or Tok if Barnette had journeyed upriver in a different geological era.

The floodplain — that broad, scoured flat through which the channel flows — is actually part of the river. Perhaps it is inundated only once a year or even once every hundred years, but it still belongs to the stream. During breakup, ice jams plug the channels, often covering large portions of the floodplain and occasionally diverting channels to new areas.

Terraces form when the river cuts down below a former floodplain. This usually happens when less debris is fed into the river, allowing the channel to incise itself, but it would also occur if the land were suddenly elevated or if sea level abruptly dropped. The Parks Highway travels along many different terraces through the first 30 miles of the Nenana Valley. Spectacular examples, resembling giant gravelly benches, can be seen by looking across the valley. These terraces were formed as past glacial oscillations changed the supply of sediment to the Nenana River.

*Gravelly Fans.* Alluvial fans are broad, fan-shaped slopes of sand and gravel

## Alluvial Fan

*Mountain streams, such as this one in Denali National Park, carry large amounts of coarse gravel in a constricted channel. When these streams enter lowlands, they dump their gravel loads in channels that are forever shifting back and forth across the fan-shaped landform called an alluvial fan. (Courtesy of Robert Thorson)*

left by rivers and streams. You can find them where rivers descend from highlands and drop their heavy loads at the mountain front, or near the mouths of large tributaries within mountain valleys, where smaller streams produce sediment at a faster rate than the master stream can remove it. Beautiful examples of fans can be seen along the Alaska Highway near Kluane Lake in Yukon Territory and at the mouths of most tributaries in mountain valleys. You may have seen small ones below gullies at construction sites. The entire vicinity of Tok — for 10 miles in all directions — is built on one enormous alluvial fan that drained former ice sheets south of the Alaska Range.

Streams and rivers usually flow through mountains in confined channels that are steep enough to carry the sediment that runs into them. At the mountain front, however, the slope suddenly decreases or the channel is unconfined, so the water spreads out, loses its velocity and drops its load. Because any channel is likely to become quickly plugged with debris, the river is diverted to the left or right, where a new channel is formed and plugged again. Throughout thousands of years, a broad alluvial fan is built that radiates outward from the valley mouth.

Alluvial fans are thickest and coarsest at their points of origin. Continued deposition in this fashion can build great wedges of gravel outward along the fronts of entire mountain ranges. These wedges join together and with time they are gradually filling the great valleys of the Interior, those of the Tanana, Kuskokwim and Yukon rivers.

# Ice on the Rocks

Ribbons of ice descend into the Interior from the mountains of the Brooks and the Alaska ranges. At present there are no glaciers in the rolling highlands of the Interior, but they were once widely distributed above elevations of 5,000 feet; they would reform in only dozens of centuries if the snow line dropped a little. Glaciers form only in frigid areas where more snow falls each year than melts, resulting in a gradual buildup that converts snow to pure ice through compaction and refreezing. They flow down-valley because ice behaves almost like putty under its own great weight, and they slide along their beds like great icy toboggans. In the upper reaches of a glacier more snow falls than melts, whereas in its lower reaches of clear, banded, striped and debris-covered ice, the reverse is true. The position of a glacier's snout is controlled by the balance between downward flow of ice from its upper reaches and rate of melting at its lower end. In snowy, cold decades, glaciers advance like inexorable white bulldozers. During warm periods they waste away and they run out of fuel. Occasionally they surge and move hundreds of feet per day, only to stagnate in place until the snow builds up again.

Drive down the Richardson Highway to Black Rapids Glacier overlook. Before you lies a ribbon of ice that snakes its way down from Mount Hayes. The snout is covered with rocky mud and stripes of mud trend gracefully up the valley. The glacier not only occupies this valley, it carved it! In fact, the Delta Valley, where you stand, was carved by an even bigger glacier. The turbid gray color of the river in the foreground is caused by high concentrations of silt and clay, called glacial flour, which were milled from the mountains by ice abrasion.

Glaciers are the sharpest and fastest means of sculpting magnificent scenery, because they can rapidly carve deep gashes in otherwise gentle valleys, create broad troughs by persistent grinding, form innumerable lakes by scouring and deposition, and generate broad, braided streams that drain from them. Glaciers erode by grinding their beds like sandpaper and by plucking out large rocky blocks which they deposit far off as isolated boulders called erratics. This debris is carried within and on the ice, like bales of hay moving down a conveyor belt. The gray, rocky ridges in front of Black Rapids Glacier are called moraines. These moraines were deposited by the glacier and reveal that as little as 50 years ago, the glacier's front stood well beyond its present limit. The ground on which you stand is also a moraine, for only several thousand years ago Black Rapids Glacier surged across where the trans-Alaska pipeline and Richardson Highway are today. At normal speeds, Alaska valley glaciers could cover a football field in a year; but Black Rapids, a surging glacier, advances at many times that rate in fits and starts.

Farther down-valley near Donnelly Dome, you see a broad, hilly area dotted with lakes and scattered with piles of windswept gravel. This area formed when the gravel-covered glacier of the last Ice Age stagnated and gradually disappeared. To the north, the highway runs straight as an arrow over the old river bed that drained the ancient dying glacier. The modern Delta River has cut deep below its old course, leaving the terrace on which the highway is built.

A common misconception is that glaciers literally retreat uphill. This cannot

## Glacier Growth

*Glaciers develop when snow accumulates faster than it can melt. At least four annual snow layers are visible in giant snow blocks, called seracs, in the top photo. When snow becomes too thick in the upper parts of a glacier, it compacts into ice and flows slowly down-valley where it melts (bottom photo). Rock debris eroded by the ice is gradually exposed as lateral and medial moraines. (Top, Bradford Washburn; bottom, courtesy of Robert Thorson)*

happen because gravity cannot reverse its course; however the terminus or snout of a glacier can withdraw while the ice is forever moving forward.

In the highland country of the Interior, glaciers formed, accomplished their work, disappeared and reformed at least four times in the past. Glacial episodes here were in phase with global ice ages that regularly alternated with warm intervals over tens of thousands of years. Mounts Harper and Prindle in the Yukon-Tanana Upland were centers of accumulation, where glaciers radiated from the summits like spokes from a wheel. The Beaver Mountains near McGrath and the Kokrine Hills and Ray Mountains near the Koyukuk River, were also local centers of repeated glaciation. The area near Fairbanks was apparently never glaciated, because the surrounding hills were not high enough to support ice fields. The Fairbanks area looks different from the foothills of the Alaska Range largely because it was never carved by ice.

*Gusty Winds.* The effects of wind on the landscapes near Fairbanks cannot be missed. The yellow silt, called loess, that mantles the bedrock hills was blown upward from gravelly meltwater rivers of the Tanana Valley as billowing clouds of dust. At Gold Hill, between Fairbanks and Ester, more than 150 feet of loess is visible. No matter how dusty it was, the silt probably did not accumulate fast enough to suffocate the ancient vegetation. In fact, these plants probably helped to anchor the soil, allowing such great thicknesses to pile up. This silt blanket thins northward from the edge of the Yukon-Tanana Upland, indicating that its source was to the south. Other extensive loess deposits are found along the Yukon, Kobuk and Kuskokwim rivers.

Once deposited, the silt was washed down-slope, overloading the valleys with muck and transforming them from gravel streams cutting bedrock to quiet meandering courses through boggy, plugged valleys. Goldstream Valley is an excellent example of such a muck-choked stream. The muck froze as it accumulated, preserving within it the remains of a wide variety of animals and plants, many of them now extinct. Loess burial of the hills and valleys near Fairbanks smoothed the landscape to its present curvature, healing many of the more jagged scars from previous erosion.

Gusty winds moving across the dry meltwater channels also blew up clouds of sand and heaped them into great dunes that were common near ancient glacier-fed rivers. At one time these areas were inland sand seas not unlike the Sahara Desert. In the lake-dotted terrain of the Nenana and Delta valleys, winds were locally so strong that even the coarsest sand was blown away. Left in its place was a litter of stones, sculpted into weird shapes and polished by the abrasive sand. These faceted gemlike stones, called ventifacts, are preserved as evidence of the tremendous winds that drifted over the land in the not-too-distant past. Jack Warren Road near Delta Junction is an excellent place to start a ventifact collection.

*A Myriad of Lakes.* Alaska is speckled with several million lakes that formed by many different processes. Most interior lowland lakes formed when ice lenses melted under the hot summer sun. The thousands of lakes you can see on a plane trip toward Lake Minchumina are mostly irregular and less than 20 feet deep. In fact, moose tracks are visible on the bottoms of many. Some of these lakes are black, while others are blue. In the turbid, azure lakes, sediment is

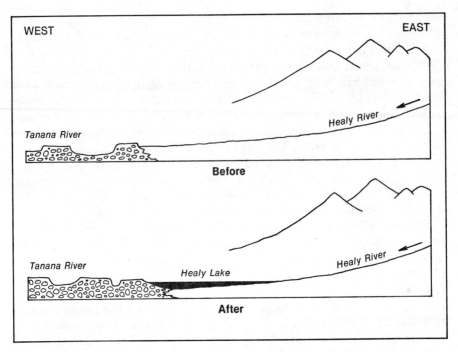

*Healy Lake formed when the Tanana River blocked the mouth of its tributary, the Healy River. The Tanana carries much more sediment than all of its tributaries to the north. Consequently, when the Tanana builds up its floodplain, it dams the mouths of tributaries such as the Healy River, creating a broad, shallow lake.*

swirling around as parts of the lake floor collapse beneath your view. Thaw lakes form because any surface puddle absorbs more heat than the nearby frozen, tussock-covered silt. Ponds grow until they drain or stabilize and fill with sediment. Once the material freezes again, a new cycle can begin and repeat itself with endless variations. The position and size of a lake may change each time, but the character of the terrain does not.

Lakes are formed in many less common ways. Let's imagine that you are canoeing down the lower Porcupine River near Fort Yukon. If you take the wrong channel you may end up in a quietwater slough with stabilized banks and no downstream exit. The slough that you have just entered is on its way to becoming a lake, as soon as the upstream end is plugged with river mud. Miles of these long, snakey lakes lie along major rivers of the Interior, reminders of where the channel used to be.

On another trip you might pull into the Harding Lake turnout on the Richardson Highway. Looking eastward, you see a valley carved into the hills and to the west you see the gravelly Tanana River; Harding Lake stands at the junction. This lake, as well as Healy, Quartz and many others in the region, was formed when the Tanana River built itself up higher than the mouths of the valleys which fed into it. This drowned the junction, forming a broad, shallow lake that grew slowly up-valley as the level of the Tanana River rose with gravel. The Chena River runs lazily through Fairbanks because it has such a slight downstream slope. A slight but rapid buildup of the Tanana floodplain gravel would back up the Chena to create a broad, shallow lake below the tops of the city's buildings.

In mountainous areas, more permanent lake basins can be scoured out of bedrock by glaciers. Lake Iliamna and Lake Clark are excellent examples. Deep lakes, like Walker Lake in the southern Brooks Range, formed when piles of glacial rubble dammed valleys through which rivers flowed. In areas like Donnelly Dome, the Yanert Fork region and near Wonder Lake in Denali National Park, there are broad areas with thousands of lakes. These formed where earlier glaciers stagnated in place, burying ice blocks that eventually melted, leaving steep-walled depressions that filled with water and created small lakes in abundance.

All lakes are temporary things in the geological perspective. They are doomed to eventual destruction because their basins collect the local sediment and fill during relatively short spans of time. Most isolated lakes, like Ballaine and Smith lakes near the University of Alaska campus, fill with brown, peaty muck, the remains of plants and algae that fall to the bottom and cannot decompose for lack of oxygen. Lakes in valley bottoms, like Walker and Paxson lakes, fill rapidly as streams build deltas into their inlets. Walker and Chandalar lakes probably measure just one-fourth to one-half of their original length some 13,000 years ago.

Evidence of former lake levels can be seen in abandoned shorelines and piles of beach sediment now long dry. Much of the Copper River Basin was flooded with a gray, glacier-dammed lake during the last Ice Age. What is now Gulkana may have once had giant icebergs floating overhead. Rounded beach gravels well above Harding Lake's present level reveal that it used to be higher. As you read this sentence a lake somewhere in the Interior is probably beginning to drain and another may have started forming, proof of the ephemeral nature of most lakes.

*A Prelude.* You have now been introduced to the many characters in the performance called "Landscape Origins in Interior Alaska," and have learned how the theater was constructed. Stay with me, because the performance is yet to come. Stream erosion, a lead character, is sometimes torrential and sometimes placid. Another lead character, glaciers, grind their way through each act. Frost action and weathering occur in every scene and embellish the roles of other performers. Wind and lakes come and go as they please. All of these characters work together as parts of a machine fueled by gravity that sculpts the scenery we see. Look out your window, or reflect on a past trip and try to see these performers in action. What you see or remember now is the end of the performance, for these characters have been playing their parts since the earth was born. Let's go back to the beginning of time and watch the landscape of the Interior evolve.

# A Journey Through the Past

A good way to begin a tour through interior Alaska's past is to drive the Taylor Highway to Eagle and float a few miles down the Yukon River to any high river bluff. There you camp for the night below some of the oldest known rocks in central Alaska. In the flickering glow of the evening fire, your mind drifts from the present to the ancient rocks behind you and you try to imagine what happened almost a billion years ago when these rocks were being formed.

The rocks behind you were laid down hundreds of feet below the Precambrian sea off the ancient coast of North America, in a time when algal scum was the most advanced life-form. For many thousands of years, layer upon layer of mud and sand gradually settled on the sea floor, forming alternate beds of pebbly, sandy and limy material as the ancient shoreline drifted back and forth. The addition of each mud layer compressed the sediments more and more tightly, until they became rocks. Once solidified, the deeply buried rocks were carried northward as part of North America from a fragmented supercontinent to the south. Ocean basins and mountains of the present time did not yet exist.

During the next 325 million years of the Paleozoic Era, deep layers of sediments continued to accumulate. Again and again, the rocks were lifted from the primordial sea, then sank beneath it. They also acquired the scars of previous landscapes, scratches of ancient glaciers and marks of long-vanished sunny beaches. By this time, the seas were inhabited by strange, jawless bony fish and enormous clams. The sea teemed with shelly life. Dominating the land were forests of tree ferns. To the south, fragments of ocean crust, ancient volcanic islands and slices of other continents were being created independently of one another; they would later be transported northward and jumbled together to create the Alaska we know today.

The next 170 million years encompass the Mesozoic Era, when great reptiles roamed the earth. During this time the major assembly of Alaska took place, as the juggernaut of plate tectonics crunched several mini-continents together into a single mass. The Yukon-Tanana Upland and the rocks northwest of Livengood slid northward against North America as they were carried on top of the Pacific Plate. As the plate slid beneath North America along the edges of long-vanished ocean trenches, the rocks were scraped from its surface to remain as part of Alaska. These terranes were later sheared into fragments and slid along great faults until they reached their present positions, at least 300 miles north of where they formed.

This transformation happened slowly. The events of the last few paragraphs took place during a span of earth history more than 2 million human lifetimes long. There is no way of knowing what Alaska's landscapes looked like then; it is as if we can only see the basement rocks of houses long since gone. But we do know that Alaska's landscape had many features that are still found here today, including mountains, volcanoes, streams and seacoasts.

The ancient core of Alaska, that stable westward part of the continent between the Yukon and Porcupine rivers, was squashed like a bug between the Brooks Range and terranes arriving from the south. The Brooks Range bore the brunt of the collision, as it was sliced up and folded like an accordion during the great compression. By the beginning of Mesozoic times, the marine sediments near Livengood and the strongly metamorphosed rocks beneath Fairbanks had slid northward along great faults to arrive at their present locations. To the west, fragments of North America apparently broke off and mixed with the amalgamating patchwork of terranes. However, the geology of western Alaska is poorly known at best.

The next major event in the evolution of interior Alaska was creation of the Alaska Range. These mountains consist of dozens of individual small terranes that were bulldozed to their present location as southcentral Alaska was added to the mainland; this happened gradually, between late Mesozoic and early Tertiary time. Details of what happened after the rocks arrived are poorly known. But we do know that the Alaska Range was raised south of Fairbanks at least twice in the distant past.

The compressional forces that lifted the Alaska Range also affected the crust to the north. The rocks here were folded, slid and sheared, and they thickened the crust, shortening the original crust into one-half or one-third of its previous length. Two processes occurred: one was like spreading out a deck of cards and then pushing the cards together, sliding them atop one another, shortening and thickening the pile. The other was like pushing a rug against a wall, creating folds as the rug shortens. These are the kinds of subterranean pressures that acted on the earth's crust below the Interior during the arrival of the Alaska Range.

During and after their arrival, rocks of the Alaska Range were slivered into fragments that were later stretched out along the Denali Fault. To the west, large slices of the continent were shoved up, gliding over the rocks of the Interior until reaching their present position. To the east, in the Yukon-Tanana Upland, great masses of molten rock formed, melting their way upward as cores of volcanoes, now represented by the domes around Fairbanks. These intrusions continued during millions of years of slow mountain growth, finally dying out during late Mesozoic time, about 85 million years ago. Rocks next to the granite intrusions were fractured and baked into different forms, like fragmented glazed pottery. During final cooling, cracks and fissures in the surrounding schist were filled with gold-bearing veins of quartz, which are now the source for placer gold.

Initial raising of the Alaska Range is recorded by the gigantic accumulation of tilted rocks known as the Cantwell Formation, which can be seen in the walls of Nenana Canyon between Denali National Park and Cantwell. This formation is thousands of feet thick, consisting of terrestrial sediments laid down in early Tertiary time as rubble from rapidly rising mountains. It represents an earlier version of the Alaska Range, now forever gone from view. Later uplift cemented and sliced the Cantwell Formation into dozens of massive fragments, as new mountains were made from mountain rubble in the endless recycling of earth materials.

The final fragments added to mainland Alaska include the Chugach Range and Prince William Sound area, thick sequences of volcanic and gray sedimentary rocks that first arrived only tens of millions of years ago. Rocks of these mountains look like those forming in the ocean bottom near Japan today. As the descending Pacific Plate crunched slowly into southcentral Alaska, the sediments were scraped off and folded into mountains. Modern movement along the Denali Fault and recent earthquakes in the Interior probably result from continued uplift of these southern ranges.

The surface rocks we now see in the Interior are not the same as the ones that arrived here during ancient geologic times. Thousands of feet — perhaps even miles — of rocks have been stripped off since their arrival; we are looking at the roots of old mountain ranges long since sculpted away. The same holds true for all of Alaska's mountains except the youngest — the Chugach and Aleutian ranges. We can only imagine the many landscape scenes that are now gone forever, just as the present scene will be obliterated with the passage of time.

## The Modern Landscape Takes Shape

*The Story of the Coalfields.* The oldest features which remain on the modern landscape are of the Cenozoic Era, the last 65 million years. Broad interior basins that originated during early and middle Tertiary time began collecting debris from adjacent eroding highlands. Many, such as the upper Yukon Basin, are still receiving sediment today. Perhaps the best known interior basin contains the coalfields near Healy, a sedimentary pile that records the history of the northern Alaska Range. Walk up any gully above Healy Creek to look at the deposits and the story will unfold layer by layer.

At the beginning of the story, the schist bedrock was deeply weathered to thick, clay-rich, golden soil that now forms only in warm, moist climates. For hundreds of feet above the soil, layers of coal up to 40 feet thick alternate with buff-colored sand, gravelly sand and clay. The coal originated in swampy lowlands of a broad alluvial plain, traversed by broad, winding rivers. Composition of the sandy gravels and patterns of the fossilized sandbars reveal that the rivers drained southward through the remnant core of already-eroded mountains. The Alaska Range, as we know it today, clearly did not exist when the coal was being laid down about 30 million years ago, or the rivers could not have drained southward.

Many of the coal seams have self-ignited in the past, making large slow-burning underground fires that baked the underlying clay into a red bricklike pottery called clinker. This explains why local residents call these the "hills of fire." Fossils in the clinker indicate that giant sequoia forests with many deciduous trees, like maples and oaks, covered this area and presumably much of the Interior. It may be difficult for modern residents to imagine Fairbanks having a climate and landscape like northcentral California, yet geological evidence reveals that it did.

At some time during the late Cenozoic, perhaps as recently as 10 million years ago, the style of deposition at Healy changed completely. Lake beds overlying the coal indicate that something — presumably a rising Alaska Range — blocked southward drainage and formed a vast lake where the foothills stand today. Thick volcanic ash beds in lake sediments indicate that explosive eruptions accompanied this final uplift.

The lake beds are capped by great thicknesses of gravel laid down by alluvial fans and rivers that shed debris northward. These rusty-stained gravels reveal that the rising Alaska Range had become high enough to reverse the southward drainage that formed the underlying coal beds. As it lifted this final time, the coal beds were fractured and bent into gently dipping folds now visible along the highway on the east side of the Nenana Valley. The older basement rocks on which they rest were locally thrust upward to stand as resistant outer hills of schist such as Rex Dome. Young intrusions like Sugarloaf Mountain, a black spine surrounded by acres of white rubble, are the necks of old volcanoes whose outer slopes have eroded away. Sugarloaf is visible to southbound travelers about four miles east of Nenana Gorge. Rock fractures surrounding these old volcanoes were pumped full of molten rock, which crystallized as dark veins (dikes) of basalt that appear to hold the schist together like reinforcement rods in concrete. Several of these black dikes, about 10 feet thick, can be seen close up as you travel through Nenana Gorge near Windy Bridge. Above all of these intrusions and up-thrusted basement rocks, the youngest gravels were tipped northward as the range front rose like a giant wedge, creating the modern valleys through which glaciers could later descend.

*Ancient Ice Sheets.* Glaciation of the Alaska Range began sometime during late Teritiary time, earlier than 2 million years ago. Glaciation here was more recent than in areas farther south, such as the Wrangell Mountains and the Yakutat area, where large glaciers developed more than 10 million years ago. As you wander the foothills between the Toklat and Delta rivers, you will see

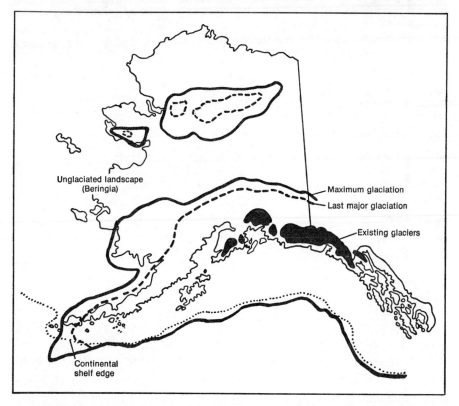

Unglaciated landscape
(Beringia)

Maximum glaciation

Last major glaciation

Existing glaciers

Continental
shelf edge

*Glaciers today are small in comparison to their former size. The shaded areas show modern glaciers, the dashed line shows the extent of ice at the peak of the last Ice Age, and the solid line indicates the maximum extent of glaciers at any time in the past. Except for small, isolated glaciated regions in central Alaska (not shown), the Interior and exposed western continental shelf were never covered by glaciers, and thus provided suitable habitat for plants, animals and possibly humans. (Diagram modified from one prepared by T.D. Hamilton, 1982.)*

## Rock Jointing

*This aerial depicts a bedrock valley wall that is now breaking apart into joints. Several thousand years ago this area was a smoothly scoured rock hillside. Removal of rock and ice during and after glaciation caused the hillside to expand slightly outward, fracturing the rock into millions of blocks which average about three feet across. (Courtesy of Robert Thorson)*

automobile-sized blocks of granite protruding from the tundra. These boulders, derived from the youngest Tertiary gravels, could have been carried here only by the ancient ice; rivers are simply not capable of moving such large boulders that far. These early glaciers were hundreds of times larger than the modern ones and much bigger than those of the last great Ice Age about 20,000 years ago. Broad glacial lobes may have extended over the area of modern foothills to within 20 miles of Nenana. Why were these ancient glaciers big enough to rim the southern Interior in a wall of white? Perhaps it used to snow more, or perhaps the Alaska Range was higher or broader at that time. We simply don't know.

To the north in the late Tertiary, the Brooks Range was also thickly mantled with ice caps, and the rolling hills and low mountains of the Interior may have been covered as well. Again these extensive northern glaciers were perhaps caused by larger mountain ranges or heavier snowfall in a wetter climate. The Arctic Ocean may not have been covered with pack ice until about a million years ago, so it could have supplied moisture to the Brooks Range as the open Pacific does to the Chugach and Wrangell mountains today.

*The Interior Highlands.* The highlands that dominate the Interior between the Alaska and Brooks ranges began taking on their present form during the last 10 million years. During this time thousands of feet of rocks were stripped from the slopes. Lofty mountains of an earlier age north of Fairbanks have been reduced to their present appearance by a temporary victory of erosion over tectonism.

We might ask ourselves why, if erosion has been going on so long, is the Interior still so rugged? Why hasn't it been weathered down to a low, rolling plain? There are several possible explanations. Perhaps the original mountains were very high and erosion will ultimately reduce them to a flat lowland; we may simply be looking at a middle stage in their destruction. It is also possible that the highlands are being maintained in their present form; removal of rocks by erosion may be causing the landscape to rise, creating a true equilibrium. A final possibility is that modern tectonic forces continue to bulge the Interior slowly upward over broad areas, as streams do their best to break down the rising hills.

*The Great Rivers.* The three great rivers of interior Alaska, the Yukon, Tanana and Porcupine, changed drastically as the landscape evolved toward its present form. The Yukon Flats, a triangle-shaped basin between the settlements of Venetie, Circle and Stevens Village, is underlain by a thick sequence of Tertiary clay. Apparently the whole basin was warped downward by tectonic forces, creating an enormous muddy lake that existed until the outlet near Rampart eroded deeply enough to drain it. The ancient Yukon River was probably different from the river we know today. Geologic studies in southern Yukon Territory hint that the ancestral river drained southward to the Gulf of Alaska during Tertiary time. Strong mountain building along the coast may have defeated this southern drainage, so the river was forced to shift its course toward the northwest, where it sliced its present narrow canyon between the Canadian border and Circle.

If this scenario is true, the Interior acquired the Yukon at the expense of southeastern Alaska. Recently some politicians have suggested routing the Yukon southward to the Lower 48, attempting another theft of Yukon waters. Tributaries such as the Charley and Fortymile rivers, adjacent to the Yukon Canyon, gradually lengthened themselves southward to the Alaska Range and eastward into Yukon Territory. High terraces carved above the canyon have been gradually warped by mountain-building forces, but these have not been enough to divert the Yukon.

The Tanana River has also changed greatly during the last several million years. The upper river may have drained southward through the ancestral Alaska Range before its most recent uplift. Once blocked, it must have been diverted westward around the growing mountains and against wedges of alluvium that spread into the great Tanana-Kuskokwim flats. The abrupt edge of the Alaska Range foothills between the McKinley and Delta rivers marks the southern rim of this newly formed basin.

The land south of Fairbanks and Nenana used to be a range of low mountains, only slightly lower than nearby ridges along the Parks Highway. The mountains are still there, but now entombed by several thousand feet of gray gravel, shed northward from the rising range to the south. An oil well at Nenana penetrated more than 2,000 feet of gravel, indicating how much sediment covers this ancient landscape. Wood River Buttes and Japan Hills are the highest summits of the mountains buried below; they simply protrude above the gravel

## Drainage Basins

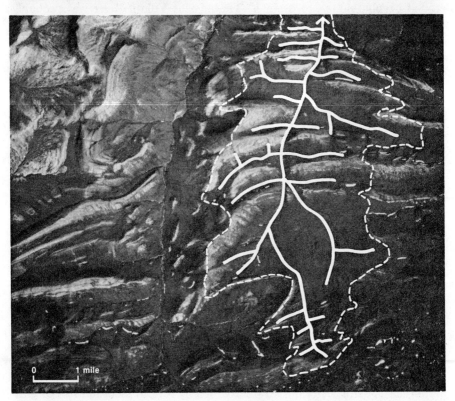

*As water drains off the landscape, it is carried away by a system of tributaries that merge into larger channels to form a drainage basin. The top aerial of the Yukon-Tanana Upland shows the dentritic (leaflike) pattern that develops when surface rocks are uniform in strength. The bottom photo of the northern Brooks Range shows a more irregularly shaped basin in which the valleys develop along belts of weak rock. (Both courtesy of Robert Thorson)*

fill. As gravel built out toward the north, it pushed the Tanana River hard against the crystalline upland, cutting spectacular cliffs at river level such as Shaw Creek Bluff. If we consider the landforms beneath the surface, these cliffs are really notches high on the flanks of buried hills. The southern edge of the Yukon-Tanana Upland is destined to migrate northward as more and more gravel is dumped into the basin.

East of the Delta River, the Tanana cut into an elongated depression between the Yukon-Tanana Upland and the Alaska Range, doubling its length as it extended toward Canada. The south-flowing tributaries of the upper Tanana are now short, cascading drainages which lengthen toward the Yukon. With each passing year, more and more Yukon water is diverted into the Tanana, which perhaps will eventually cut right into the upper Yukon drainage. If this happens, the upper Yukon will become a tributary of the Tanana; but none of us will be around to see it.

The Tanana River also extended itself southward during the last few million years. Two of its larger tributaries, the Delta and Nenana rivers, begin as glacial meltwater south of the Alaska Range and flow northward directly through the range to join the Tanana. How could these rivers have lengthened themselves directly through the Alaska Range? The answer involves the ancient ice sheets, which were biggest on the southern side of the range, where Pacific moisture nourished them. Lobes of ice drained northward from these ice fields through low spots in the range, carving deep valleys across its backbone. When the glaciers disappeared, the Delta and Nenana rivers continued to follow this northward course.

The Porcupine River is a grand example of a recent theft of Canadian waters. About 30,000 years ago the Porcupine was a small, sluggish stream that flowed from the Canadian border to the Coleen River, which drains from the southern Brooks Range. At this time large networks of streams in central and northern Yukon Territory ran into the Mackenzie River. As the great ice caps of central Canada spread westward they blocked the Mackenzie drainage, impounding lakes in Yukon Territory. The lakes rose until they spilled westward into Alaska across the lowest divide, quickly carving narrow Porcupine Canyon with their heavy flood of water. The canyon was cut so deeply that when the ice cap melted, drainage from the Canadian side was permanently diverted through Alaska. Compared to its beginning as an Alaskan stream, the Porcupine has now increased its water volume more than fivefold; its canyon is a scenic by-product of this piracy.

*A Short Review.* You now have a sense of the larger elements of landscape evolution that occurred in the Interior during Tertiary time. The land buckled with tectonic forces, basins and ancient lakes were created and filled, major rivers were rerouted and ancient ice sheets oscillated back and forth in time. Most changes proceeded gradually, but some were punctuated by violent, perhaps even catastrophic, events. During these major changes in landscape evolution, erosion by countless streams proceeded inexorably, lowering the masses of rock that used to be high mountains. Streams shifted their positions as they cut downward, creating hills of similar appearance in different places at different times.

## Finishing Touches

*The Pleistocene Ice Age.* We have now reviewed the long term evolution of the landscape through the end of Tertiary time, about 2 million years ago. As we move forward to the Pleistocene Epoch, we witness a time of profound global climatic changes that caused cyclic expansions of ice sheets and mountain glacier systems. Herds of woolly mammoths, giant bison and solitary saber-toothed cats traversed the scene. Existing glaciers in the Brooks and Alaska ranges expanded to great proportions, then shrank back during milder interglacial phases like the one we are experiencing today. Glaciers also radiated outward from central summits of the Interior's highlands, but these were small in comparison to those of the bordering ranges.

Evidence of at least four Pleistocene cycles of glacier growth and wastage is preserved in landforms and sediments throughout the highlands. Steep, V-shaped valleys were carved to broad, U-shaped troughs by the grinding, scratching ice. Great amphitheaters called cirques were hewn from mountain peaks at the valley heads. Piles of glacial rubble were dumped at the snouts of stabilized glaciers, forming cross-valley embankments that dammed rivers and created narrow lakes. Glaciers also freshened the topography by steepening slopes and stripping the valleys of accumulated rubble.

Large glaciers sprawled northward from the Alaska Range toward the Yukon-Tanana Upland, but never quite reached it. In most valleys, glaciers only poked into the foothill belt, but in the Delta Valley ice spilled forward from the mountain front as a large rounded lobe on the Tanana Flats. Huge fanlike networks of bare gravelly channels issued from the melting snouts of hundreds of glaciers. Fluctuations in melting intermittently flooded the channels with turbid gray water, leaving sandy silt to dry in the sun and the wind. Dense, chilled air above the ice rushed persistently down-glacier as a river of air that warmed and became drier during its descent.

This combination of cold winds blowing over drying river beds set the stage for new possibilities of scenery. The gusting winds swirled up the dirt and separated it into sand that bounced along the ground and silt that billowed great distances as clouds of dust. Moraines and low-lying hills beyond the reach of streams were abraded by moving sand sheets in windstorms that must have blackened the air. Sand polishing also left behind shiny pavements of gravel. Sand also accumulated in large tracts of shifting dunes that migrated downwind in beautiful crescents and elongated shapes, marching steadily over everything in their paths. In many areas a vista from horizon to horizon would reveal nothing but heaps of grayish-brown sand.

These ice-age sand dunes still cover large areas of Alaska's Interior. The first hill south of Nenana on the Parks Highway is a fossil dune, one of millions of streamlined ridges between Nenana and Lake Minchumina that were formed between about 25,000 and 12,000 years ago. The upper Tanana is choked with them as well. Active dunes along the Kobuk and Koyukuk rivers look like the sands of great deserts; they are but tiny remnants of the much larger Pleistocene dune fields. If you drive up the Taylor Highway from Tetlin Junction, you will see countless patches of gray sand exposed in road cuts over the first 10 miles.

The road winds through these ancient crescent dunes which now cloak the hills in a mantle of gray. Sometimes dunes are hard to see because they are buried under blankets of loess, which settled as the ancient winds died down. Low-lying areas between them are also commonly filled with muck and peat, obscuring the dunes even more. Fossil dunes are much more common than you might expect because we usually don't think of anywhere in Alaska as ever having been so dry.

*Filled Valleys.* Glacially milled silt from the Tanana Valley was blown northward as clouds of dust. Wherever the hills slowed the winds, the silt rained down as a gentle shower of fine dust. Gradually, accumulations from many dust storms built up as loess, now exposed as golden brown road cuts on hillsides near Fairbanks.

Rain and melting snow then washed much of the loess into valley bottoms and built small alluvial fans at the bases of gullies. Creeping solifluction lobes also helped to move the silt down what were then unforested slopes. We know that the muck deposits accumulated and froze rapidly; otherwise they would not contain the partially decomposed remains of extinct plants and animals. Because the Interior was probably drier during glacial intervals, stream flows may have been too small to carry away silt eroding into the valleys. Perhaps this explains why almost all of the small valleys near Fairbanks are filled with frozen muck, an unwanted burden to those who mine gold.

Many of the creeks around Fairbanks are pitifully small compared to the size of the valleys they drain. Coarse stream gravel, like that visible in the mine tailings near Fox, could hardly have been carried by the streams now placidly flowing over the silty muck. This suggests that at some earlier and perhaps wetter time, these creeks must have been larger streams, perhaps similar to the modern Chatanika River.

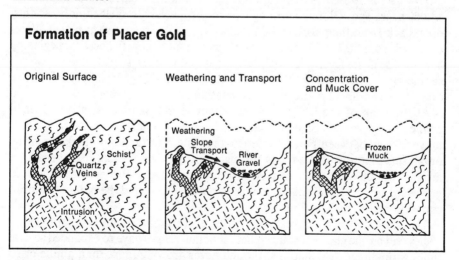

## Formation of Placer Gold

Original Surface

Weathering and Transport

Concentration and Muck Cover

Schist

Quartz Veins

Intrusion

Weathering

Slope Transport

River Gravel

Frozen Muck

*Most placer gold found in the Interior was derived by weathering of schist that contained gold-bearing quartz veins and transport of the gold to valley bottoms. Because gold is virtually indestructible and heavy, it concentrates in stream bottoms and remains. Most placer deposits are covered by a thick mantle of frozen muck which miners must wash away before they can get at the gold-bearing gravel.*

These ancient gravel rivers helped to create the placer gold responsible for the founding of Fairbanks. After weathering on the hillsides, fragments of lode gold moved down-slope where they were broken up by turbulent streams. Dense flakes and nuggets shifted their way down to the base of the gravels to rest on the floors of ancient valleys. We know the gold deposits are old because the bedrock on which they lie is strongly weathered and some of the muck above the gravel is almost half-a-million years old. Luckily, gold is almost chemically inert; otherwise it would have long since weathered and washed away. Gold-bearing gravel also occurs in the rock-cut benches on the valley walls. These benches, now long obscured by muck, record a time when the creeks had not yet completed the job of excavating these familiar valleys.

The thick frozen muck deposits, a burden to mining and construction, contain a wealth of prehistory. Within the fetid, gooey mess exposed in mining cuts are buried forests, old reddish soils and fossil ice wedges; each is a clue to former times. Observing these features, interpreting their significance, ordering the sequences in which they occur and correlating them from region to region permit geologists to reconstruct a picture of the lost ice age worlds.

The vivid white layers and streaks in the muck at Gold Hill and other localities are layers of ash carried to the Interior from distant volcanoes. These layers are composed almost entirely of bubbly fragments of glass, signifying catastrophic eruptions more violent than the 1912 explosion of Mount Katmai. By comparison, the 1980 eruption of Mount St. Helens was a mere puff of cinder. Although the Interior has but a single volcano (Prindle Volcano near the Charley River), multiple layers of ash indicate that periodically the region was inundated by choking falls of white abrasive powder. No one knows where and when these falls originated, but they probably will occur again.

*Toward the Present.* An abrupt change in climate occurred about 13,000 to 14,000 years ago. Global warming caused the glaciers to melt rapidly, so they drew back from their former limits and eventually stagnated in place. Water unlocked from the ice flowed into the rivers and ultimately the oceans, beginning a major rise in sea level. This inundated continental shelves all around the world, submerging great areas that were once dry land. During glacial periods, these areas emerged again as parts of the continents.

At the peak of the last glaciation, about 18,000 years ago, a broad plain connected Alaska and Siberia. Terrestrial plants, animals and perhaps humans moved freely between North America and Asia, but the land blocked marine organisms that now move freely through Bering Strait. Global rise of sea level around 14,000 years ago converted the Bering Land Bridge into a watery graveyard for terrestrial species unable to move and severed the Asian-American connection for the last time.

The last 4,000 or 5,000 years have seen a return to a slightly cooler climate. Valley and cirque glaciers in the higher mountain ranges have re-expanded several times with climatic oscillations, though never growing more than a mile or so from the present limits. Our immediate ancestors probably saw slightly larger glaciers throughout the world as the 20th century began. Glaciers did not form in the rocky hills of the Interior's highlands during this interval, but the summits may have been shrouded in snow throughout the summer.

*The Reasons Why.* As you read this sentence, global climates are changing in ways we do not yet understand. Are we poised on the brink of another Ice Age, or can we expect the climate to change only slightly for decades to come? The record of the past cannot yet give us an answer, in spite of our scientific effort focused on the problem. However, we do know that the average global climate during the past half-million years is similar to the one about 12,000 years ago, when vast ice sheets still covered much of Canada and Scandinavia; in other words, we are living in an exceptionally warm period. This is an ominous thought when we are locked in the grip of a subarctic winter.

The global climate may never be in a true state of equilibrium. Instead it oscillates between the colder and warmer states of glacial and interglacial periods. The causes of ice ages are still unknown, but many factors are becoming increasingly suspect. Among these are the position of our planet in relation to the sun, the amount of heat given off by the sun and the amount of volcanic dust and gas in our atmosphere. Significant climatic changes and renewed glaciation will almost certainly occur in the future, providing that we do not overload the atmosphere with carbon dioxide. Excessive amounts of this gas in the air could maintain the earth in an unstable state of increased warmth, like the planet Venus. Predicting when and how climate will change on the earth is not only a great mystery, but important for long-term human planning. Our present understanding is that the subarctic will warm significantly, the midwestern United States will return to dust bowl conditions and the best prairie farmlands will move northward into the plains of Canada.

## Ancient Visions: A Conclusion

We have traced in detail the origin of interior Alaska's landscapes and the processes that gradually shaped them to modern form. Now it is time to review this great span of geological evolution, compressing millions of years into a few moments. To do this, you might imagine yourself in each of the scenes described in the following paragraphs, perhaps even closing your eyes to visualize the changing primeval terrain near Fairbanks. The scenes are described in chronological order, but each covers a shorter period of time than the one before, like film speeding up.

The scene is dark. The time is latest Precambrian, more than 600 million years ago. None of the animals familiar to you have evolved and no mortal mind is aware of your presence. You are deep beneath the sea, far south of present Alaska, perhaps off the coast of where Vancouver Island will someday stand. A gentle fall of gray sediment gradually buries you up to your neck, locking you into the ocean floor.

In the next scene, perhaps tens of millions of years later, you are buried thousands of feet below the sea floor in a layer of sediment now compacted and cemented into rock.

Several hundred million years later, in Mesozoic time, you are buried even deeper, under pressures so great that the rock is now plastic. It oozes and recrystallizes to shiny mica as it is squashed between slowly colliding continents.

Toward the end of the Mesozoic Era, perhaps 100 million years ago, you are riding northward at inches per year in the basement of a migrating continent. Later you feel the earth quake and rumble, not once but thousands of times as the massive terrane crunches into North America and intermittently slides northwestward along great continental faults. During the collision, majestic mountains are raised above you, only to be tumbled to the sea by rivers that will vanish like the mountains themselves. A flat wedge of continent, scraped off the top of a colliding block, is thrust over the schist that binds you deep within the earth. Rocks of the Alaska Range have now arrived as ancient mountains which will also be destroyed before this scene is finished.

In the next Mesozoic scene, the rocks beneath you melt and move upward as molten blobs of liquid granite. As the intrusions begin to cool they shoot off veins of gold through fractures. In early Tertiary time, before 50 million years ago, the ancient Alaska Range is being eroded down to stubs. You have now arrived at your final destination in the central Interior and the surrounding landscape has been welded permanently to North America. Yet neither the rocks that hold you nor the place where they were formed look as they will appear in the final scene.

You have now watched 95 percent of the film, which began with the oldest rocks in the Interior. If the film had started at the beginning of geological time, 4.6 billion years ago, it would have taken nine times longer to reach this point. By the next scene, early in the Tertiary, interior Alaska had been assembled as a patchwork of large continental fragments. Ancient landscapes have come and gone, and all that remains from these times is the foundation from which the later terrain was carved.

In the next scene, about 40 million years ago, the mountains north of Fairbanks are covered with a warm, temperate forest — permafrost, glaciers and frost action are completely unknown. Streams relentlessly wear away the rocks above you, transforming the tall mountains to subdued highlands. The Yukon and Tanana rivers begin developing the valleys in which they now flow, but much of the Tanana still drains southward to the Pacific. As the rocks overhead are removed, you are lifted upward by buoyant forces within the earth. You are rising closer to the surface on which you will eventually stand.

Sometime between about 15 and 8 million years ago you feel the earthquakes which accompany the final rebirth of the Alaska Range. The rocks around you are fractured by great forces and showered with volcanic ash. Gone forever are the coal swamps to the south, replaced by a large lake into which great fans of stream gravel are dumped by mountain torrents from the young Alaska Range.

In latest Tertiary time, between about 5 and 2 million years ago, you are entombed within rock perhaps 100 feet below the surface. Your earliest human ancestors are prowling the savannahs of Africa. Great walls of glacial ice descend northward from the Alaska Range and southward from the Brooks Range. The landscape above you changes character as tundra covers the surface and frost becomes a dominant force in the deepening chill of glacial times.

Warm and cold periods alternate during the next several million years of Pleistocene time, as you are brought steadily closer to the surface. Instead of the heated depths, you are now surrounded by ice that forms in delicate veins and huge lenses. Solifluction lobes glide down hillsides, snowbanks remain throughout the summer and lacelike networks of stony ground grow and disappear with the seasons. The ground cracks again and again as it shrinks from bitter winter cold.

Nearby, the Chena River is now set in its course as a rushing tributary of the distant Tanana. A great basin forms to the south, as foothills of the Alaska Range are raised. Sheets of gray gravel spill northward and bury the surrounding hills, filling the Tanana Flats. As the gravels continue to shed northward, the rising Tanana is shoved hard against the Yukon-Tanana Upland, carving cliff-like gashes on the hillsides and converting the Chena from frothy to placid waters.

You are now watching the climax of the last Ice Age, about 18,000 years ago. Emerging headfirst from your long burial, you glimpse the last fleeting minutes of our geologic calendar. Your body is still firmly held because these rocks are not yet eroded from the landscape. Glaciers poke through the foothills to the north and south. Howling winds pile sand into dune-covered seas and intermittent dust storms are everywhere. Streams are choked with muck and rich with the bones of extinct beasts. Distant eruptions cloak the midnight sun in darkness, leaving glassy ash that glitters in the morning light.

In the final scene, about 13,000 years ago, you are only knee-deep in rock as you watch the glaciers disappear. Spruce and birch forests migrate slowly northward and ice-rich bogs develop in the sodden flats. The ground at your knees lowers, slowly oozing away as a saturated slurry of rock waste and mud. Frost chisels away at the rock around your ankles and transports the rubble down-slope.

The modern scenery near Fairbanks slowly takes on its present form as you step from the earth . . . and walk on a landscape that will change before you are gone.

## The Final Note

As you look back on the hypothetical images described in this chapter, I hope you realize how ephemeral landscapes are during the enormous span of geological time. They are but temporary glimpses, caught in a ceaseless battle between the creation and destruction of continents. Climates come and go as continents are shifted about and each leaves its imprint on the land. Perhaps you can also imagine future scenes, because the Alaskan landscape is now changing at rates and in ways similar to those of the past. I hope that what you have learned about the geologic evolution of the Interior will help increase your sense of wonder as you travel about our magnificent land.

# Pleistocene Rhymes and Seasonal Reasons

### Natural History of the Interior

#### By R. Dale Guthrie and Mary Lee Guthrie

*Editor's note: R. Dale Guthrie is a professor in the biology department at the University of Alaska, Fairbanks; his wife, Mary Lee, is a self-employed writer.*

## Beginnings

Our little girl, just turning three, is afraid of "monsters" in the winter dark. We try to explain to her that there are no monsters around, just the animals she knows: the small redpolls and chickadees that visit our winter feeder, fluffed up against the cold, and the occasional moose that wanders through the yard, leaving its tracks in the garden, and that they won't hurt her. There is just the snow and the white hares slipping around looking for some willow twigs to eat. There are no monsters now.

We don't tell her that once there were real monsters on our ridge: enormous woolly things moving through the semi-dark, their white tusks gleaming in the moonlight. And there were lions too, larger than any we know today, roaring in the darkness. Surely some little girls who lived on this ridge in that distant time saw the silver reflections of those animals' eyes returning the campfire light. For such little girls there were monsters in the dark and maybe there are deep memories of those times that can't be erased from children's fears. A few unseen monsters may not be altogether bad; they keep one appreciating the safe hearth of home.

We have seen these monsters, not in distant memory, but in thawing banks of mud and muck where they were buried tens of thousands of years ago and frozen before they could completely decompose. On a cloudy day we fought mosquitoes and picked still blood-red meat out of cold muck and washed clean the soft dark and auburn hair that had not seen the light of day for 300 centuries. We would like to tell you about these Pleistocene giants and some of the other animals that lived in the Interior — not so long ago in the earth's time yet barely within imagination's sight — just during the chapter of the earth's story before our own.

The Pleistocene history of interior Alaska is more interesting than that of many other areas. Not only was this an ice-free refuge when much of the north was buried under massive glaciers, but a record of those times is found in numerous fossils, exceptionally well preserved in the thick loess deposits. This fossil record is especially good for the latter part of the Pleistocene and on up to the present, the time span of faunal and floral history we will cover in this chapter.

First we will describe some major features of the late Pleistocene habitat, including the large mammals that once occupied the Interior. We want to share a few stories about how remnants of this time were preserved and later discovered. Also, because most species of large mammals that lived here during the Pleistocene no longer exist, we will discuss ideas about when and why they became extinct.

The present plant and animal communities of interior Alaska are very different from those found here during the Pleistocene, so we will describe those ancient times as a background to better understand the conditions in which we live today. We will then look at the character of interior Alaska's modern environment in a collage: summer fires and their profound effect on the taiga landscape, the 10-year-long, boom and bust cycle of snowshoe hares which so dramatically affects wildlife, the brief summer bloom of insects as typified by mosquitoes, the seasonal richness of salmon runs, and nature's strategies for surviving winters just under the belt of the Arctic Circle.

## The Mammoth Steppe

There are many stories in traditional Athabaskan lore about how things got to be the way they are — how the eagle got its white head, or where the moose came from — and in a way the story we are about to relate is like these. Origin questions are asked in every culture. We all wonder at life...wonder, and try to peer behind the curtain of things as they are now, to see before and beyond the edge of our own view, past even what our ancestors have seen.

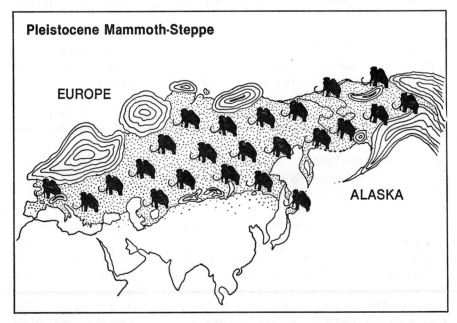

*The mammoth steppe. During most of the Pleistocene epoch, northern portions of Eurasia, including Alaska, were arid with a vegetation pattern different from todays'. Although there were differences in plant and animal species throughout this vast landscape, there were characteristics which connected this entire biome. The woolly mammoth was one of the important large mammal species occupying this habitat. Judging from the anatomy of these mammoths, they were well adapted to the cold and dry northern climate and vegetation.*

It is so difficult to imagine the Interior much different than it is today: vast stretches of spruce forest splotched over a waterlogged landscape. Even in the rocky uplands of the Tanana Hills, one has only to drop down into the slightest swale between crests to feel the squish of tundra muskegs. It is not easy hiking country; you have to pick a route carefully to avoid the soggy areas. Marshlands of the Tanana Flats between Fairbanks and the Alaska Range are a vast bog where water glistens among the thickets and tussocks. Even in the upland forests the understory is clogged with deep green moss, and a summer haze of horsetail rushes rises over punky trees downed decades ago.

But this was quite a different landscape during the last glacial episode, which ended roughly 14,000 to 11,000 years ago. We say roughly because the change was not abrupt. That early landscape was converted to today's through a jerky series of changes lasting thousands of years. From bits and pieces, we are beginning to reconstruct what the Interior may have looked like before glacial conditions disappeared. We'll tell you a little about that evidence later on.

Twenty thousand years ago there were no trees of significance on the landscape of the Interior; low vegetation stretched as far as the eye could see. There was, in fact, a dry grassland extending across interior Alaska westward to northern Asia, and from there it reached farther across Europe to southern England or western France. The plants and animals of this grassland were not all the same from one end to the other, but they were similar in many respects. The Russians call such treeless grasslands *steppes,* and the single mammal most often associated with this steppe was an elephant specially adapted to the Far North — the woolly mammoth. Thus this area has been characterized for easy reference as the "mammoth steppe."

What we now call Alaska was not really a biological part of North America then. Alaska was separated from the southern part of the continent by the coalescence of the Cordilleran and Laurentide ice sheets. Alaska and the unglaciated parts of Yukon Territory protruded like a giant thumb northward out of these immense sheets of ice. The ice-free Alaskan Interior was connected to Asia by a broad land mass exposed by lowered sea levels. So much water was tied up in the glaciers and ice sheets that sea levels dropped more than 300 feet during the glacial episodes.

Alaska has been linked to Asia by this land bridge across the Bering Sea at several times in the past. This link is revealed in the fossil record by the abrupt appearance of Asian mammals in the Americas. In fact, these waves of Asian faunal immigration are often used to mark units of geological time. Likewise, Alaska has been separated from Alberta and points farther south several times throughout the Pleistocene. As the ice closed off contact between north and south for several thousands of years, paired species of animals evolved on either side of the ice sheets. For example, bighorn sheep and Dall sheep are a product of one sheep species being pinched into two isolated segments for a long period of time. Looking north and south along the line where these two sheep species come together, one can see this same pattern of paired species among ground squirrels, pikas and other animals.

Alaska has thus been like a revolving door, at times opening to the northwest and Asia via the Bering Land Bridge, and at other times open to the southeast and the rest of North America. During the last few million years, at least, this revolving door never allowed direct communication between Asia and the Americas for a significant length of time. The conditions that opened the land bridge from Alaska to Asia were the same ones that closed the route between Alaska and the rest of North America. This opening and closing of colonization greatly influenced the fauna and flora of both the Old World and New World. During interglacial episodes when forests were present in Alaska and

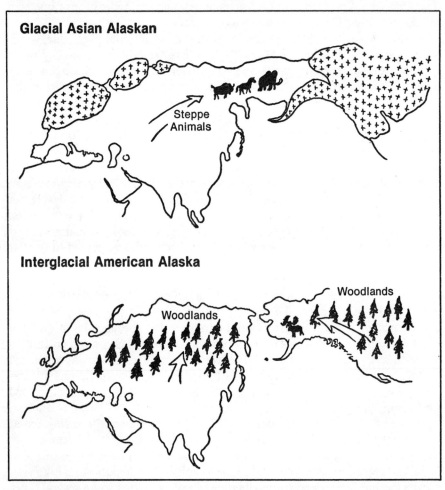

*Interior Alaska was a biological revolving door between Asia and America. During the glacials Alaska was part of Asia, because it was cut off from the rest of America by continental ice sheets. The lowered sea level exposed the continental shelf and thus connected Alaska to Asia, resulting in an east-west flow of flora and fauna during these times. However, because there were few or no trees around during the glacials, species with close connections between Alaska and Asia tend to be the more open ground species. During the wetter, warmer interglacials or interstadials, Alaska was part of America and separated from Asia by open water in summer and ice in winter. For some species like arctic foxes, which can travel over winter ice, this was no barrier; but for many other plants and animals, this constituted a major barrier. When Alaska was connected to America, the biota was mainly woodland; thus woodland species are similar between Alaska and Maine, for example. This turnstile connection adds considerable interest and diversity to Alaska's fauna and flora.*

northern Asia, sea levels were up and the door between the continents was closed. Thus, animals and plants associated with woodlands have few close relatives across this bridge. For example, species of spruce, tree squirrels, porcupines and beavers are quite distinct on opposite sides of the Bering Strait today. However, species which were on either side during the glacials, when sea levels were lower, had relatively free communication and are very similar — caribou, grizzlies, ground squirrels, lemmings and others. Thus Alaska had a truly Asian character during the glacials, sharing many details of fauna and flora as well as climate.

Glacial climate in the Interior was different from that of today. It may have been colder, but certainly there was more wind and less moisture. We know from the mammals that lived in Alaska during the glacials that there could have been little snow cover. What snow did fall was probably re-sorted and packed in drifts, much as it is now in mountain pass areas of Delta Junction and Healy. With so little moisture there must have been clear weather most of the year, with high cumulus clouds building in the summer and sparkling starlit nights in the winter. The clear skies would have made summers quite warm with deep thaws, but by the same token winters would have been cold with the loss of heat to the black night sky. On the other hand, winter winds, which we seldom have today, would have upset any tendency for heavy colder air to accumulate in the lowlands. So the glacial climate may have actually been warmer in the lowlands and cooler in the uplands.

It was in this glacial climate that the great deposits of loess accumulated — the fine, silty dust, produced by grinding glacial action, which underlies much of the modern Interior's landscape. The loess deposit is 90 feet deep on the ridge where our house sits just behind the Musk Farm north of the University of Alaska, and it is far deeper in other spots. So although summer skies during the glacials were clear, the haze of airborne silt must have created some colorful sunsets, lasting for hours as the summer sun rolled around the evening sky. The glacial loess figures importantly in our story of the Pleistocene, for it is in this silty book that most of what we know is written. The dusty silt entombs creatures and preserves them for the future.

## Pleistocene Animals of the Interior

Nothing does more to jolt a person into realizing that interior Alaska was quite a different place during the Pleistocene than to review the cast of large mammals who lived here. These animals certainly don't belong in today's landscape. We have spent considerable time camping and hunting in different parts of the Interior and more than once, during a quiet time glassing over distant slopes, have commented on how we would feel if a small herd of woolly mammoths were to round the bend down-valley. They were here. Mammoths did round that bend not too long ago. What a sight they must have been: tresses of soft, dark hair more than a yard long moving with the breeze, white tusks contrasting with the dark of their pelts, their bodies flowing up the valley with their smooth, slow gait. And people, not too different from ourselves, did hunt, butcher and eat woolly mammoths.

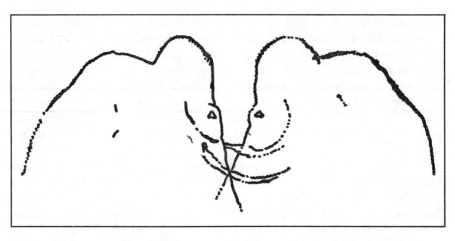

*The bison, horse and mammoth on the cave walls of Spain and France belong to much the same fauna which lived in Alaska's Interior at the time of the last glacial. Musk-ox, caribou, saiga antelope, wolf, lion, brown bear and elk likewise were pictured on those same caves and were also living in Alaska during the last glacial. Some of these pictures can tell us about how these animals looked and how they behaved. For example, these two bull mammoths from a drawing in Rouffignac Cave in the Perigord region of southcentral France seem to be fighting in head-to-head combat, as elephants fight today.*

For several reasons, mammoths are a good introduction to the extinct Pleistocene animals of the Interior. Mammoth mummies found in the Far North and cave drawings of mammoths in southern France — the two ends of their geographic range — have given us a good idea of how these extinct animals must have looked. They were about the size of Asian elephants, the common circus kind, but shorter in length and longer in leg; that is, they were higher at the shoulder in proportion to their size. Furthermore the shoulder was considerably taller than the rump, giving them a rather strange shape for an elephant. In many respects, they were like modern elephants: for example, they had two breasts up between the forelegs and the males had no external scrotum, the testes being inside the body cavity. The skull, and hence head, was high-domed and relatively short from front to back. Unlike modern elephants, their long prehensile trunk (actually an evolutionary extension of the proboscis or nose) ended in a handlike tip which they probably used to gather snow to drink when there was no free water in winter. Mammoths also used this special device to feed on herbaceous vegetation.

There are a lot of stories that the oversize mammoth tusks were devices for clearing snow, but if the tusks were used for that it was not their main purpose. Elephant tusks evolved as weapons for use against other members of the same species. In fact, two beautiful ivory carvings found in archaeological sites in France clearly portray a pair of mammoths fighting with their tusks. Female mammoths had small tusks, which became smaller, until the females had virtually none just before the species' extinction. The small tusks of female mammoths would have been a severe handicap if tusks indeed functioned as snow rakes; furthermore, African elephants have large tusks and there is little need for snow removal there.

All living elephants are organized into matriarchies; the females take care of the young and form large bands of aunts, mothers, grandmas, daughters and young males below reproductive age. Other males hang out in bachelor bands, or, as they get old and surly, live as isolated bulls. It is most probable that mammoths behaved in similar ways.

Winter was probably a rough time for mammoths. There are large growth rings on the roots of fossil teeth, marking the time when growth slowed in the fall and stopped during most of the winter. Living elephants require a minimum of four bales of grass hay a day and plenty of water. They cannot tolerate severe droughts because so much food is put through their systems so quickly that a lot of water is lost, passed through with the feces. Elephants have a short gut transit time for their food, less than 12 hours. Unlike bison or moose, which survive by digesting food of medium quality thoroughly, elephants eat great quantities of rather poor quality food, pass it rapidly through the gut and take whatever is most easily digested.

Mammoths were undoubtedly similar to elephants; it seems that such large land animals all share the same strategy and operate on large quantities of low quality food. Finding the equivalent of four bales of hay every day during the long northern winters would not have been an easy task. Mammoths must have been nomadic or they would have quickly eaten all the grass in any one valley.

Stomach contents found in frozen mammoth mummies have shown that the animals were mainly grass eaters. Grass is a good staple food for elephants. Its dead stems and leaf blades remain aboveground in the winter. These winter grasses are essentially carbohydrates, without much in the way of other nutrients. It is to the grass's advantage to have these dead portions removed, so the new shoots are unshaded in the spring. Also, the herbivores' manure recycles nutrients more quickly than if the dead grass simply decomposed during several years.

Although dead grass contains few toxins, the stems and leaves are laced with minute crystals called phytoliths, essentially little bits of glass the grasses use in the summer to defend their tissues from some herbivores. Mammoths, however, were well adapted to handling these substances. Plant phytoliths are abrasive and cause the teeth of animals eating them to wear quickly, but mammoth teeth were high-crowned with complex flattened loops of enamel, making them resistant to wear. These teeth evolved in response to the plant phytolith defenses, eventually getting so large that the animal needed only one on each side of the upper and lower jaw. As each tooth wore out, it was replaced from behind by a new one. A mammoth wore out six sets of these teeth in the course of its life — 24 teeth in all. This complicated process of tooth replacement has been mapped so we can age a fossil by which set of teeth it was using at the time of death and by the amount of tooth-wear.

Thanks to this information, we know that woolly mammoths had a long life expectancy, something like that of humans before the industrial revolution. Few mammoths died in middle age. The fossil mammoths we find reflect the pattern of deaths that most often occurred: they were the very young, the teenagers (leaving the protection of mom) and the elderly — a survivorship curve similar to that of humans.

The mammoth is not the most common late Pleistocene fossil. That place

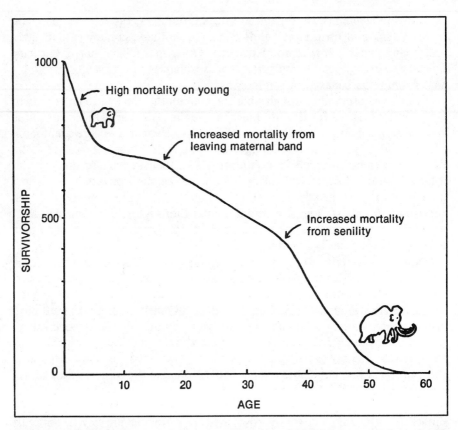

*The diagram shows the survivorship curve of mammoths from the Fairbanks area. Individual cheek teeth of mammoths can be aged because these mammals use six sets of teeth serially through their lifetime, as do living elephants. Their absolute ages within any tooth wear state can be determined by the annulae on the roots of the cheek teeth. Beginning with a cohort of 1,000, newborn mammoths experience their most difficult times during the first year or two, when they depend most on the cow. Once able to feed on their own, and well-protected by their mothers they seldom suffer major injury or death. When they mature and move out on their own, however, adolescent mammoths, particularly males, experience a rise in the likelihood of death. After this period, the survivorship curve is a long, sloping plateau with few deaths until senility begins to increase the mortality rate.*

is held by a little reddish-buff pony, not too different from the modern wild horses of central Asia, which are probably now extinct in the wild but are still bred by zoos. The fossil horses varied widely in size throughout the Pleistocene, but 45 to 50 inches would be a good average height for them. Imagine a solidly built horse as big as a medium-sized Shetland pony but with relatively small hooves, an upright mane and a rather heavy head. The bones of these horses are most common in the valley flats, so perhaps they preferred areas where they could see their predators at a distance.

One of our favorite characters in the Pleistocene cast is a large bison, the steppe bison, as it was called in the Old World. Like the mammoth and horse, this species ranged across Eurasia. One of the animals most commonly pictured in the cave paintings of Spain and France, the steppe bison differed slightly from living bison but was undoubtedly its ancestor. Horns of the steppe bison were quite large and the animal lacked the pantaloons, or black leggings, on the forelegs of modern bison. The steppe bison's bonnet was not as well developed, nor did it have a woolly wattle under the chin. This bison was a grazer, as were mammoths and horses.

The tooth crown enamel patterns of all three Pleistocene animals are quite complex, an adaptation to the rapid wear caused by grass phytoliths. Unlike the Alaskan mammoth and horse, the bison did not become extinct at the end of the Pleistocene. We have identified them from paleontological and archaeological sites scattered through the Holocene, the last 10,000 years. The most recent specimen found thus far lived about 500 years ago. It is difficult to picture Athabaskans hunting bison in interior Alaska, but this should not seem so unusual, because during historic times other Athabaskans hunted them farther south, where the grasslands met the boreal forest.

The little saiga antelope is another member of the Pleistocene fauna that would seem out of place on the modern Alaskan landscape, but they are not extinct; they live today in the southern part of the Soviet Union, in Kazakhstan and Uzbekistan. A saiga antelope weighs about as much as an American pronghorn, but neither are real antelopes in the African sense. The saiga is more closely related to musk-oxen or sheep; all three are members of the same phylogenetic group that became adapted to living on open grasslands. Saiga have small hooves and can run rapidly over flat or rolling open country, which is how they escape their predators. Their tan-yellow coat matches the color of dead grasses on the

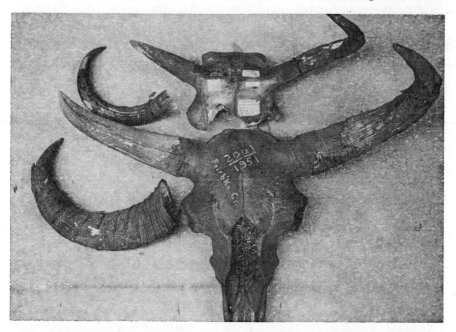

*These ancient bison skulls were found in a muck bank near Fairbanks. The upper is a female; the lower a male. They show the great sexual dimorphism of this species. The horn sheaths are still on both skulls, but the left ones are removed to show the bony horn core underneath. (Courtesy of Dale and Mary Lee Guthrie)*

open country where they live. One of the saiga's more curious characteristics is a long proboscis, especially during the rutting season, when the old males' noses become large and pendulous, making them look like cartoon characters. Like other bovids (cattle, sheep, goats, musk-oxen, etc.), saiga have horns made of keratin, but they are clear, with an almost amber tint. Only the males are horned. Female saiga are unusual for northern bovids in that they customarily twin, hiding their young out in the open and visiting them just a few times during the day to nurse. During the zenith of the mammoth steppe, these small animals were found all the way from England and France across Eurasia to Alaska and Yukon Territory.

The bonnet-horned musk-ox was another fascinating creature of the Alaskan Pleistocene. It was about the size of a small bison, and although it was a distant relative of modern musk-oxen, the two animals were built quite differently. The bonnet-horned musk-ox gets its name from the way its horns were fused at their bases, which (in older males at least) produced a large boss or bonnet from which two sharp horns projected and hooked upward as in living musk-oxen. Judging from the way the skull was engineered, the males fought by clashing with their heads. As in musk-oxen of today, these horny bosses must have cushioned the impact, along with the pneumatization of the skull cap.

Bonnet-horned musk-oxen were also found south of the continental ice sheet, as far east as New Jersey. And while there is evidence that they died out on the East Coast just before 11,000 years ago, the few dates from Alaska suggest that they might have died out earlier in the Far North. We don't know why, but for some reason bonnet-horned musk-oxen never reached the Old World. The stomach contents of a mummified young female found near Fairbanks indicate that they ate willow twigs during the winter — as do most populations of living musk-oxen.

There were even camels in the Interior during the Pleistocene. These Alaskan camels belonged to a species that roamed western North America, from Mexico all along the western Rocky Mountains and up into Alaska. These were large animals, the same size as living Old World camels. Only a few dozen specimens have been found in Alaska, but like many other Pleistocene fossils, these were found in widely scattered locations across unglaciated parts of the state. One camel bone, for example, was found on the North Slope.

Camels are eclectic in their dietary habits. Although they have a massive molar battery to eat grass when it is available, they also use their agile, split upper-lip to pluck off and eat a particular bit of vegetation they desire, much as we might use our opposing finger and thumb. This versatility makes camels quite adaptable to a variety of different diets.

The camels' unique build is due to their special gait: a pace, or rack, as it is often called in five-gaited horses. The hind leg and foreleg of one side move — in the same direction and at the same time — like two people walking in step, one behind the other. This is not a common mammalian gait because it is relatively unstable; the camel's body has to swing from side to side, like a rolling ship. But for a long-legged creature the pace is relatively efficient; giraffes are pacers as well. To compensate for its instability, the camel's toes are splayed and have long flat pads. We have enough fossil bones to know that the Alaskan camel's toes were constructed in a fashion similar to those of modern camels and must, therefore, have paced on the mammoth steppe.

Some of the Pleistocene mammals, such as Dall sheep, moose, elk, caribou and musk-oxen, are more familiar, but these species were not the star players they are today. It is hard to know exactly how numerous the various animal species were during the Pleistocene because of the many variables and quirks involved in preserving and finding fossils; but certain species do occur very rarely in the fossil record. Some of these include mastodon, stag moose, yaks and ground sloths.

The mastodon, a large elephantlike proboscidian, had teeth that indicate it probably browsed on shrubs and trees of the boreal forests. Alaskan fossils of this species have been found, but not dated; most likely mastodon lived in the Interior only during the warmer interglacials. The stag moose is probably closely related to the living moose and, at least in Eurasia, it must have been ancestral to the living moose. However, both species seem to have existed contemporaneously south of the continental ice sheet in North America.

Yaks came to Alaska from their center of evolution in the high mountains of Asia, but they did not get south of the ice sheets into the rest of North America. Yaks are a cold-adapted version of cattle which evolved earlier in the warmer Eurasian lowlands and did not colonize Alaska. Normally, bison fill the high-latitude, high-altitude cattlelike niche. Why yaks were able to squeeze into that niche in Alaska for some time during the Pleistocene is still an unanswered question.

Ground sloths are not easy to describe. There are no modern counterparts to use for rough analogies to these Pleistocene giants. They originated in South America and are remotely related to the living tree sloths. Alaskan ground sloths belonged to a large group of species that were relatively common during the Pleistocene. They were round in overall shape, had relatively short faces, powerful arms and long claws. Some species probably used their claws for eating, but certainly all must have used them for defense as they were quite slow and otherwise defenseless. Deep deposits of ground sloth feces have been found in caves in the American Southwest. These deposits, which date from the late Pleistocene, seem to consist mainly of fragments of shrubs. Based on this, it seems likely that Alaskan ground sloths, like the mastodon, lived here during one of the warmer interglacials.

Extinct carnivores in the Pleistocene deposits are just as curious as the herbivores. The strangest must certainly be the gigantic short-faced bear. This animal was as large as the Kodiak brown bear but built quite differently. It had a rather short snout or muzzle, which explains its common name. Unlike the brown bear, it had short stubby claws, but its legs were rangier and longer. It still isn't clear just what ecological role this bear played in the spectrum of predators. Some paleontologists have proposed that it was a more active predator than living bears, which tend to be scavengers, rodent diggers, or salmon feeders.

With the possible exception of wolves, the most common large mammal predators here in the late Pleistocene seem to have been lions. These northern lions also lived all across the north of Eurasia and were apparently a common acquaintance of early hunters in France.

Pictures of lions appear on cave walls and on bone and antler implements. These pictures, drawn from life, let us see what the fossil bones can only suggest. The late Pleistocene specie lacked the large mane of African male lions and had instead a small mane on the top and bottom of the neck. The tail was not tipped with a conspicuous tuft, but was furry along its entire length, like the tail of a house cat. When animals live polygamously, the males are quite showy and dramatically different from females. One can understand the showy African males because they rule a pride of several smaller and plainer females. The lack of a mane in Alaskan lions may be explained in terms of their inability to get enough food in any one area to support a large pride. It is likely that the Pleistocene prides were small, or that these Alaskan lions lived relatively solitary lives as their tiger relatives do today.

A few bones of one species of saber-toothed cat have been found in Alaska. Unlike some other saber-toothed species, this northern form was relatively small, somewhere in the range of a mountain lion. Its canine teeth were longer than a lion's, flatter in cross section, and serrated along the inside edge, much like a bread knife. The large cats we know today — lions, cheetahs and tigers — kill their prey by strangling, clamping their jaws on the victim's throat or snout. Saber-toothed cats apparently did not kill that way, but used their long canines to penetrate areas of the neck where large herbivores were vulnerable. We can tell from the structure of fossil skulls that these cats had small jaw muscles and thus a weak bite. Their strong muscles were in the neck, giving saber-toothed cats the ability to drive their long canines deeply into their prey — stabbing the victim, probably while it was still on its feet. Saber-toothed cats had relatively short, powerful legs and a bobtail that must have made them look quite different from lions or other cats living today.

Cheetahs closely related to the living African and Asian species lived all across the Far North during the Pleistocene. They first entered North America via Alaska sometime in that time period. Cheetah bones have not yet been identified from Alaska, but only recently have we identified their bones from Pleistocene deposits in northern Asia and North America. The collections of fossils from Alaska deserve to be re-examined with cheetahs in mind. Cheetahs are not abundant in their ranges today and perhaps were never numerous in Alaska either, so they would be predictably rare as a fossil.

Two unusual carnivores among the smaller Alaskan Pleistocene animals are the badger and ferret. Today the nearest badgers are found hundreds of miles to the south, in the area of Edmonton, Alberta. The Pleistocene badger was a larger animal, but still closely related. The Alaskan ferret does not seem to have a close living relative, but undoubtedly it occupied the same niche as the black-footed ferret in the Great Plains. The black-footed ferret is now quite rare because of the great reduction in prairie dogs (which are actually ground squirrels) by cattle ranchers. Arctic ground squirrels were probably the main prey of the Alaskan ferret. Ground squirrel bones and their fossil nests are fairly common in the Fairbanks muck, although nowadays these little animals are not found in the Fairbanks area.

Pleistocene carnivores which still survive in the Interior include the red fox, wolf, wolverine, weasel, lynx, mink and marten.

# Pollen: The Living Dust

It is difficult to study the plants of Pleistocene times because, unlike mammals, they do not leave bones behind, but fortunately some plants do leave their pollen. Because plants cannot go out looking for mates like animals, they must resort to a more passive courtship. Many plants rely on insects to transport male germ cells to the females. They allow the insect to take some of their pollen for protein, and they lure it with little nectar sacs of sugar water for calories (this is why flowers taste sweet) and with scents that can be detected from a long distance (this is why flowers are fragrant). But not all plant sex life is so contrived. Many just release jillions of little germ cells in the hope that by saturating the air they will fertilize a female of the same species. To survive during their journey, wafting along in the air currents, these pollen grains have a specially constructed shell made of a waxy material, impenetrable to fungi and decomposers. The abundance and preservability of these pollen grains are a windfall for paleoecologists.

These microscopic particles fall as dust everywhere during the pollinating season. They are the reason many people with hay fever have such a difficult time in summer. Year after year, pollen grains accumulate in natural traps like ponds and lakes, sinking to the bottom along with real dust particles and the remains of plants and water animals. Throughout time, pollen particles become an important part of the sediments. If after a thousand years the climate changes and different species of plants occur in greater abundance in that region, the shift is usually revealed by the percentages of various plant pollens in the accumulating sediments.

Palynologists — scientists who study pollens — probe such lakes and ponds with a special device that allows them to get a continuous core all the way to the bottom of the sediments. The cores are taken back to the laboratory in tubular carriers, numbered by depth and orientation. The sediments are sampled at intervals all along the core. Then the samples are treated with a series of reagents, the main one being floric acid, to remove the silt particles and almost everything else but the pollen grains, whose waxy covering is invulnerable to the acid. These are stained and placed under a microscope. Each plant group has characteristically shaped pollen. Some, like grasses, exhibit little variability among members of the group. Others, particularly the tree genera, are quite characteristic and are identifiable even to the species level. The palynologist then identifies a prescribed number of pollen grains in each sample.

When these results are plotted vertically as percentages of plant groups, they form a profile, showing which were relatively dominant and which were rather minor. If there is a major change in percentages along the profile, the palynologist can go back to the sediment core, which has been kept in a freezer, and remove a large organic sample for radiocarbon dating. Episodes of climatic change, or at least changes in regional vegetation, can thus be delimited chronologically. When numerous studies of this sort have been done in a general region and a consistent pattern emerges, the data is considered reliable enough to characterize the nature and timing of changes that have occurred in the vegetation.

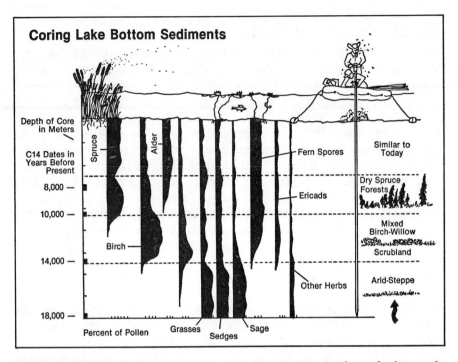

*This diagram shows pollen samples taken in pond sediments. A core is taken as far down as the corer can penetrate. The core sections are then numbered and taken back to the laboratory where small samples are prepared by dissolving away all material except the resistant waxy pollen. The pollen is then identified and percentages of the different types are determined for each sample taken along the core. When these percentages are plotted, scientists get an overall view of the proportions of the different pollens through time. Organic sediments for Carbon 14 dating are taken from the core at the points where critical changes occur in pollen proportions. The information that emerges from this data is used to reconstruct when and what kind of changes occurred in the vegetation patterns.*

A number of palynologists have worked in interior Alaska and adjacent areas, including Yukon Territory, and have been able to tell us something about the kinds of vegetation that occurred during the glacials and how they changed with the increased moisture and warming of the Holocene. During the last glacial, the main pollens present included grasses and sedges, wormwood or sage, a variety of forbs and some willow. This is called the herb zone, because there are no tree pollens of any major significance. Coming up through our pollen profile, this herb zone lasts until about 13,500 years ago, when a major change began to occur. The striking thing about this second zone is the higher percentage of birch pollen, and hence it is called the birch zone. A bit later, northern berry bushes such as blueberry and cranberry became abundant, so this could be thought of as the shrub zone. At about 11,000 years ago cottonwood or aspen has a strong peak, and slightly later spruce shows up in abundance. At about 8,000 years ago, alder begins to occur in significant quantities. This last zone, called the spruce-alder zone, continues to the present.

One interpretation of these pollen percentages is that the dry, cold glacial steppes of the herb zone were mainly grass and sage, although certainly they must have varied with altitude and from area to area. At the beginning of the birch zone, however, dwarf birch and the berry shrubs began to show up in abundance. These are plants that thrive on moist cool soils.

The long lag-time before spruce and alder trees occurred in the Interior following recession of the glacial ice may be due to their absence from all of Alaska. It would have taken some time for them to colonize northward. It looks as if poplar may have survived in ice-free areas, so it would have been an early arrival, with spruce following soon afterward. Alder took longer, not reaching its farthest limit on the Yukon Delta until 5,000 or 6,000 years ago. The amount of spores from moss, sphagnum and fern increased during the birch zone and became abundant during the spruce-alder zone.

Thus, Fairbanks went from a grassy, low-herb landscape 14,000 years ago to a thick, patchy shrubland soon afterward, and graded into a spruce forest at about 10,000 years ago. This, of course, is not the end of the story. Sometime in the future, palynologists will see our point on the pollen profile as just a squiggle in the spruce-alder zone. And someday the spruce will again die out in the Interior; the Tanana Flats and the slopes on Chena Ridge will no longer support anything but low profile grasses and forbs, for everything we have learned about the past indicates these long-term cycles of change are not at an end. Much of the study of these cycles of forest and dry grasslands is written in the archives of the Fairbanks mud.

## Archives in the Mud

Glacial ice creeping northward along the valleys from the Alaska Range worked the rocks in its path like a giant milling machine, plucking up boulders and grinding them into the rounded cobbles so characteristic of glacial till deposits. This glacial action also produced smaller pebbles, sand and tiny particles of silt and clay. In the summer these milled products were continuously disgorged into the outwash deltas and rivers on the flats.

The mass of ice in a glacier tends to cool the air above it, and as this cooled air descends along the glacier's slope it picks up speed, creating a strong down-valley wind. This cool wind sweeps the sand into dunes and carries finer particles high into the air as dust clouds which deposit the silt miles from its source. When this glacial silt settled out over the Tanana Hills it must have looked like dust along a dirt road in the summertime, coating all the vegetation with a thin buff sheet until it was washed off by the next shower. Such dust didn't look like much, but throughout thousands of years it accumulated to form thick deposits of loess.

This is why Fairbanks can be so dusty during a dry summer or so muddy during spring breakup. Deep deposits of talcumlike dust mantle the landscape of the Interior. The angular, microscopic form of the particles allows them to stand in vertical banks that seem to defy gravity; sand and larger stones cannot hold that erect posture. But the loess banks will hold only when they are dry, which Fairbanks usually is. If a cut bank is given the slightest angle, however, a trickle of water acts like a fire hose. The small particles easily move into solution and away they go downstream, to the valley bottoms where the water slows and the particles settle out as mud fans. Anything in the path of this mud is covered, and once organic remains are buried their decay is eventually stopped by the cool soil. Bones, pollen, leaves, seeds, roots and other organic remnants are thus sealed against time, preserved for perpetuity and the curious interests of paleontologists.

Suppose a Pleistocene horse, old and near starvation, finally dies. Because of its weakness, the animal is most likely to be moving down-slope, not climbing ridge tops. Its carcass would be scavenged by large carnivores, ravens, jays and insects until only bare bones are left. They are not still assembled in the skeleton but scattered all over the landscape. Most of the spongy bones like ribs, foot bones, ends of long bones and vertebrae are chewed by wolverines and wolves for their marrow. Likewise, the delicate bones of the face are usually bitten off for the soft tissue they enclose. However, the dense, thick skull bones of larger mammals are seldom completely opened and eaten through. A variety of scavengers may chew on them, but these skull bones, as well as the shed antlers of caribou and moose, lie around the landscape for several years. Eventually they crack and begin to come apart; weather causes them to flake and they become no more than minerals absorbed into the soil from which they ultimately came.

Occasionally, however, the silt being washed down the swales is deposited over these bones and they are preserved. We have no good idea how often that happens. It must be less than one time in a thousand and probably less than one time in ten thousand, so only a small percentage of bones are ever preserved. But all animals must die sometime, and if enough of them are living where silt is being deposited, throughout many centuries some bones will be preserved.

The term fossil is a loosely used word meaning anything that is very old. It does not necessarily imply a replacement by minerals, as is the frequent case for fossils whose age goes back millions of years. Fossil bones from the Fairbanks area are fresh looking, although they usually are stained by the dark organics of the soils burying them and may vary in color from deep cream to the darkest black. They usually contain much of the original proteins that bonded the bone minerals together and many still have dehydrated marrow inside the cavities. Occasionally the tendons still are attached, like dessicated strings bonded to the bone. Sometimes there are even hooves on the feet and dried skin clothing the bone. More rarely, complete mummies of entire animals are found.

Silt that is moved and redeposited downhill is quite different in appearance from the tan loess on the upper slopes. This reworked silt, known locally as muck, is rich in organics that washed down with it, and when wetted it looks quite black. Paleontologists can separate the silt from the organic materials incorporated with it by placing a bucketful of muck into a box with a screen bottom. When this muck is washed in a flowing stream, the silt goes into suspension again and falls through the screen, which is just a bit finer mesh than a window screen. What is left behind is a mass of plant material dating from the time the silt was deposited. Plant fragments usually amount to one-fifth to one-tenth of the volume of the screened silt. These are dried, taken back to the laboratory and searched under a dissecting microscope.

Among the plant fragments, one can find the teeth and bones of mice and

## Creation of a Mummy

Old mammoth dies
in winter

Partially decomposes
and freezes

Is scavenged the
remainder of the winter

In spring, partially covered
with silt from downslope
wash

Continues to decompose some
next year or two but becomes
buried further in cold ground

Over the millenia as
sediments accumulate the
annual thaw rises above it
and the mammoth is
preserved frozen

*Frozen mummies of large mammals occur when an animal dies in an area in which silt is being deposited rapidly over frozen ground. Adult animals usually die during winter. Frozen mummies always show some decomposition, if for no other reason than it may take a day or more for the body, with its insulating coat of hair, to cool. Mummified carcasses in the North also normally show some degree of scavenging from predators before they are buried. Most seem to have been buried during the first summer season, probably by large amounts of silt transported down-slope by run-off from spring rains. As the permafrost level moves up to meet the new surface, the carcass is frozen in place.*

shrews that once lived in Pleistocene Alaska. Most of these are ancestors of the modern animals, and they look different because they are in an earlier evolutionary stage. Some, like the collared lemmings, have evolved rapidly and their different evolutionary forms can be used as a rough indicator of the age of the sediments. Others, like the brown lemmings, are conservative and their tooth characteristics, for instance, have changed little in the last million years. There are also the shiny black exterior skeletons of beetles. These tiny remains have proven to be an important tool in reconstructing past climates.

Occasionally pebbles of polished white quartz turn up in the washed screens. For a long time they remained a mystery. How did these pea-sized, rounded pebbles get mixed in with the airborne loess and where did they come from? The pebbles turned out to be gizzard stones of Pleistocene grouse and ptarmigan. Many birds use gizzard stones in lieu of teeth to grind up their rough forage. Carnivores eating these bird species carefully avoid the gizzard, for obvious reasons. Once we found a compact cluster of these polished pebbles deposited in the peat, all that remained of a bird that had died and lain undisturbed while the carcass decomposed thousands of years ago. Here were the gizzard stones, fresh as the day they were last used.

But some large gizzard stones, which range up to an inch in diameter and seem too big for any living birds, are still a puzzle. They are the only clue we have to a large and now extinct bird that once lived here. Like so many things from the Pleistocene, we can hold these pebbles in our hand, a solid clue, close enough to touch, suggestive of strange animals that we can almost see and of others we may never imagine — all of them gone.

Covered with this muck, Pleistocene fossils lie beneath the ground all across the Interior, so anyone living here has no doubt walked over some of them. Like walking unknowingly across an abandoned graveyard, we tramp daily over the bygone glories of the Ice Age. Hidden under the surface are mummies of mammoths, some of which likely saw the first people who entered this hemisphere. Perhaps one of these mammoths has a projectile point embedded in its flank; such fossils have been found from other places and times. Somewhere down there are the floors of the early hunters' camps, a book full of information about their lives written in flakes of stone and garbage.

The story of the past is beneath our feet, but usually we have only small fragments of this wealth to work with. Understanding this story is a task for Sherlock Holmes, with no books to tell us exactly how to begin or even what questions to ask. Since we can't see beneath the ground, we have to wait for excavations to expose the past. Some of the best sites have been discovered in holes dug for house foundations or garbage pits. Road cuts, mining activity and construction projects all inadvertently provide access to information. Usually the exposures are natural products of wandering streams and rivers, carving sediments and creating new cut banks, sectioning through the past.

Snow and ice that have accumulated all winter begin to thaw as the spring sun slowly brings the landscape to the melting point. Finally a critical threshold is reached and breakup is underway. Runoff lifts the stream ice from its shoreline anchor, until it crushes and grinds downstream. The force of this moving ice and the high spring waters scour and wash the cut banks, so the river is different

*A mammoth skull erodes from an Alaskan riverbank. (Courtesy of Dale and Mary Lee Guthrie)*

every year. Because large mammal fossils are heavier than the surrounding silt, these bones are left behind, high-graded like the gold nuggets in a miner's sluice box. Usually the fossils are not found directly below the exposure from which they emerged, but are scattered on the first few gravel bars downstream. Although such bones can be identified and dated, they provide less information for paleontologists than those taken directly from the sediments in which they've been buried. This is because the surrounding sediments contain a wealth of paleoecological information, such as pollen, seeds, small mammals and insects.

The richest Pleistocene fossil localities found along rivers in the Interior lie where the rivers loop toward the hills and cut into thick fans of sediments coming down silt-filled valleys. These localities are characteristically dark in color from the high proportion of organics they contain. As a result of these same organics they have a unique odor, the smell of ancient life and death, partly decomposed, frozen before fully composting and uncorked after millennia. The smell is really quite hard to describe: it is not unpleasant, something like dank soil, but with an acid sweetness.

A typical cross section to these exposures immediately tells us something about the past climate. The topmost strata are usually thick peats with roots and layers of compressed sphagnum like pages of a book. Since this level is interwoven and tougher than the underlying silt, it usually is undercut and overhangs the layers below, carrying with it trees which bow deeply toward the stream before they tumble down-slope during some spring breakup. Beneath this peat is a deep layer of organic silt. Usually there are massive ice wedges within it — as much as 33 feet (10 meters) across and equally deep — their faces gleaming like giant crystal facets. The surfaces of this ice are often covered by thin layers of wet silt. Ice wedges are more resistant to thaw than the silty areas between, resulting in a huge scalloped effect. Animal and plant remains found in this zone of silt and ice usually fall within the range of radiocarbon dating, going back some 30,000 years and somewhat earlier. This is the peak of the last glaciation, and it is within this zone that most bones of large Pleistocene mammals are found around Fairbanks.

Beneath this zone is another peaty layer several feet thick with tree roots and limbs and twigs. Its age dates at the outer range of radiocarbon dating, from 35,000 to 40,000 years ago. This is an interstadial: a warmer and wetter period which occurred within the last glacial. During this time trees recolonized the North and along with them came animals adapted to a more southern climate. Turkeys and spotted skunks reached as far north as Yukon Territory. Fossils of ground sloths and mastodon found in the Interior are still undated, but undoubtedly they lived here during one of these warm, wet periods.

Farther down the section there is more silt from another cold episode, and beneath this is another forest bed and peat deposit from the earliest interglacial, which we know dates at around 100,000 years ago. In some places there is more silt beneath this layer, dating from still earlier glaciations. This oldest layer is quite variable, and it contains some of the most unusual animals: large pikas the size of rabbits, enormous horses quite unlike the little ponies from more recent glaciations, moose with short noses and broad-palmed antlers stuck out on a shaft a half-yard long on each side. But even at this early date there are animals any of us would recognize, for example, caribou and bison.

But if stream cut banks were our major source of fossils, we would know considerably less than we do. At the turn of the century something happened that would greatly influence Alaska's Interior for centuries to come — miners found gold. Large supply boats could make it up the slow-moving Tanana River because of its gentle gradient. The current changes near the place where the Chena River meets the Tanana, because Pleistocene uplift of the Alaska Range has made the gradient relatively steep and the river shallower above that point. This place where the supply boats stopped because of shallow water was for decades Alaska's largest city, Fairbanks.

Gold was to be found in the gravel placer deposits in most valleys, but under many yards of silt. Valley gravel accumulated early in the Pleistocene, but late Pleistocene silt then covered the old stream-bed gravels and gold. To reach the gold beneath this overburden, the early miners dug tunnels down through the frozen silt during the winter and bucketed the gravel into a pile; then, the following summer they sluiced the gravel to extract the heavy particles of gold. This laborious technique prevailed for a decade or two until the big mining companies came in. At this point the exposure of Pleistocene fossils gathered momentum.

The large mining companies, particularly Fairbanks Exploration Company, bought up many of the smaller claims and built dredges to more efficiently process the placer deposits. To operate these dredges, the entire overburden of silt had to be removed from on top of the gravel. A complex system of ditches and pipes was constructed to wash away the silt. Thousands of Pleistocene fossils were uncovered in the process of the miners' washing operations.

## Mummies, Miners and Scholars

Long before the Europeans explored the Far North, Natives had watched bones of large animals emerge from eroding riverbanks, but these were not the bones of the animals they hunted and ate. Some of them had long white teeth, and occasionally a complete carcass, strange in scale and proportion, emerged. Who were these creatures? Obviously they did not live aboveground or you would see them, so they must have lived underground. And when they mistakenly emerged along stream-banks they died, for the ones found there were always dead. Such were the explanations given to the first Europeans who entered the North.

Generation after generation, thousands upon thousands of individual animals live and die leaving no trace. Just a few are preserved by some curious turn of nature, and of that few we happen to find only a handful. Thousands of years ago a large boulder fell from the roof of what is now called Shanidar Cave, in Iraq, killing an old Neanderthal man. During countless hundreds of generations, other people camped and hunted from the same rock cave, but they left few traces. Only this one man's bones have been found. The same is true of animals as well. A young mammoth gets stuck in the mud on a tributary of the Kolyma River in Siberia. Its frantic mother tries to rescue it, but the baby sinks even farther and goes under. Thousands of young mammoths died every year in those times, but they were left to be dismembered by scavengers,

*Hydrologic mining operations like this one uncovered the remains of many extinct animals in Alaska's Interior. (Courtesy of Dale and Mary Lee Guthrie)*

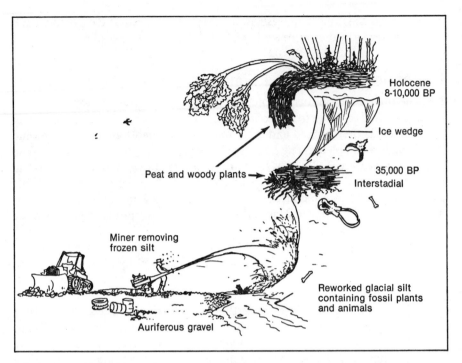

Holocene
8-10,000 BP

Ice wedge

35,000 BP
Interstadial

Peat and woody plants →

Miner removing
frozen silt

Reworked glacial silt
containing fossil plants
and animals

Auriferous gravel

*This drawing shows a characteristic muck exposure in Alaska's Interior. Miners must remove the Pleistocene silt overburden from gold-bearing gravels. To accomplish this, miners wash the muck with jets of warm, run-off water from summer rains. These jets wash away the muck which thaws each day at the surface of the frozen ground. This mining activity exposes sediments which contain fossil plants and animals. There are often fossil beds of woodland plants from past interglacials. Glacial sediments, on the other hand, are homogenous frozen silts with no woody plants.*

their bones weathering to dust with no trace remaining of their brief lives. Only this baby mammoth is different, like another young mammoth from Dome Creek north of Fairbanks. Enzymes and bacteria began decomposition, but the cold mud quickly chilled the warm tissues and slowed their activity. Winter came; the mud was frozen. Next spring more mud flowed over the body and the thaw didn't reach the baby mammoth. Nor did it the next year, nor the next, as more sediment was deposited. The young mammoth was frozen in perpetuity.

Pleistocene mummies from Alaska and Siberia are as close to immortality as the earth can offer. Most other fossils preserve because the bones are replaced with minerals and retain little of their own tissue. But mummies of the Far North are deep-frozen and have been for tens of thousands of years. Finding one is a little like breaking the seal on an Egyptian burial chamber — it gives us a chance for a special look at the past because of the wealth of preserved detail. Often the animal's last meal is in its stomach, and the last bite may even be in its mouth or wedged in the crevices of its teeth.

These mummies are not easy to describe to someone who hasn't seen them. They are a disappointment to people accustomed to cartoon portrayals of a smiling mammoth in a cake of blue ice or horses frozen mid-stride when the deep freeze hit. The real mummies are bathed in mud and hardly recognizable.

The early miners turned their hydraulic guns on the mummies to clean them up, and in so doing they washed away the most interesting information.

Preservation of Pleistocene mummies in the Interior depended on rapid deposition of deep mud over the dead animal before it was completely scavenged and decomposed, or on the animal being trapped in an environment which provided the same protective covering. Several sites in Siberia appear to be traps of this later sort, where there are lots of bones with parts of the mammoths still preserved. These sites are thought to have been old oxbows where individual animals occasionally broke through the drier surface into underlying mud. They might take only an animal or two every decade, but with enough time they became veritable mammoth cemeteries.

Alaska has had its share of Pleistocene mummies discovered: two large male bison, a female bonnet-horned musk-ox, several moose, one mammoth and parts of a number of large mammals — usually legs and feet — have been found here. There are also mummies of mice, ground squirrels, hares, lynx and a pika.

Looking at the carcasses of the large mummies, most appear to have died in winter, had their red meat partially or almost completely scavenged and then became covered during spring runoff. If such a carcass lasts through one summer, it is usually well-flyblown and little fly pupa cases are everywhere around the bones and in the bone canals. Alaskan mummies which have the skin and meat preserved show none of this, so we can say that they did not stay above the surface through summer.

It is an extraordinary experience to watch a bison's head with giant black horn, then left ear and neck emerge as one carefully picks away the thawing muck, to know that this animal roamed and fed along the ridges here — long before there had ever been a human track in this hemisphere. What do you want to know about those times; what could the bison tell us? If we could have seen the spring thaw as the bison saw it, or the cooling Septembers from the eyes that a raven plucked out before the burial, we would probably be shocked, for the puzzle of Pleistocene Alaska is not very readable. But that bison mummy is a fine piece with which to begin.

When the 1900s had barely started, word crackled across the country — by telegraph and newspaper — of gold aplenty in Alaska. Ships brought men by the thousands, not just men with dreams, but self-reliant men who had used imagination and baling wire to keep the dirt farm going. Traces of the creativity and can-do of these early miners, thousands of miles away from manufacturing centers and supplies, can still be seen in the Interior. Their lives are intertwined with the information we have about the extinct animals of Pleistocene Alaska, because with picks and shovels they began the massive excavations for gold which have fortuitously uncovered great numbers of Pleistocene fossils.

What did these miners think of the giant bones of strange animals that washed out of the muck? Robert Service missed this grist for his poems, and we have lost whatever tall tales were told over biscuits and moose meat about the elephant tusks and the varied skulls, teeth and limb bones that emerged from the week's diggings. There must have been some interesting stories. You can see shadows of them by talking to some of the old miners who caught the end of that era. Remember that many people at the time thought the world was only a little more than 4,000 years old. Louis Agassiz's Glacial Theory and the whole notion of an Ice Age were new ideas, still being developed and only slowly achieving solid acceptance.

There were horses too, horses living wild on this continent, yet there was no record of horses when the first Europeans arrived. Certainly the miners' horses could not range wild in the Interior's hills, and even most stock horses did not last the winter. The snow was too deep to get down to what little grass existed. The old miners still argue that the climate must have been nearly tropical for these ice age animals to live in the Far North; elephant tusks and lion skulls seem to be proof of that.

Travelers to exotic lands are always incapable of totally portraying their experiences to people back home. Marco Polo ended his chronicles with the comment that he had seen so many strange things he could not begin to completely picture them for the reader. In a farmhouse outside a little town in Illinois there is a large mammoth molar, its surface polished to a high gloss. The man who brought it back when he returned to take his place on the family farm must have had something of that same sense, remembering the wavering lights in the night sky, the odd smell of the muck, the giant moose with antlers spreading farther than a man could reach and the remains of all the other creatures uncovered in the mud. He had seen things too strange to tell.

From the late 1920s to the end of the 1950s, hydraulic hoses in placer mines all over the Interior were washing away millions of tons of silt, uncovering remains of Pleistocene fossils at a tremendous rate. Aside from the miners' ordinary interest in these remains, there were others whose concern was far more

*Otto Geist examines mammoth bones and hair in a hydrologically mined bank at Ester, a few miles from Fairbanks. (Courtesy of Dale and Mary Lee Guthrie)*

serious. Notable among them were two colorful and largely self-trained scientists — Otto Geist and Childs Frick. These men were responsible for saving literally tens of thousands of Alaskan fossils from being lost in trash heaps or dispersed to the private market.

Otto Geist arrived in Alaska in the early 1920s. The son of a Bavarian antiquarian, he was a natural collector. His strong interests and ability in natural history had led to scientific expeditions in the Alaska wilderness and to friendships with Olaus Murie and his wife Margaret, as well as Charles Bunnell, then president of the Alaska Agricultural College and School of Mines, the infant University of Alaska.

Childs Frick, a son of the steel millionaire Henry Clay Frick, was the other member of this strange team. He had become fascinated with mammal fossils and pursued his hobby with substantial interest and resources, collecting specimens from around the world. Such a hobby was not unusual at the turn of the century; another famous New Yorker, Teddy Roosevelt, had similar passions as a collector and used his wealth and influence to help finance operations at the American Museum of Natural History in New York City. Frick sponsored fossil collecting expeditions throughout the Western Hemisphere, enlisting some of the best field collectors of the day to help with this work. Like Frick himself, most of these collectors were self-trained.

Charles Bunnell and Neil Rice, who was president of Fairbanks Exploration Company, were convinced that someone should salvage the growing number of exposed fossils. Rice contacted his friend Frick, who financed an expedition to Alaska led by a curator of paleontology from the American Museum, Peter Kaisen. Geist accompanied the expedition, and from Kaisen he learned how to preserve and identify fossils. When Kaisen returned to New York, Geist was engaged as the collector in residence.

Frick then offered to finance the further collection of fossils in a joint venture with the University of Alaska. He paid Geist's salary and provided lab assistance for cleaning and packing the fossils, which were then boxed and shipped to New York. Through philanthropic connections, Frick acquired space for them in the American Museum of Natural History. The Frick collections were just upstairs from the rooms where George Gaylord Simpson and other members of the regular paleontological staff worked, but tensions between the two groups kept them from spending much time with each other's collections.

One bad feature of Frick's paying for fossils was that he did not want the heaviest bones, nor was he interested in certain bones, like vertebrae. Also, Frick did not want broken bones; he mainly asked for skulls and particularly for good skulls. In retrospect, these biases in the collection are unfortunate because many of the questions most interesting to us today can be answered only with more complete collections and with fossil bones that have been modified by carnivores. Without adequate storage facilities or funds to ship these rejected bones to New York, Geist built a fossil fence around his house in Fairbanks. (The fence disappeared after Geist's death in 1963.)

But on the whole the association between Frick and the University of Alaska was a fine arrangement. Fossils that Geist collected along the creeks and shipped to Frick in New York were given secure storage and study. Upon his death Frick endowed the American Museum of Natural History with a new wing to house the fossil mammal collections, a great portion of them from Alaska. The Frick Collection staff was integrated into the vertebrate paleontology staff and a new era of cooperation began at the American Museum. The general decline of mining activity and the resulting decrease in number of fossils sent to New York ended the Geist-Frick association in the 1950s. Since then many large mammal fossils found in the Interior have been acquired by the University of Alaska Museum on the Fairbanks campus.

## Extinctions

The fauna and vegetation of interior Alaska changed remarkably in response to periods of glacial cold and interglacial warming throughout the Pleistocene. But the series of changes occurring around 12,000 years ago seems to have been unique. In earlier climatic changes many animal species died out in certain places. They suffered local extinctions, but survived in other regions and recolonized when the climate again supported an environment in which they could thrive. But around 12,000 years ago, local extinctions of many large mammal species expanded to the point of total species extinction. This was perhaps the case with some birds as well, but we know much less about birds because they have delicate bones and no teeth, leaving us with few clues in the fossil record.

In one region after another, mammoths failed to survive until finally they became extinct everywhere. There would never again be woolly mammoths, no matter how widespread the conditions to which they were adapted. These wholesale extinctions affected not only Alaska; they were as great, or nearly so, in the rest of the world. Complete extinctions like this attract the attention of scientists, who wonder about the ecology of past environments.

There are as yet no exact dates on the timing of these extinctions, but the best estimate is sometime between 11,000 and 12,000 years ago. It is unlikely that all these species died out at exactly the same time. They do not seem to have died in a sudden cataclysm, as we will discuss in a moment. We can say with some certainty that in sediments younger than 11,000 years we find no traces of woolly mammoth, bonnet-horned musk-oxen, saber-toothed cats, lions, short-faced bears, sloths, horses, saiga antelope, camels, or any of the other extinct Pleistocene species. More recently than 11,000 years ago, in addition to the familiar caribou, sheep and moose, we also find bison and elk, which seem to have persisted in the Interior almost up to historic times.

Currently there are two contending theories which purport to explain these extinctions. Both have the backing of considerable evidence and each eloquently accounts for both the timing of the extinctions and the kinds of species that became extinct.

One theory proposes that people first came into North America around 12,000 years ago. These early groups were hunters, specializing in large mammals. Their hunting camps and the bone litter from their kills are scattered in many archaeological sites all across Eurasia. According to this theory, the animals of northern Asia and North America were not adapted to this new kind of predator and were quickly killed off. Hunters would have been eager to take the largest mammals in these new territories and their effects would have been greatest among the more reproductively conservative species such as the mammoth.

Archaeological evidence for such a theory is strong. According to some archaeologists, the earliest remains of humans in northern Asia date to just before 12,000 years ago. In Alaska they first show up abundantly just after that time. Also, the kill sites of early people in the Great Plains and Siberia from about this same time contain remains of mammoths, uncontestable evidence that mammoths were hunted and used as a food resource. So this theory is a serious contender for a best accounting of the extinctions.

However, there are no Alaskan archaeological sites with associations of man and the large mammal species that became extinct before 11,000 years ago. But this is controversial. There are some bones from Alaska and Yukon Territory which could be interpreted as evidence that humans were present in these areas 80,000 to 100,000 years ago, although this interpretation is doubted by many scientists. Nevertheless, we shouldn't be surprised to find evidence of association between humans and the now-extinct species, because both seem to have been here around 12,000 years ago.

The other theory that attempts to account for the late Pleistocene extinctions points to major ecological changes occurring at about this same time. The pollen record shows a marked change about 13,500 years ago, when birch pollen begins to increase dramatically. This has been interpreted as an indication of a moister climate which resulted in an increase in shrubs like willow and dwarf birch. At about this time the dominant Pleistocene mammals, particularly the mammoth, horse and bison, seem to decrease in abundance. The latest date for mammoths occurring in Alaska is around 13,000 years ago, but before unquestionably accepting that time, we need dates on more specimens. In fact, we suspect that mammoths continued to exist beyond that time.

Mammoth, horse and bison fossils show a diminishing body size, dating from the time of this increase in shrubs and even earlier. Mammoths at the edge of extinction were almost tuskless compared to the gigantic three- to four-yard-long tusks of mature males in an earlier era. Likewise, bison horns began to decrease in size from their immense proportions during the peak glacial toward the small blunt horns of living bison. These size reductions and the ones in other species — even the species that did not become extinct like caribou, moose and musk-oxen — suggest that the range was deteriorating. In the North, such large mammals have a limited resource of dietary nutrients to devote to reproduction and their own growth. When there is a new pinch on resources, animals usually respond by cutting back on the nutrients they devote to growing to their maximum genetic potential. This is why families immigrating to North America from areas where protein is in short supply normally see an increase of several inches in body size among the first generation to grow up with a protein-rich diet.

These reductions in body size, and the climatic and vegetational changes occurring at this critical time, point to an ecological change as the cause of the extinctions. There does not seem to have been much snow in interior Alaska during the glacials. That changed after 13,500 years ago, when the weather began to slip toward the present conditions marked by little winter wind and snowfalls regularly accumulating to a yard or occasionally a yard-and-a-half. Such deep snow covers critical survival food for grazers like bison, horse, saiga and mammoth. Bison that have been reintroduced into the Interior can live here only in areas which are blown clear of snow.

In addition to increasing snow depths, the character of the vegetation began to change. Instead of forbs and grasses adapted to drier conditions, the woody plants began to come in with their greater concentrations of defense chemicals. These required considerable moisture to flourish. Plants like mosses decompose slowly, as do the toxic parts of spruce and broad-leafed evergreens like Labrador tea, which began to dominate the vegetation. These plant parts accumulate and insulate the soil so the permafrost level rises, which restricts the amount of nitrogen and other nutrients available to plants. The cooler soils and limited nutrients reinforce selection for kinds of plants that can tolerate these conditions; that is, plants so well protected by toxins that they cannot safely be eaten by large mammals. And so the cycle continues until there is little that most large mammals can eat. Moose are able to do well in the winter by feeding on the willows and similar plants which grow along disturbed areas like streams; they could not survive in mature spruce forests. In fact, we know of no large mammal that can. Thus, the ecological theory argues for a climatic-vegetational shift to account for the large mammal extinctions.

The matter of late-Pleistocene extinctions has engaged the curiosity and efforts of a number of researchers and certainly we know more about the problem now than we did five, 10, or 30 years ago. But a simple resolution seems unlikely. Like any historical science, we are working at a distance and with spotty data; and like most ecological investigations, the situation is probably more complex than we know.

At first glance the grasslands of the glacial past, reconstructed from remnants buried in the frozen silt, appear dramatically different from the Interior as we know it today. But the biota of the present is connected to the mammoth steppe by many species and many adaptations to conditions found in both environments. In fact, we think the present can best be seen and experienced with this past in mind. The present lies like a thin warm crust over the frozen past: a real baked Alaska.

Details of the behavior and ecology of present animals and plants of the Interior would fill many books. We've chosen just a few animals and ecological themes to highlight our sketch of the present landscape.

# Fire — The Creative Force

The boreal forests of the Interior are often categorized as taiga. On a large scale this is a fitting classification, but when we examine the various habitats more closely they appear quite diverse. For example, many hilltops are above treeline, which is reached at an altitude of around 2,000 feet in the Fairbanks area. These tundra uplands are dominated by mixtures of low-growing willow and birch species and by a variety of berry bushes. At higher altitudes herbs and miniature broadleaf evergreens are most common. These small woody plants often live to be quite old; they comprise a sort of Lilliputian forest, recognized only from a vole's-eye view. Despite exposure to sun, drying winds and steep drainages, these tundra uplands are almost always moist. Soils at these higher altitudes are shallow and permafrost is pervasive, even on south-facing slopes.

The lowlands and river valleys are also complex vegetational mixtures. The largest trees tend to grow along the streams, where good drainage and warmth of the water keeps permafrost from forming. Away from the streams permafrost is common to spotty, and habitats are generally damp, particularly considering the scant annual rainfall the Interior receives. This dominance of moisture-seeking plants thriving on only 12 inches of precipitation each year is mainly due to poor drainage conditions. Most local lakes have formed where the insulating mat of vegetation overlying the permafrost has been broken. As the permafrost thaws and settles, water accumulates; this standing water further warms the permafrost and soon a thaw lake forms. Such lakes are usually quite shallow with black organic mud bottoms.

The high latitude of interior Alaska means that our sun angle is quite shallow, even at the peak of summer. This makes exposure an important variable in determining the character of habitat for any specific location. Steep south-facing slopes are like a little bit of Colorado in the Northland. Because they tip toward the sun, such slopes catch a fuller warmth; indeed, they have often been equated with an effective latitude of 30 to 40 degrees north, compared with the true latitude of 65 degrees at Fairbanks.

Many plants commonly found much farther south will grow on these slopes. You can sit on a warm south slope during a spring day, basking in the sun amid the sound of bees visiting early flowers, while the flats below and the north-facing slope behind you are still buried in snow. Dall sheep and other animals also seek out these south slopes, where spring vegetation first emerges. In some ways, slopes like those along the Tanana River are a remnant fringe of the mammoth steppe. They are drier, they have a longer growing season, the snow melts earlier and they support a different array of plants.

Fires must have been common in the Interior when grassy habitats were widespread during the glacials. Grasslands are susceptible to fires during dry seasons. Most of the aboveground plant tissue is dead then, and it has an extremely high surface to mass ratio — matted wisps of grass are among the most easily burned natural tinders. But as woodlands recolonized the Interior at the end of the last glacial, grass fires must eventually have ceased and fires perhaps became uncommon; but not for long. Soon another kind of wildfire began — the forest fire — which now plays a key role in patterning interior Alaska's vegetation.

Most wildfires in the North are started by lightning. During long dry spells, tall cumulus clouds build in the skies, generating violent flashes of electron exchange. The instantaneous arc of kiln-hot energy ripping down a dry spruce is surefire. The fires go with the wind, leaving thousands of acres blackened, with crooked burned fingers reaching downwind into the landscape. Summer air in the Interior frequently has a haze and a slight sharpness to the smell. The smokey haze and low sun angle produce long, beautiful sunsets and sunrises along the northern horizon. Local radio stations keep tabs on the location, size and stage of different burns for those interested.

The landscape left by a fire remains grim for several years, but what we observe in the decades that follow is a flourishing growth of broadleaf plants, claiming the burn as their own for the next 50 to 100 years. It is this early successional growth of willows and berries, forbs and grasses that makes the richest habitat for many northern mammals. Minerals and nutrients have been released by the fires, soils have thawed, the insulating forest floor litter has been removed. In short, the fire has created a landscape of opportunity for new organisms with new talents. To experience and know the Interior, one must understand the important role of fire. It is a natural part of wild interior Alaska, like the silty rivers and the deep loess banks. Fire is ultimately responsible for what you see in the landscape; it is a fire-driven ecosystem.

In well-drained uplands and along rivers, spruce trees will ultimately replace birch, cottonwood and aspen. It is a common sight to see a gnarled, stag-head white birch tree being eclipsed by dark green spruce emerging from below. Eventually, if left undisturbed, most forests of the Interior will grow dark with a closed canopy of spruce.

Spruce is a good competitor on the thin northern soils. It requires little each year from the few available soil nutrients. Unlike a deciduous tree, it does not shed its needles annually but waits four years or more and then changes them subtly, not in a molt, but imperceptibly as a musk-ox sheds its long guard hairs. To live on the poor interior soils, spruce plays a conservative game. It keeps most of its nutrients aboveground in the tree itself, chancing damage. There are no reserves below ground, unlike the willow which can regenerate even if cut back to the ground. But the spruce is not so exposed to danger as one might think at a casual glance. The willow's main enemies are animal herbivores, and here spruce has a special hedge on its gamble of exposing its nutrients aboveground — it is poisonous. Concentrations of terpenes in old spruce needles and spruce bark are strong enough to kill the gut flora of moose and hares. Without these organisms these animals cannot digest the woody tissues that are the bulk of their diets. A browser can tolerate a little spruce in its diet, diluting it with other less toxic plants, but not too much. Signs of heavy spruce browsing suggest that somebody is starving.

You may rightly ask how spruce grouse, porcupines and spruce bark beetles avoid these poisons. There is an interesting story behind each of these animal species and the particular vulnerabilities of the spruce they exploit. When a spruce needle forms it has comparatively few toxins, and in fact, the tree toxins do not develop fully until the needles are more than one year old. Spruce grouse fly from tree to tree finding those with the lowest concentrations of toxins and eating the juvenile needles. Needles near the crown of the tree are usually the least protected. On this diet grouse remain healthy and fat throughout the winter.

Porcupines climb to the upper reaches of spruce trees and eat the less defended cambium hidden under the coarse outer bark. It is a good strategy. Because toxic defenses are not free to the plant, a principle governing their use is that, for any given part of the plant, the intensity of defense must be matched to the likelihood of damage versus the cost of losing that part of the plant. In the case of trees, since most big browsers can reach only the lower parts, most of the toxins are located there. The upper tree parts are least defended,

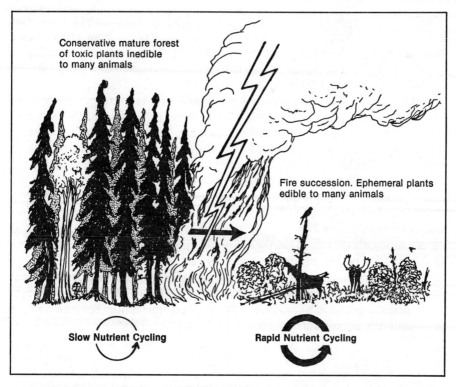

Conservative mature forest
of toxic plants inedible
to many animals

Fire succession. Ephemeral plants
edible to many animals

**Slow Nutrient Cycling**

**Rapid Nutrient Cycling**

*Fire plays a major role in the productivity of woodlands in the Interior. Most fires in the North start naturally, usually by lightning. Because spruce burns easily and has few defenses against fire, northern forests burn frequently. Most hillsides are in some stage of recovery from past fires, or what we refer to as succession back to a mature spruce woodlands. The first plants to recolonize after a burn are usually short-lived shrubs and grasses. These succession species can tolerate being eaten by mammals because much of their biomass is underground, in roots which store nutrient and energy reserves. These shrubs and grasses take nutrients from the soil efficiently and promote rapid recycling of soil nutrients. Mature spruce, on the other hand, are conservative, holding most of their biomass above the surface. They take up nutrients slowly from the poor forest soil. Without subsurface reserves, they cannot afford to be browsed much. The spruce contain toxic resins to ward off animals, but these resins also make the spruce highly combustible. Fire is thus important in maintaining a more varied landscape where mature spruce forests and succession species can live in a heterogenous mosaic.*

commensurate with the lower likelihood of being browsed above the head of a moose or hare. But porcupines can do more than stretch, they can climb.

Most of the poisons in spruce bark are volatile, so they will deter a browser before it bites. The spicy fragrance of a coniferous forest is in fact a warning from the trees — don't eat me. This volatility is increased with heat, as you know from walking through such a forest in the heat of the summer. But the intense heat of a forest fire is enough to drive virtually all of these volatile poisons out of the trees. Snowshoe hares regularly seek out and eat the charred bark of spruce after a fire, seemingly without penalty. And this is also where some spruce bark beetles come in.

Most insects dislike smoke, which is why a campfire is a good mosquito or blackfly deterrent. The reason insects dislike smoke so much is that toxins employed by the plants as insecticides are liberated by the heat and become part of the smoke. When a smoker lights a cigarette, he is volatilizing an insecticide (nicotine) in tobacco leaves to assimilate it directly through his moist pulmonary membranes. For insects, the smoke contains a concentrate of a toxin evolved to exclude them from the plant's nutrients.

But perhaps you have noticed that while campfires keep the mosquitoes and flies down, another little insect is attracted in droves by the smoke. Unless you've paid close attention you've probably missed them, because these tiny bark beetles are not offensive to humans. They follow the smoke to its source because where there is smoke there is heat, and where there is heat the offending toxins are driven off, making some spruce bark vulnerable to invasion.

While these terpenes are a spruces' ace-in-the-hole against herbivores, they do have a detrimental side. They ignite and burn easily. Just throw a spruce bough on the fire and hear the explosive *whoosh*. And therein lies the source of our story about fire in northern woodlands. Some researchers have even proposed that petroleum deposits are, in fact, the accumulated droplets of hydrocarbon toxins from the dense gymnosperm forests of the Mesozoic, ancient forests that were protecting themselves from being eaten by dinosaurs. Whatever their origin, petroleum products are a good metaphor for the intense combustibility of a spruce forest.

## Plant Poisons and Hare Highs

When the forest fires of interior Alaska rage across the country all life in their path is consumed, yet the blackened landscape of a new burn is a fertile place. Minerals that were bound up in tree tissues fall to the ground as ash. The newly exposed and enriched soil resembles a garden plot ready for seeding, and a rich bloom of plants soon occupies the burn.

The species of plants that thrive in a new burn are quite different from those lost in the fire; they are colonizers, plants that are evolutionarily tuned to sprout, grow and set seed in the most spendthrift fashion. Fireweed is probably the showiest of these colonizers; its bright midsummer blossoms quickly turn into thousands and thousands of wind-borne seeds. Many colonizers are forbs and grasses; others are willows and berry bushes. All are characterized by a fast rate of growth, with an ability to extract nutrients from the soil quickly. And they all begin reproducing, whether by setting seed or vegetatively, without delay.

Most of these plant species were originally adapted to colonizing along shifting streams or other transient habitats. Because their habitats are so undependable, they keep many of their nutrients below ground so they can recover if breakup or another fire removes their aboveground tissue. Their strategy is to grow and reproduce — quickly — before the next catastrophe wipes them away and before the trees come in and shade them out.

It is important to understand the evolution of these pioneers, because in one way or another most mammals that live in the North depend on the succession of plants that follow a burn. Why are these plants important? It is as if the willows are wagering with nature, gambling that they can grow quickly enough to seed before they are destroyed by a physical event or eaten up. Willows, unlike spruce, don't spend much of their energy or nutrient budget on defense. For these colonizing species, resources put toward defense must be withdrawn from the growth and reproduction part of the resource ledger, and that greatly reduces their ability to take advantage of the transient habitat that is their particular niche.

Thus, more than any other plants in the North, these early colonizers with their low defense budgets are the best eating. Their relative lack of toxins makes them easily digestible, and because they grow rapidly they are high in energy and nutrients. Moose find them delectable. This is why hunters in the Interior find moose in old burns, along streams, or in the willow fingers which penetrate into the tundra. Moose are in these areas because of the special kinds of forage that grow there.

Because most of the plants that grow after a burn are low to the ground and tasty, they make excellent forage for snowshoe hares. As snow accumulates during the winter, it lifts the hares higher and higher up into the shrubs, giving them access to more food. The snow's weight also bends the limbs over, bringing yet more food within reach. Indeed, these upper limbs are best of all because they are the youngest, most nutritious and least defended with toxins. Old burns and river bottoms are therefore choice habitats for snowshoe hares.

I [Dale Guthrie] arrived in Alaska during a bright August in 1963, eager for the experience, but like every newcomer to the Far North I didn't know exactly what to expect. Although the beauty and immensity of the landscape was overwhelming, the things that impressed me most were the hares. They were everywhere. Walking through the woods that fall I startled literally dozens of snowshoe hares. When one thumped its hind feet before running, there were so many that the thumping spread to the edge of earshot. As one hare heard another, it too would thump, carrying the sound like a contagion through the woods. Hunting them was no sport. I finally tired of eating them and began to use their meat for sausage.

I could not see how anybody could starve in this land of plenty. Then, just two years later, there were almost no hares to be found. In some areas you could walk for hours without finding a single track in old snow. By chance, I had arrived during a major hare population boom. They are not always so dramatic, but that one was spectacular. The snowshoe hare cycle personifies the boom-bust character of the North.

With amazing regularity, these peaks in hare populations occur throughout the Interior about every 10 years. They may vary a year or so in different regions or sometimes even in the same locality, but the cycle is well recognized all across the North. In fact, the snowshoe hare cycle has repercussions that radiate all the way to New York City, because fur prices more or less cycle with the hares. Many of the furs sold in New York come from animals that were, in their former lives, directly or indirectly eaters of hare. Fox, lynx, wolverine and wolf become more abundant during the snowshoe hare booms, so trappers are more successful. These predators also experience steep population increases and declines as secondary cyclers. Predatory birds like goshawks, Swainson's hawks and great horned owls also increase as hare populations build. And when hare numbers decline, the predatory birds and the furbearers both turn to other

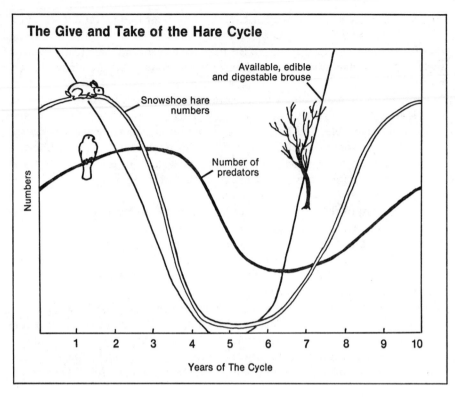

### The Give and Take of the Hare Cycle

Available, edible
and digestable brouse

Snowshoe hare
numbers

Number of
predators

Numbers

Years of The Cycle

*Snowshoe hares* undergo dramatic density cycles in Alaska's Interior. The duration of these cycles is about 10 years. Because hares are important prey to many predators, the cycle affects the abundance of many other species as well. Predators follow along, slightly out of phase with the hare cycle. When predators become abundant, grouse and porcupines are preyed upon more intensively, and thus also cycle in a 10-year pattern. The availability of edible browse with sufficient nutrients also cycles with the hares. Scientists now think that the availability of this critical browse is the main factor in hare cycles.

herbivores like porcupines and grouse. As a result, these animals become tertiary cyclers, their numbers rising and falling slightly out of phase with the hares.

Scientists have been studying the snowshoe hare cycle for decades, and some recent work has finally offered a convincing explanation of why hare populations in the North fluctuate so markedly. For years there were many competing theories to account for this phenomenon, including sunspot cycles, cyclic predator-prey interactions, genetic cycles, physiological shifts in reproduction, nutrient and energy availability and so on.

The problem that had eluded scientists was why hares continued to decline to such a deep low rather than rebound quickly. Many people had observed that the vegetation, which had been greatly affected by the abundant hares, began to recover immediately as the hares continued to decline. Why didn't the hares respond to the increasing food supply and recover at the same rate? Some scientists argued that the high numbers of predators kept them from recovering, and only when the predators were also reduced from lack of food would hare cycle swing upward once again.

New evidence, primarily the research of Dr. John Bryant of the University of Alaska, has shown that plants that are the hares' winter food do not respond passively to being eaten by hares. The massive browse damage inflicted by hares during the crest of the cycle stimulates an increased level of toxins in the plants. A heavily browsed plant responds by increasing the toxicity in older growth and in the smaller diameter, new growth plant parts that form the bulk of the hares' diet. Furthermore, the new levels of toxins do not disappear after a season but continue for up to three or four years, during which time the hares, of course, continue to decline. The casual observer sees plenty of green, delectable forage, but to the hares it is a poisonous cafeteria and they continue to act as if they are starving — as in fact they are.

Walking through a mixed woodland after the crest of a hare cycle, you see the many dead saplings girdled by hares in their desperation to find suitable food. Not only is the most recent damage there, but also the healed scars and dead trunks from the last hare population boom. If you look carefully, damage from the previous boom, 20 years ago, can even be seen. Hares seem to be a prime factor in thinning the close-growing young woodlands into more open successional forests.

Because hares appear to be mainly nutrient-limited rather than calorie-limited, they do not put on major reserves of fat like other northern mammals. Energy foods are abundant for them and they are always well fed, but they can die of nutrient starvation even with a full stomach. Hares do most of their digesting in a side branch of the gut called the cecum, related to the vestigal human appendix, but the hares' cecum is more than two feet long. Microorganisms in the cecum produce a variety of complex vitamins essential to the animals' health, but apparently hares are unable to digest these vitamins through the cecal wall so they do a peculiar thing. Even people who have spent their entire lives in hare country are probably unaware of it. In the morning before laying up for the day, a hare will hunker over with its head between its legs, and squirt the contents of the cecum into its mouth and eat it. This way of gaining access to those necessary vitamins sounds peculiar, but it seems to work well.

The 10-year cycle of hare abundance and scarcity epitomizes other long term boom-bust cycles in the unstable ecosystems of the Far North. One can depend on spring coming after the long winter, but not too much else. This high contrast in the annual cycle of seasons is both a metaphor for and foundation of other boom-bust cycles. Spring sunshine returns with unbelievable suddenness from the cold darkness of winter. White hares quickly molt to brown and the air begins to hum with life — mosquitoes are a sure sign of spring.

# Spring and Mosquitoes

Mosquitoes must not have been a serious pest during the glacials. The arid climate, lack of woodlands, light winter snows and strong winds of the glacial periods must have been difficult for most kinds of insects. There were probably very few pools of standing water. Conditions are certainly different today, when the Interior has a fully deserved reputation for hordes of mosquitoes.

Spring comes on with a disquieting rush in Alaska's Interior. One week there is snow on the ground and freezing nighttime temperatures, the next week water is running everywhere and migrant birds have arrived. Leaf buds open, the landscape turns green and the young of the year are born: Dall sheep lambs, moose and caribou calves, fox and wolf pups, their arrival timed to take best advantage of the short growing season. The brief summer affects cold-blooded animals in an even more intense way. To develop, grow and reproduce within the four months from breakup to autumn freeze, the multitude of invertebrates that live in Alaska's Interior must be in a hurry. As a result, insects bloom like the algae in the warming ponds. Even before all the snow patches are gone the air is abuzz with activity. There are many interesting stories to tell about invertebrate lifestyles and strategies in the North, but we have chosen to take a closer look at an insect you can't help but notice, one that epitomizes the brief summer bloom of insect life, the mosquito.

Interior Alaska is an immensely congenial place for mosquitoes because it offers ample quantities of the two things they need to develop and flourish: water and food. The first phase of the mosquito life cycle is aquatic, because the females lay their eggs on or near water. Because frozen ground does not allow melting snow to percolate down to the water table, spring runoff is captured in millions of little pools. Bogs and muskegs make the lowlands a miserable place for people, as they are almost impassable, but for small aquatic creatures they are a splendid incubator, warmed by a 24-hour sun. Another reason mosquitoes flourish is that the bloom of microorganisms in these little pools provides food for the growing larvae.

Like summer flowers, mosquitoes do not all bloom at once. There is a succession of emerging species, each staggered slightly from the other. The first out are the big, slow-moving bombers of the genus *Culiseta*. Females of this species overwinter beneath the snow and emerge while it is still melting. They are never so abundant as to be overwhelming. With their dangling legs and blur of wings, the *Culiseta* alight gently and slowly probe around with their bloodsucking proboscises. These early mosquitoes give you a false sense of safety, one which is soon destroyed.

Females of the genus *Aedes* lay their eggs during late summer, in little rafts or imbedded in the mud. These eggs remain snow-covered for most of the year, but when the snow melts they develop rapidly. The large *Culiseta* mosquitoes have hardly abated when the *Aedes* species, small-bodied and aggressive, begin to emerge. By mid-June they finally become so rash that there are no preliminaries — just the mad attack of a blur not much bigger than a gnat buzzing onto your forehead, sucking blood before you can swing your swat. There should be standard numeral ratings for mosquito abundance. For instance, Stage 5: must walk with eyes slit and talk through teeth. There are occasions around the end of June in the lowlands and sometimes on warm, quiet days in the open tundra, when only a head-net can provide a modicum of peace from the swarms of mosquitoes.

There are 27 different species of mosquitoes in Alaska. Most require at least one feeding from a warm-blooded vertebrate to lay a full-sized clutch of eggs; however, there are some interesting specializations. Adult members of one species feed only on a little wood frog. The female mosquito needs proteins she obtains from vertebrate blood to produce eggs, so only she does the biting. The males hover around warm-blooded animals, like kids around a corner soda fountain, trying to locate a female, but they don't need to eat. They just run on stored energy until they expire. Females can lay some eggs after drawing sap from plants, but in this case they produce fewer eggs or eggs that hatch poorly. They need the nutrients available in vertebrate blood.

How did female mosquitoes ever get into the strange business of sucking blood from animals? One theory suggests that they were first feeders on fruit and sap. Their tubular proboscis has a bladelike device, a bit like an apple corer, that the mosquito uses to penetrate the tough plant cuticle. A thin saliva is secreted down this tube and the nutritious plant fluids, thus diluted, are sucked up. The sweet taste of sap cues the mosquito that it is on the right track. The taste of amino acids and glucose in blood, however, provides the same sweet flavor, allowing the mosquito to become a carnivore rather than herbivore. The sharp proboscis penetrates the tough outer layer of vertebrate skin just as it does the cuticle of plants.

Mosquitoes have a good sense of smell, and heat sensors like a ground-to-air missile. And they are fast; it is difficult to outrun them. A dash across the tundra usually gives only a few seconds, respite until they track you down, like blue-tick coon hounds following a hot trail. Nowadays, mosquito repellents allow us to enjoy Alaskan summers, but before these were available the Indians, and later miners, had to resort to smoke from fires. Under severe mosquito conditions it was common to carry a smudge fire in the bow of the canoe, letting the smoke sweep back over the paddlers to hold down the haze of mosquitoes.

Dragonflies are the main predators of adult mosquitoes; in fact the Koyukon Athabaskan name for dragonfly *(tl'eeyh ahona)* translates as "mosquito hawk." They increase until by the end of summer they are a common sight. We have a large west-facing chimney that runs several stories up the side of the house. The afternoon sun warms the stone and makes the chimney a spot where dragonflies like to overnight. They collect there as evening comes on, and the chimney ends up looking like the flight deck of an ancient aircraft carrier clotted with airplanes.

Mosquitoes have time for only one generation in the interior Alaskan summer, so when all the individuals hatched in one year have emerged, usually by the Fourth of July, they begin to disappear rapidly. Some run out of reserves, some are eaten by dragonflies, but they all disappear almost as quickly as they came. By the first of August only a few survivors are still humming.

## Gambler Trout

The formation of glaciers during the Pleistocene affected many different plants and animals, but probably none more than northern members of the trout family. These fishes had adapted to cold northern streams by being a most active predator, ready to seize an insect when it fell to the surface or overtake and eat smaller fish. This active predatory life produced a powerfully muscled body with torpedo contours.

But Pleistocene glacial activity clouded the streams with silt, and the water became uninhabitable for creatures which had been the trout's food. Scientists believe these conditions pushed some trout downstream, to freshwater deltas where rivers emptied into the ocean. In these delta feeding areas the fish gradually adapted to the higher salinity of the sea, then later moved into the sea itself. But these particular trout never adapted to laying their eggs at sea where there were too many predators. After they matured, the trout made a long journey back to reproduce in cold riffles in the upper reaches of the rivers that were their ancestral homes. This journey and this fish, the salmon, form a significant part of the story of interior Alaska. Without salmon or similar migratory fish as a dependable staple resource, there would have been far fewer Athabaskan people in the Interior when the European explorers arrived here.

Successive episodes of glaciation during the Pleistocene blocked and separated different drainages, even continents, and produced a complex array of Pacific salmon species. Three of these species make spawning runs up the rivers of interior Alaska: chum, king and silver. As young fish, these salmon begin a wide arc of migration that loops round the Bering Sea by the shores of Asia. During this time they feed on large plankton in the surface waters and grow at a fantastic rate. Several years later — prime, sleek and heavy with roe or milt — the mature salmon begin their return into the delta of their home stream.

Moving upstream in the fresh water, salmon lose their marine parasites and begin following the smell of home. Each little brook is chemically distinct from every other brook, and salmon remember the smell of the one in which they were hatched years earlier. They keep to the stream edges where the backwaters and eddies help their travel. Flying in a small plane over clear stretches of a salmon stream, you can see the silvery-green ribbons of fish moving upstream. As the salmon near their ancestral breeding grounds, they begin an irreversible transformation into their fighting colors and weaponry. The males begin to discolor, turning red in the case of the king salmon, and their underjaws hook out in a menacing clasping vise, ready for other males who would challenge their spawning areas.

Each male seems to know which spots the females will favor. He selects one of these spots, establishes a territory there and defends it from other male intruders. When a female chooses his spot, she begins her nest by digging a hole in the loose gravel, turning on her side and gouging her tail into the bottom, letting the current sweep the debris away. When ready she lays some of her many eggs and at the same time the male sprays them with milky white semen. Eggs tucked neatly into the depression are now covered by the female, using the same tail movements to stir the gravel upstream so it will settle onto the nest. These little pink balls, the size of small peas, rapidly begin to look like miniature salmon. As the fish develop they stay protected beneath the gravel, living on the large yolk that the female salmon built from the fat of the sea. With this yolk sac attached they are called "alevins." Finally, they emerge from the gravel as "fry" to feed on microorganisms, insect larvae and copepods. At about two inches they are called "fingerlings," and in the case of the chum they begin to migrate to the sea in their first year. King salmon stay on and grow larger before heading for salt water. Back at sea the cycle begins again, as it has since the Pleistocene.

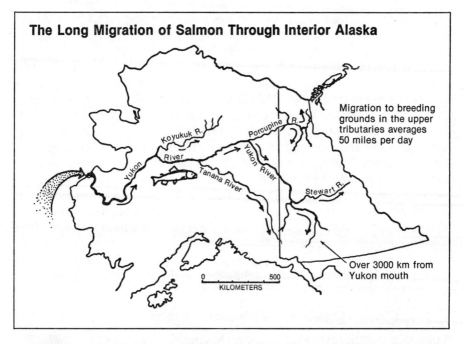

**The Long Migration of Salmon Through Interior Alaska**

Migration to breeding grounds in the upper tributaries averages 50 miles per day

Over 3000 km from Yukon mouth

*Many residents of the Interior eagerly await the migration of salmon through their homeland. This is one of the longest migrations of fish to their breeding grounds in the world. Three species of salmon pass through the Interior: king, chum and silver. The fish average about 50 miles a day, and some travel more than 1,800 miles. All salmon die after breeding. The young salmon slowly work their way downstream to the ocean, swing into the Bering Sea, then migrate back upstream as adults to complete the cycle.*

Once the females have laid all of their roe and the males their milt, they do not have the genetic information to live. Unlike Atlantic salmon, these Pacific species do not return to the sea, but lie gray, half alive and half dead, in the slow waters at the foot of the riffle. In a few days the spent salmon will furnish the attending bald eagles, gulls and bears with enough energy and nutrients to help raise their young.

Why these salmon always die after a single run is a fascinating evolutionary problem. Reproduction might be likened to gambling. Is it better to have one grand try at getting rich or better to be conservative and play cautiously? The best bet depends on what is to be gained and what is to be lost. The successful salmon, having made it from egg to sea and then back again to the spawning grounds, is lucky indeed, for most of his cohorts succumbed to the many dangers along the way. The chances of reproducing and going through the cycle again successfully are also remote. So we could say that salmon had an evolutionary choice: the individual fish that were capable of returning to sea could only have done so by laying fewer or smaller eggs. In other words, energy allocated to longer survival and return to the sea would have left them with fewer resources for reproduction. Individual salmon that put more of their body resources into a greater number of healthy eggs must have had a greater impact on the following generations. Thus the one-shot gamble was selected. Like an annual plant that must live and set seed in a single glorious season, pulling all of its resources from its own tissue to convert them to seeds, the Pacific salmon lives one grand cycle and dies.

The importance of salmon to the people of pre-European Alaska cannot be overemphasized. Ecologists speak in terms of carrying capacity and productivity of different landscapes. The northern Interior ranks near the bottom in productivity of foods which people can consume; relying on the terrestrial resources in this country is a sometime thing. When snowshoe hares were at their cyclic low and caribou and moose were undergoing one of their episodic lows, the Interior was a lean place indeed. But summer runs of salmon brought rich marine resources to the heart of the Interior in the very form it was most needed: protein-rich steaks and energy-rich fat. The fish camp thus became an important part of the native people's yearly rounds. Salmon runs were comparatively predictable and reliable, and the fish could be dried for the long winter, both for use as human food and as fuel for sled-dog transportation. Thus these free-wheeling, on-the-go gambler trout created by the Pleistocene became a cornerstone of human subsistence in the Interior.

## Cold, Cold, Cold

In summer, interior Alaska is a lush green landscape. Much of the lowland is so thick with vegetation it is virtually impenetrable. Birds are singing everywhere and there is an inescapable whine of insect wings in your ear. But if this picture doesn't fit the non-Alaskan's image of the place, just wait until winter. The sun sinks lower and lower every day until it barely clears peaks of the Alaska Range. Snow that began accumulating in October takes on the blues and magentas of the low sun. The wind ceases to blow and cold milks the moisture from the air in flickering crystals that fall to the ground, known locally as "diamond dust."

In such stillness the colder, heavier air slowly slides to the valley bottoms producing inversions; such spells drop the mercury to temperatures of minus 50 degrees almost every winter. The story of how northern plants and animals have adapted to this extreme cold is fascinating and has been the subject of many books and scientific articles.

The most obvious way to avoid freezing in such weather is to move south before winter arrives. Most of the bird species seen here in the summer leave for the winter. Every New Year's Day the Audubon Society sponsors a bird species count all over the United States. Fairbanks birders participate, with a note of humor, searching in the thin light of midwinter for the dozen or so familiar species that constitute the whole of our winter bird list.

Like other residents who overwinter here, however, those few birds that do stay often have interesting stories. For example, the tiny redpolls, with bodies no longer than your thumb, spend the short January days eating birch seeds as fast as they can stuff them in. Birch seeds are small but nutritious, and they are available all winter long because the paper birch strategy for seed dispersal is to scatter seeds on the snow and let them wash away during breakup to some exposed soil farther down the drainage. Chickadees and redpolls, maintaining their internal temperature at 97 degrees during a cold snap of minus 50 degrees, are thus sustaining a temperature differential of 150 degrees across their little margin of insulating down.

The winter raptors (hawks and owls) and mammalian carnivores fluctuate radically with the hare cycle, but the big black ravens always seem to be here. They cruise along, rowing through the dense cold air, *whish-whish-whish-whish,* craning their necks in every direction. Studies at the University of Alaska have shown that at minus 50 degrees they still maintain a normal metabolic rate. Their bare feet are kept warm by regularly flushing the tissues with blood at about the time ice crystals would begin to form, then letting them cool down and warming them again in a repeated cycle. At minus 70 degrees ravens in laboratory cold chambers began to fluff up their feathers and pull their heads tight against their bodies.

No mammals leave the Interior for farther south except humans and the little brown bat. A few of these little bats come up for the summer to take advantage of the big insect bloom. Their main problem seems to be that they are nocturnal feeders and there is not much night in the North during the summer.

Some plants, like lichens, avoid winter problems by simply getting rid of their water altogether; others dehydrate the cell contents and put the water in spaces between the cells. For insects the solution seems to lie in finding the least-cold spot (we can't bring ourselves to say warmest), and then enriching the cell contents with some sort of antifreeze (glycerol).

These alternatives aren't open to warm-blooded creatures like birds and mammals, which must maintain their body temperatures. Northern animals must therefore be well insulated. Unlike the coats of the same species farther south, the downy undercoats of northern furbearers are dense, which is why their pelts are prized all over the world. Many northern mammals and some birds have special circulatory adaptations. Blood circulating back toward the heart from their limbs is warmed by new blood coming from the heart, so very cold blood is not taken into the core of the body. This process helps keep the animals' limbs and feet from freezing and helps maintain core body temperature.

There are also behavioral strategies for handling winter life in the Interior. One is to hibernate, like ground squirrels, in some spot that doesn't get severely cold. Another is to have a dependable, energy-rich food source throughout the winter months, like the one snowshoe hares find in the twigs of deciduous plants. The main strategy, however, is to eat so much food during the summer and autumn that accumulated fat stores will compensate as the animal descends the energy slope of the long winter. Thus, by late autumn, most northern animals are carrying important supplies of fat.

Some animals lay up stores not on their bodies but in caches. The pika hoards willow leaves, dried in the open and then stashed under rocks in areas where snow drifts in the hills. The archetypical storer, the red squirrel, lays up bulky middens of spruce cones in prime territories. Usually these big midden piles, complete with a burrow in the middle to hold the squirrel among its wealth during the cold days of winter, have enough reserve cones to last for three or four years. The reason for this can be found in the erratic nature of white spruce cone production — the spruce trees may fail to produce cones for several years in a row. In those years only the squirrels on the best territories survive, making these areas well worth the hard effort devoted to their defense.

There are a few places where a mammal can avoid the full intensity of midwinter cold. One is under the water and another is under the snow. Deep streams and lakes do not freeze to the bottom, and even though the water which remains is near freezing it is much warmer than the air. Beaver and muskrat and water shrews thus escape the sharp spikes of cold under the ice.

Warmth collected in the ground from the preceding summer slowly radiates outward all through the winter. However, the snow acts as an insulator and slows that flow of heat. This movement of heat from the ground creates a crystalline layer at the base of the blanket of snow, called the subnivian space. It is not easy for small mammals to travel in this space. Fortunately for them, grasses and sedges do not grow like woody plants but have their meristematic, or growth, tissue at the base and not at the tip. Voles and lemmings clip and eat this nutritious base of the grass stem, leaving the more fibrous tops. Shrews zigzag through this subnivean space rooting for hibernating insects. All is well in the winter for voles under the snow: It is comparatively warm, their main enemies — the predatory birds — are no longer a threat, and they fatten on winter-cured forage, berries and seeds. All is well indeed, except for their winter nemeses, the little snow weasel and the larger black-tailed ermine. Hunting mice in the white crystal caverns is their specialty.

Humans coping with such cold must face the same constraints and have traditionally responded to the long northern winters with similar strategies. They have stored food in caches and as fat, used well-insulated clothing and made warm shelters from the cold. Their low population density in the North during traditional times reflects the frequent hard times and occasional bounty of this land.

## Living Amid the Past

The immense plates of stone that comprise the foundation of interior Alaska date back millions of years. Most of these were formed in a time before humans, or anything like humans, lived. No human eye ever saw a dinosaur. It is easy to get lost in fossil history. There is so much of it and both the numbers and names can be enormous, but you cannot really find your way without your imagination. It is a bit like visiting the ruins or a Neolithic tomb in the British Isles and realizing that this tomb was a ruin when Roman soldiers stopped by two millennia ago to eat their lunch. In fact, the tomb was even a ruin to the Druid farmers who worked the valley 1,000 years before that.

Prehistory sometimes gets compacted and blurred when our tour bus through time travels too quickly. This chapter has not been a tour to the distant ruins. We have only been talking about the topmost icing, the fine powdery dust that forms the shallow mantle on top of the hard rock ruins of interior Alaska — the last part of the Pleistocene.

Pleistocene mammals of the mammoth steppe were here when humans arrived. These first Alaskans made their tools from fresh white mammoth ivory, worked the skins of these furry ice age creatures into clothing and listened to the roar of lions coming through the winter night. But the mammoth steppe was already changing. There is only tenuous evidence of people being in the Far North before woody plants began to recolonize the Interior at the end of the last glacial, about 13,000 to 14,000 years ago. Perhaps some of these changes allowed humans to colonize the North.

The windy, woodless mammoth steppe which existed during the last glacial may have been too harsh for humans. Certainly the availability of large mammals to eat was not a limiting factor. Large mammal resources existed in the Far North long before signs of human habitation. But as woody plants came back into the North, they would have furnished a critical source of heat and material for tools. Large mammals of the mammoth steppe were disappearing at the time the woodlands recolonized northward, but the same climatic changes that allowed these plants to survive would also have been more hospitable to humans.

Thus, early people of the Interior found a landscape unlike ours in many ways, and certainly they experienced much that we would find strange. Yet, climatologists tell us that the difference between a full glacial climate and that of today was at best a matter of a few degrees. Perhaps even more likely, the glacial conditions were a matter of seasonal shifts in cold, wind and moisture patterns within the year rather than dramatic changes in year-to-year averages. Small climatic changes which persist for a long time do occasion large changes in vegetation and animals.

The ancestral people most surely understood the dramatic effects of wildfire and of wildlife cycles, felt the June plague of mosquitoes and perhaps puzzled over the mysterious giant red fish that appeared in the streams as adults, then spawned and died. They must have known much of the same Interior we know — the silty rivers and their steep loess banks, baked-Alaska permafrost and the boom-bust, yin-yang extremes of the seasons. The seasonal rhythms of the Pleistocene still rhyme through the present.

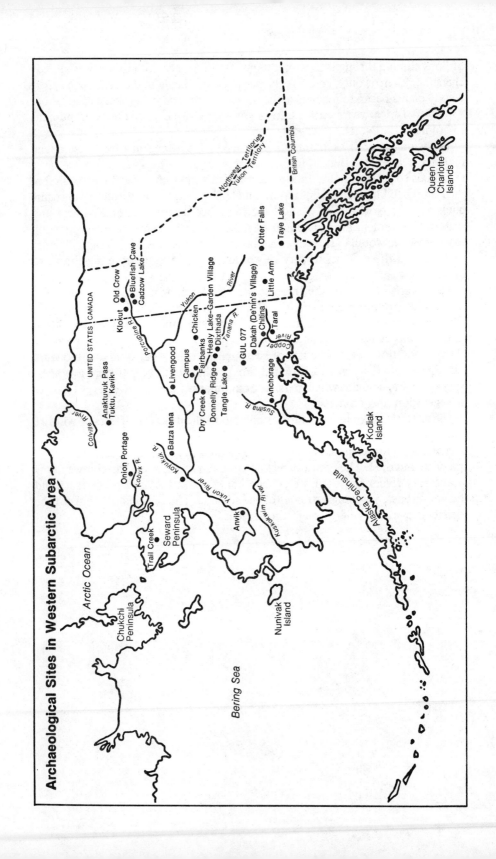

# Archaeological Sites in Western Subarctic Area

# Footprints on the Land

### The Origins of Interior Alaska's People

#### By Jean S. Aigner

*Editor's note: Jean S. Agner, Professor of Anthropology at the University of Alaska, Fairbanks, has participated in archaeological and anthropological surveys throughout Alaska.*

## The Old Woman's Tale

It was a summer evening, in a grove of willows somewhere near the center of a great northern land mass, 15,000 years before this land would be called Alaska. But already there were people here, little nomadic bands, with one or two dozen members in each, scattered through the expanse of grassland tundra. People had camped in this spot before, and they would use it many more times throughout the centuries to come.

There were three tents in the camp, made from animal skins drawn over wooden frames and held down by large stones. In the open area between them, fish were drying and a communal hearth burned low. An old lady sat beside the campfire, soaking up its warmth as she lost herself in tales of the past. A group of young boys listened intently while she spoke, their skeptical expressions half-hidden in the dim glow. The woman, who had recently joined their band, told of a giant hairy beast that towered over the hunters and had great curved tusks longer than the height of two tall men. She made no claim to actually having joined in the kill; it wouldn't have been seemly anyway because such hunting was the exclusive domain of men. She could have helped to butcher and dry the meat, but she didn't even claim this. The old woman said only that long, long ago one of her ancestors saw the last living elephant killed.

But the youngsters still wondered about her story. Did she just say it happened far in the past so no one their group might encounter would contradict her story? Nevertheless, it was exciting to hear someone tell of such a large, meaty and surely dangerous prey. They saw no reason to doubt her stories that bison and horses once abounded in the meadowlands, since a few herds still remained. But even these animals were half the size the old woman described. Wasn't that evidence that her stories were only for children? In spite of their doubts, her evening tales drew them.

Adults in the group were not the least skeptical of the old lady's accounts. Everyone knew that in ancient times the animals had been much larger; all the stories said so. What's more, several people in the band had relatives, who knew of others, who had actually seen the giant animals — not alive, but in the ice. A couple of hunters from a band near the north fork of the river had been unlucky enough to slip down a sink hole, and while waiting for rescue they had pressed their faces against the ice along one side. Literally staring back through a murk rather like frozen muddy lake water was a huge bison. Its head and horns were at least two feet broader than any living bison. Although no one had ever seen an elephant in this way, there was ample proof that stories about them were true. Each year leg bones of these giant creatures washed out of the banks of the big river to the south. Perhaps next spring the young boys would find some of these bones, and then the stories would take on a new meaning.

In fact, the old lady's tales, as well as those of the hunters trapped in the sink hole, were all true, right down to the 14-foot tusks on the elephant and the massive head on the bull bison. It is also likely that earlier people of northeast Asia and Beringia — ancestors of the people who would occupy interior Alaska and the rest of North America — successfully hunted elephants, oversized bison and large horses sometime between 40,000 and 15,000 years ago. All of these animals gradually became smaller as the climate turned harsher. By 15,000 years ago the horses were quite small, standing lower than a person's head. By 10,000 to 12,000 years ago, people living in Alaska or northeast Asia no longer encountered even the small elephants (mammoths), and horses had also vanished from the Alaska side. There were fewer bison than ever, and caribou were now the only common large mammals. Sometime later, the forest spread north to the Interior and familiar animal forms like moose, beaver, brown bear and muskrat came along with it.

In the rest of this chapter we are going to talk about the origin and history of Alaska's indigenous people. We'll start with a discussion of how archaeologists work, how they dig a site and learn from it. Then we'll talk about Alaska's first people, where they came from, how they entered Alaska and where their descendants are today. This will lead us to the history of Alaska's Athabaskan people, who are probably descendants of a second migration. They encountered very different surroundings from their predecessors and had to adjust to rapidly changing temperatures and landscape after they got here. Finally we will trace the increasing population of interior people throughout the next 7,000 years, until they become archaeologically identical to historic Athabaskans.

## Archaeologists at Work

We know that human beings have lived in Alaska for at least 12,000 and perhaps more than 30,000 years. Archaeology is the way we learn about these people — when they were in a particular place, where they came from, where they went and what happened to them during hundreds of generations. Sometimes it can even tell us if these early groups were the ancestors of modern people. From evidence uncovered by archaeologists, we know about the way ancient interior Alaskans made summer and winter houses, how they fashioned their stone and bone tools and how they changed and perfected tool design and style throughout the years. We also know what they used their tools for, and we can even conjecture whether they were mainly used by women or men.

Sometimes people changed their tools gradually throughout long periods — just as knives, forks and spoons have kept their basic shapes for hundreds of years, but many different styles or patterns have been developed. At other times people gave up a tool suddenly and accepted a new design, just as slide rules are obsolete because we now use hand calculators. Thus, tools unearthed by archaeologists tell us about changes with time. Different tools may also show how certain groups of people developed their own particular preferences. This

*This photo shows the excavation of the Colorado Creek mammoth by a University of Alaska team in 1983. The precise, straight walls are important for mapping exact location of remains both horizontally and vertically. A tripod used for mapping is at upper right and a screen for sifting soil hangs from ropes at left. (Courtesy of Jean Aigner)*

*Cleaned for photographing, mammoth bones lie as they were uncovered at the Colorado Creek site. Before the bones are removed, each is numbered and its location mapped so the site can be reconstructed on paper for interpretation later. (Courtesy of Jean Aigner)*

*Archaeological excavation is meticulous and painstaking work, in which every bit of stone or bone is mapped and saved as a possible clue to the lives of early people. Work in Alaska's Interior goes on regardless of weather because the warm season is short and the ground is frozen during most of the year. (Courtesy of Jean Aigner)*

*The archaeologist's tools reflect the care needed to properly excavate a prehistoric site. Most digging is done with trowels, not shovels, and for detailed work the soil is removed with brushes, whisk brooms and dental picks. (Courtesy of Jean Aigner)*

can be helpful in trying to trace groups through the archaeological record they leave, especially when they are conservative about keeping some tools for long periods of time.

Archaeologists use several basic principles in doing their work. First, they understand that human behavior is patterned. For example, they find that the placement of tools in the ground and in relation to one another is a key to understanding how they were used and what activities they were used for. Second, archaeologists understand that all objects or artifacts made, used, broken, discarded, and lost provide clues about past human behavior, so they collect and study every item they find in a site. Third, archaeologists understand that people occupy areas for periods of time, and in digging the ground they know that the deepest artifacts are the oldest. In other words, younger remains are left or deposited above older ones as human refuse collects in the ground. Archaeologists carefully record the positions of buried items in relation to surface level and subsurface strata. By strata they mean differently colored or textured soils, which themselves may indicate something about time.

Archaeologists use a number of special tools in their work. Surveying equipment is essential to chart the location, size and makeup of sites (places of past human activity), and to map out artificial features like house remains or graves. Soil testing equipment and soil descriptions are used to identify changes in the earth they dig through. For example, an abrupt color and texture change in the earth may reveal buried soil where ancient people found a good camping spot.

Archaeologists try to recover all of the items in a site, so they prefer to dig with small tools such as trowels and dental picks — shovels are rarely the excavator's choice. Further, it is surprising how many artifacts can adhere to small clods and go unnoticed, so the dirt is often sifted through a fine mesh screen. Items are carefully mapped to show how far below the surface they lie, what soil layer they are in and where they are located within the regularly laid out excavation pit or area. The goal is to be able to later reconstruct the exact location of every artifact in relation to every other one, as well as to the surrounding soils. Each object removed from the ground is cleaned with small brushes, numbered and cataloged so it can be studied later. Artifacts from different layers of soil are kept separate because they probably reflect different time periods. Comparison of items from different layers may reveal similarities or changes throughout time.

Thus, archaeology is a systematic study of the material remains (tools, houses and food refuse) of human behavior in the past. Every object an archaeologist finds in a site, or receives from a collector, is the product of some ancient activity. Much archaeological insight depends on the context in which the artifacts are found, their positions in time or space. For this reason, archaeologists are careful to map the exact location of every flake in the ground, and they are dismayed at casual collecting because the loss of context means a loss of knowledge about the past.

*The Owl Ridge Excavation.* The easiest way to understand how archaeologists work is to look at an example. In summer 1977, archaeologists discovered and made a preliminary excavation of an ancient site along the Teklanika River, probably the remains of a camp used nearly 9,000 years ago. The official site name is FAI 091 High Ridge –1.

Neither the packhorses nor the University of Alaska archaeology team looking for ancient sites were enthusiastic about pressing through alder thickets to the edge of a bluff overlooking the river. But once there, a quick shovel into the loose surface soils produced stone flakes that proved ancient people had stopped at this place. Further digging near the edge, where the thaw reached down several feet, revealed a deep deposit of windblown silt and fine sand, known as loess. This suggested the possibility of great age for any flakes found deep in the ground. However, nothing was uncovered except a boulder about two feet below the surface.

The boulder meant little to the archaeology student who found it, but the team geologist suggested that humans were involved in bringing it there. With his encouragement, a pair of archaeology students helicoptered to the ridge in 1982 for a two-week study. The students wished to find out how large the deposit of flakes was and see whether they could uncover flakes associated with boulders deep in the loess, proving that they were brought there by people. They thought the name Owl Ridge, after a feathered companion who watched their daily progress, was more appropriate than the original designation.

Peter Phippen and his assistant Karen Sturnick fixed the location of the site on their quadrangle map of the Fairbanks area. Next, they surveyed the bluff, drawing a contour map, locating the original shovel tests and spotting likely places for more tests. These were marked out as squares on the ground. Using trowels to remove the loess and passing it through a small mesh screen, they opened new pits, each a square meter in size. It was slow going because soil away from the bluff edge had thawed only about 18 inches deep by late August and the sun melted out only an inch or two each day. So they worked on several squares at once in round-robin fashion. Near the bluff edge, about three feet down, Peter and Karen found more flakes, and they carefully troweled the loess away to expose the flakes for mapping.

One pit produced flecks of charcoal at a depth of about 39 inches. The depth was similar to that of the early flakes, suggesting both were about the same age. Peter and Karen carefully picked out pieces with tweezers, placed them in a small plastic bag and labeled it. There was enough charcoal to date the flake level at older than 9,000 years. They had discovered a new culture level at Owl Ridge below the level of the boulder.

Each flake they uncovered, near the surface or deeply buried, was measured and mapped as to vertical depth and exact horizontal position in the pit. When more pits are opened in the future, it might be possible to understand activities that occurred at the site from the distribution of these tools. It was also important to keep the upper, younger artifacts separate from the deeper, older artifacts. They represented different visits to the bluff, with perhaps a long time between.

In several test pits, Peter and Karen located eight more large boulders, from the second visit by ancient people, which seemed to form a semicircle. Between two of them they found several broken flakes and material to test for dates. If the site was shown to be very ancient, they might obtain funds to undertake

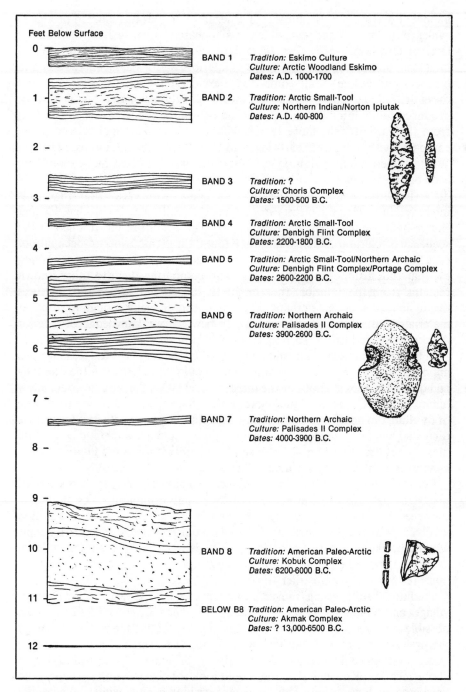

Feet Below Surface

| | | |
|---|---|---|
| 0 | BAND 1 | *Tradition:* Eskimo Culture<br>*Culture:* Arctic Woodland Eskimo<br>*Dates:* A.D. 1000-1700 |
| 1 | BAND 2 | *Tradition:* Arctic Small-Tool<br>*Culture:* Northern Indian/Norton Ipiutak<br>*Dates:* A.D. 400-800 |
| 2 | | |
| 3 | BAND 3 | *Tradition:* ?<br>*Culture:* Choris Complex<br>*Dates:* 1500-500 B.C. |
| | BAND 4 | *Tradition:* Arctic Small-Tool<br>*Culture:* Denbigh Flint Complex<br>*Dates:* 2200-1800 B.C. |
| 4 | BAND 5 | *Tradition:* Arctic Small-Tool/Northern Archaic<br>*Culture:* Denbigh Flint Complex/Portage Complex<br>*Dates:* 2600-2200 B.C. |
| 5 | | |
| 6 | BAND 6 | *Tradition:* Northern Archaic<br>*Culture:* Palisades II Complex<br>*Dates:* 3900-2600 B.C. |
| 7 | BAND 7 | *Tradition:* Northern Archaic<br>*Culture:* Palisades II Complex<br>*Dates:* 4000-3900 B.C. |
| 8 | | |
| 9 | | |
| 10 | BAND 8 | *Tradition:* American Paleo-Arctic<br>*Culture:* Kobuk Complex<br>*Dates:* 6200-6000 B.C. |
| 11 | BELOW B8 | *Tradition:* American Paleo-Arctic<br>*Culture:* Akmak Complex<br>*Dates:* ? 13,000-6500 B.C. |
| 12 | | |

**This diagram** *shows the buried sequence of cultures found at the Onion Portage site in Alaska's northern Interior. This depiction summarizes the cultural strata found there and the cultural changes through time. Archaeological cultures are defined in terms of diagnostic tools such as those shown along the right. Complex may be synonymous with culture in northern archaeology, and it is tightly defined by geographic distribution and duration. Tradition indicates a culture or related cultures that persist through longer periods of time.*

a longer excavation of the bluff. No other interior sites this old had produced evidence of rings or shelters, which this appeared to be. In fact, the boulder level of Owl Ridge proved to be 8,000 to 9,000 years old, making this an important addition to our knowledge of interior Alaska's prehistory. Peter and his faculty agreed he should complete the excavation in 1984, aiming to expose the entire boulder feature and collect all associated flakes and tools. That work produced no additional boulders but did substantially increase the collection from the earliest visit, more than 9,000 years ago. The materials could be compared with those from early levels of Dry Creek, which is discussed below.

Peter's meticulous work is typical of modern excavation techniques, but there is no one correct method for archaeology. This is because today archaeologists dig a site with methods appropriate to the goals of the excavation. Peter was interested in tracing the history of cultures that existed at Owl Ridge. He and Karen made a number of small vertical excavations or test pits to uncover the sequence of cultural remains, and they found three thin zones of occupation, each separated from the next by a zone without any artifacts. By describing the materials from each cultural zone and comparing them to other known remains from the Interior, they might fit it into the sequence of cultures throughout this region. Perhaps they would also be lucky enough to discover materials that added something entirely new to our knowledge of interior Alaska's culture history, such as the use of skin tents some 9,000 years ago.

In their careful excavation and mapping of artifacts at Owl Ridge, Peter was anticipating a larger scale excavation that would tie together all the pits they had dug. Major excavations of the three cultural layers they found would allow him to interpret activities from the tools they found and to discover what type of dwelling the boulders represented. Understanding what activities took place there and what the area looked like at the time would allow them to conjecture more about life at the site — for example, whether it was a fall hunting camp, a summer fish camp or a winter village.

Reconstructing the lifeway represented by a site requires detailed study of materials, patterns or combinations of tools, and examining clues about site size, season of use, activities represented and the particular cultural tradition involved. Much of the conjecture is based on our knowledge of modern people who hunt, gather and fish for a living. This is why archaeologists must learn as much as possible about the present native people of a region, so they can interpret remains from earlier times.

Traditional Athabaskans moved around throughout the year, living in camps, villages and temporary stopover places. Thus, when Karen and Peter found a possible tent ring overlooking a river, they knew that this site was one of many the prehistoric group would have used during the course of a year. Interior resources simply did not allow hunter-gatherers the luxury of year-round villages at one location. Knowing this, they could look for other sites the group would have used such as caribou hunting camps, fishing camps, winter villages and even temporary food caches.

*Challenges of Interior Alaskan Archaeology.* As the Owl Ridge example suggests, archaeologists face a difficult task in understanding past lifeways of interior Alaska. Because stone artifacts are so tangible, we are usually tempted

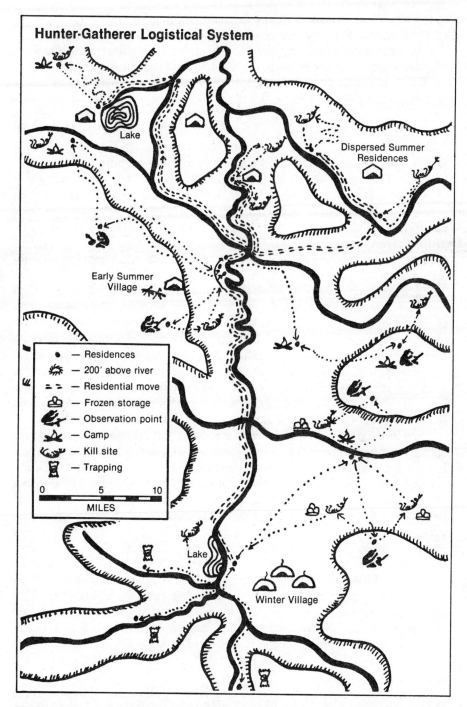

# Hunter-Gatherer Logistical System

**Lake**

**Dispersed Summer Residences**

**Early Summer Village**

| | | |
|---|---|---|
| • | — | Residences |
| | — | 200′ above river |
| = = | — | Residential move |
| | — | Frozen storage |
| | — | Observation point |
| | — | Camp |
| | — | Kill site |
| | — | Trapping |

0        5        10
MILES

**Lake**

**Winter Village**

*The hunter-gatherer* logistical system shown here is idealized but based on information provided by people of the Interior. Note that a wide variety of types of sites contributed to the total settlement system used by a family and its related band members —residential camps, storage caches, locations of animal kills, lookouts and others. Numerous examples of each would be used during the year by members of just one small band. Traces of many would be lost entirely in a few seasons.

to focus on them exclusively. Many discussions of interior prehistory emphasize tool traditions, tracing the distribution of certain styles in time and space. While this is a valid approach to the past, it often neglects more interesting questions surrounding the people who made the tools. What did they use them for? Which ones were meant for processing skins? Which were for butchering large game? Which were used for catching and cleaning fish? Did men, women or both sexes perform these tasks?

A difficult but not insurmountable problem confronting archaeologists who wish to understand the lives of interior people is the high degree of mobility they needed to survive. They undoubtedly favored all-purpose tools that were portable. This meant they were lightweight and made of fragile materials — skin, bark, grass, or even bone — that do not preserve in the acidic interior soils.

It is also difficult to trace particular groups far back in time here, because cultural or political units did not remain stable. Within a few hundred years, artifact styles may change as different people move around within a region. Under these circumstances, family or group traditions in toolmaking may not last long or be easy to trace through time.

Studies of archaeology in Alaska's Aleutian Islands, where I have worked since 1962, present an interesting contrast to the Interior. The rich Aleutian environment brought economic wealth and social stability, so people could live in large, permanent villages and own many personal items such as elaborate houses and specialized tools. Localized Aleut traditions were maintained for long periods because families lived in the same villages for generations. Children were taught to make tools the way their own community did and to decorate items in the family style. These items were made for permanence, so they tend to preserve well in the ground and become part of the archaeological record.

Therefore, continuity and change are obvious and easy to trace in Aleutian sites. This is a contrast to the meager remains found in Alaska's Interior, where it is much harder to put together a picture of prehistoric cultures and lifeways.

Our knowledge of stone tools found at various times and places throughout the Interior allows us to reconstruct the sequence of cultures that have existed here during the past. In other words, we know enough to tell one group of people, or prehistoric tradition, from another. This is done here in the same way it would be in California: for example, we can identify the early Russians in California by the complex consisting of their forts and trading posts, Cyrillic alphabet and Russian Orthodox crosses. The earlier Spanish are recognized by their missions, agricultural fields, Roman alphabet and Catholic crosses. This approach does not attempt to describe early Russian or Spanish-American culture, nor to compare their systems of government or religious beliefs. It simply identifies each in terms of diagnostic traits. Yet, increasingly, archaeologists realize that these aspects of lifestyle are reflected in the materials ancient people leave behind.

Our current understanding of interior prehistory allows us to say something about the sequence of archaeological cultures based on the kinds of objects we find and their occurrence in buried sequences. At this time we cannot say much about the day-to-day life and material content of those cultures. Nevertheless, we can use our knowledge of traditional Athabaskan societies to suggest the general characteristics of past cultures and guide future research. This is possible because we know the Interior's climate and resources have been relatively stable for the past 8,000 years. Luckily, the material from several archaeological sites has been studied in enough detail to make comparisons with the traditional lifeways and material goods of people like the Athabaskans. They appear to support biological and linguistic studies which also suggest that interior people have been here for a long time — longer than the coastal Eskimos, for example, but not so long as Indians of the United States and eastern Canada. This information is critical to understanding interior prehistory, and I will return to it throughout the chapter.

My interpretation of interior Alaska's prehistoric record is influenced by my own work in the Aleutians which reveals that people lived in the same area and maintained the same kind of adaptation for 8,000 to 9,000 years. As far back as we have preserved skeletons, some 4,000 years, the people can be identified as Aleuts. And I believe that the material remains take Aleut prehistory back another 3,000 to 5,000 years.

Archaeological materials from interior Alaska do indicate a long continuity in adaptation — that is, similar kinds of economic pursuits and settlement patterns. My assumption, drawn from the Aleutians, is that this likely also reflects continuity in customs. In other words, if we use all the available archaeological, biological and linguistic information, we can learn at what point the early inhabitants of interior Alaska can likely be called Athabaskan. I should note that different archaeologists have their own ways of defining prehistoric cultures. For example, some emphasize stone tools more than I do and make little use of information about human biology, language or adaptation. Thus, other archaeologists who have studied interior Alaska's prehistory have come up with different identifications from the ones I will present here or have refrained from making them altogether.

Because there are so many questions about Athabaskan and interior prehistory still to be answered, I will try to look at the general patterns we have discussed thus far — overall change in material culture and long-term patterns of cultural adaptation. The information I present is drawn from excavations done during the past 60 years, but keep in mind that even now large areas of Alaska are little-known archaeologically and new information is coming in all the time. The general course of interior prehistory is fairly clear, in my opinion, but the details are likely to change.

Many sites discovered in recent years were found during surveys made in conjunction with large-scale construction projects, as federal and state laws require assessment of project impacts on cultural resources such as prehistoric and historic sites. Examples of major surveys in the Interior in the last 15 years include those made along the trans-Alaska oil pipeline, the proposed natural gas pipeline and in the proposed Susitna Dam area. Other sites have been found by members of research projects whose specific aim was to discover evidence of the first people to reach interior Alaska. Archaeologists have also located sites with the help of bush area residents such as Athabaskan villagers. The important Healy Lake site, where cultural remains cover a span of 11,000 years, is one of these.

We are certain from dated sites in the Interior that human prehistory in Alaska goes back about 12,000 years. Some archaeologists would triple this time-depth, based on recent biological, linguistic and geological hypotheses, or on conclusions drawn from present archaeological information. Others would prefer a more conservative 20,000-year date, and a few others are comfortable only with an antiquity of about 12,000 years for humans in the entire New World. This last is most unlikely. I now turn to the story of the migration of Alaska's first people and the evolution of interior cultures during the thousands of years that followed. As you will see, this story has been literally pieced together by archaeologists from a half-century of detailed, meticulous research.

## The First People: Ancient Migrants of Beringia

*A Bridge Between the Continents.* The first people of interior Alaska arrived hundreds of generations ago, perhaps even more. Arrived is hardly the word

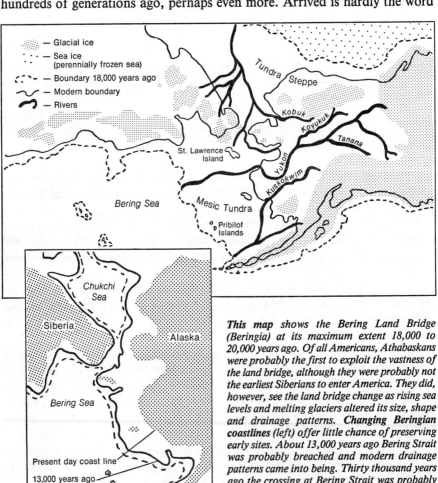

*This map shows the Bering Land Bridge (Beringia) at its maximum extent 18,000 to 20,000 years ago. Of all Americans, Athabaskans were probably the first to exploit the vastness of the land bridge, although they were probably not the earliest Siberians to enter America. They did, however, see the land bridge change as rising sea levels and melting glaciers altered its size, shape and drainage patterns. Changing Beringian coastlines (left) offer little chance of preserving early sites. About 13,000 years ago Bering Strait was probably breached and modern drainage patterns came into being. Thirty thousand years ago the crossing at Bering Strait was probably a narrow neck of land, but Alaska's Interior was somewhat larger and certainly richer in resources than at any time later.*

for it; they did not step off a train and set up camp. Rather, small groups of people who made their livelihood from subsistence hunting and gathering pressed gradually eastward from northeastern Asia. They moved slowly across the low-lying land known as Beringia, or the Bering Land Bridge, which was actually the shallow coastal shelf of the Bering Sea plus northeast Siberia and Alaska. This entire area became dry land several times in the past, when worldwide climatic cooling formed great sheets of ice and locked up the earth's water. Most of this plain lies beneath the Bering and Chukchi seas today except for the highest hills, which are now St. Lawrence Island and the Pribilofs. At times during the last 100,000 years Beringia was one of the earth's largest coastal shelves.

We cannot be sure when bands of people began their expansion north and east out of Asia. A conservative estimate would place the movements 750 generations ago (15,000 years) and there is reason to believe it could have been nearly twice that. Well-dated archaeological evidence shows that Siberian people lived from 18,000 to 15,000 years ago at 60 to 65 degrees north latitude, far enough north to move out across the Beringian lowland.

The ancient plants and animals of northeastern Asia and eastern Beringia (including Alaska and Yukon Territory) were similar at the time of these earliest movements out of the Old World, but they were different from those of today. This means that ancient hunting and gathering activities were not just like those of present-day native Asians and Alaskans. Let's consider what these early people would have encountered in the way of climate, landscape and animal life. The earliest times when people were pressing northward and, perhaps, eastward into Alaska would be somewhat more than 30,000 years ago, during a relatively mild interval of the last glacial period. We'll begin with the Old World people who first conquered the cold, then we'll discuss early ideas about the ancestors of ancient Americans and finally we'll start the trek across the Bering Land Bridge.

To cross the land bridge to Alaska, people had to be able to live successfully in the rigorous climates about 60 degrees north in Siberia. Archaeological work has been limited in that region, for many of the same reasons that hinder work in Alaska — low population, expensive transportation, difficult terrain and scattered sites of small size. However, archaeological finds in Europe offer clues about how long ago humans could have lived near the glacial ice, relying on advanced hunting and fishing skills and using fire, clothing and shelter to protect themselves from the cold.

Archaeologists have found a spring camp for reindeer and mammoth hunting in northern Germany (at 53 degrees north) dating from 55,000 years ago. There are indications that people living in this camp caught fish, birds and medium and small game with stone tools and simple bone spears. They were about as far north as they could go without wandering onto glacial ice itself. But we should note that no winter sites have been discovered here from this time period, and we know that year-round occupation of northern latitudes would have been necessary to cross into the New World on the Bering Land Bridge. There is good evidence for this about 40,000 years ago in Europe. However, eastern Siberia was free of glaciers during the past 80,000 years, allowing people to follow rivers north to more than 70 degrees north, if they were so inclined. And they would only have had to reach 60 degrees north to cross the southern edge of the land bridge into America.

*Acosta's Theory.* The route of early human movements across the now-submerged Bering Land Bridge was first proposed nearly 400 years ago by a Spanish scholar, but prevailing ideas about world history caused rejection of his theory. Why? Europeans discovered the Americas late in the 15th century, but only with circumnavigation of the world did the Spanish realize the Americas were continents separate from Asia. In the prevailing religious views of the day, all the world's people had descended from the sons of Noah — but this only included the Europeans, Africans and Asians. Finding that the Americas were not part of Asia meant that Church writings of the time, including the Bible, did not refer in any way to occupants of the newly discovered continents. Who, then, were the Americans?

By the late 16th and early 17th centuries, scholars of colonial Spain tried to fit the American people into their known world. Fantastic theories were advanced, accounting for the Americans as evacuees from lost continents or descendants of the 10 Lost Tribes (ultimately descended from Noah's sons). But one Spanish thinker of that time, Jose de Acosta, noted from firsthand colonial reports that Americans looked most like Asiatics; and furthermore, some American plants and animals were also like those of Asia. Explorations had proved that vast oceans separated Asia from places like Peru, Mexico and California, so the logical Spaniard hypothesized a connection between northern Asia and northern North America. Across this land connection, he suggested, simple hunting bands had trekked slowly into the Americas.

Although Acosta's speculation was correct, various aspects of his views did not satisfy the Church or other thinkers of the day. It was some time before his Asian-Alaskan connection was again considered, and not until Vitus Bering's 1741 voyage from Russia were the two regions shown to be close geographically. An actual previous land connection was not demonstrated until this century, with advances in knowledge about past climate and sea level. The discovery of Beringia by scientists interested in the arrival of people in the New World is more recent still. It only achieved full recognition as the link between the Old and New World people in 1967, with publication of a book called *The Bering Land Bridge,* edited by David Hopkins.

*The Changing Corridor.* The 25th anniversary of *The Bering Land Bridge* was observed with publication of another volume in 1982, this one titled *Paleoecology of Beringia,* edited by Hopkins and J.R. Matthews, Jr., C. E. Schweger and S. V. Young. Many North American, European and Asian scholars contributed to this update of our knowledge of the land bridge. We are now better able to assess what it must have been like for people traveling overland to the New World between 30,000 and 10,000 years ago. At various times the land bridge presented different advantages and disadvantages for travelers.

For example, if migrants required warmish weather and needed some wood along the way for fuel and housing, then the time to come was before 30,000 years ago. The climate was mild, though colder than now, northern Siberia and Alaska were much richer in animal life, and trees grew as far north as they do

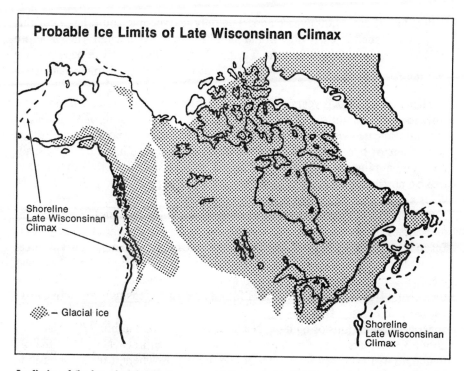

**Probable Ice Limits of Late Wisconsinan Climax**

Shoreline
Late Wisconsinan
Climax

⠿ – Glacial ice

Shoreline
Late Wisconsinan
Climax

*Ice limits of the last glacial period were especially expansive 18,000 years ago. Note that there is a constricted corridor, actually closed at certain times and places, between two major continental glaciers. The corridor was barren and unproductive, and certainly unattractive to most land mammals and humans, especially from 23,000 or 25,000 up to about 14,000 years ago.*

today. There were no dense forests, however, because the landscape was open and dry. The Beringian connection was small and narrow then, and perhaps occasionally was breached by Bering and Arctic waters. That would mean people would have needed boats for short hops and that they would have had to survive the cold at 65 degrees north in Siberia to cross into Alaska. Once in Alaska, however, they would have had open travel south.

Between about 30,000 and 14,000 years ago, it was much colder and drier than now; there were no trees at all for fuel. While the same animals were available, harsh conditions kept their numbers down. But these problems were perhaps offset by the massive breadth of land connecting the Old and New Worlds. A crossing could be made as far south as 60 degrees north though it would have been much colder than the same latitude is today. During this period huge sheets of ice covered central and eastern Canada and extended into the northern states. At times there might have been a narrow corridor between the Rockies and coastal mountains, but cold weather and sparse food reserves would have blocked people from moving southward. Warm seasons would have caused glacial melting and created lakes to barricade the way.

If the corridor was impassible between 25,000 and 14,000 years ago, it might indicate that people first crossed the Bering Land Bridge and moved southward sometime earlier. For example, a site near the southern tip of South America is dated at about 14,000 years ago. The only way people could have got this far south by such an early time would have been to move through Alaska before 25,000 years ago. Otherwise, the way south would have been impeded by ice and no one would likely have reached South America until much later than 14,000 years ago.

Then, about 14,000 years ago, the climate made a sudden and remarkable shift to warm conditions. Glaciers melted and the way south opened; but at the same time meltwaters raised the oceans and drowned the Bering Land Bridge. In just one or two thousand years the land bridge was reduced by 75 percent. Anybody aiming to travel between Siberia and Alaska about that time had to make a northern crossing (in the present area of Bering Strait), and after 12,000 years ago it could have been done only with boats. The animals and vegetation also changed, though not so abruptly as the climate. Big animals like mammoths and horses barely survived into this period; others disappeared slightly later. Bison held on still longer, and caribou made it through the change; but resources available for travelers were poor compared to earlier periods, and there was a lot less land for maneuvering. On the other hand, coastal travelers who made their living from the sea would have found Alaska increasingly attractive after 14,000 years ago.

Modern conditions of climate, sea level and plant and animal life existed by about 8,500 years ago. The land bridge was gone entirely. Nearly all the old mammals of Beringia were extinct or had moved elsewhere, except for caribou or reindeer. Forests rapidly spread north and reached their modern limits. Southern animals who found it too cold earlier or needed trees for their survival moved north, but they never reached the abundance of the great herds before 30,000 years ago.

*The Great Migrations.* By the early 1600s, Spanish conquistadors and priests had noted similarities in physical characteristics between Asian people and the Indians of North and South America. During the century that followed, biologists interested in human types learned enough about American Indians and Eskimos to determine two important things: first, both groups bore some resemblance to Asian Mongoloid people. Second, Eskimos looked more like living Chinese and Japanese than did American Indians, suggesting that the Eskimos were more recent migrants.

Throughout the 20th century, archaeologists used this two-migration theory to reconstruct peopling of the New World. The diverse languages of American Indians — some completely unrelated to others and none of them demonstrably connected to any Old World language — indicated that much time had passed since their arrival in the New World. By contrast, the Eskimo and Aleut languages are all closely related to one another and perhaps to several northeast Asian languages as well. This also indicated that Eskimos and Aleuts are relatively recent migrants.

*Ancestral Athabaskans: A Separate Migration?* Of the many American Indian groups who have been studied by physical anthropologists, Athabaskans are most distinctive. They are different enough biologically to suggest that they do not derive from other American Indians, but might have a separate Asian origin. Furthermore, while linguistic studies cannot link the Athabaskan (or Na-Dene)

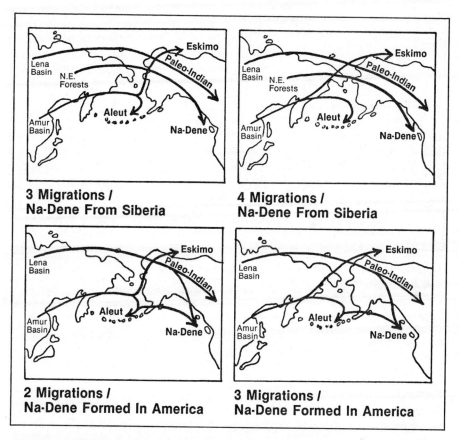

**3 Migrations /
Na-Dene From Siberia**

**4 Migrations /
Na-Dene From Siberia**

**2 Migrations /
Na-Dene Formed In America**

**3 Migrations /
Na-Dene Formed In America**

*Four scenarios for peopling the New World are indicated here. The examples at the top which bring Na-Dene, prominently Athabaskan speakers, from Siberia conform to expectations of biological and linguistic connections. The three-migration theory is followed in this chapter. The examples at the bottom suggest the Athabaskans derived from a back-migration of American Indians to Alaska. Neither biology nor language offers support for these versions.*

family to any Asian languages, neither can they connect it with any other native American language family. Linguists differ sharply in their interpretations, but one well-known expert on American Indian languages believes that all share some general underlying similarities — except Athabaskan.

Drawing from this, linguist Joseph Greenberg, dental anthropologist Christy G. Turner and human biologist Steven Zegura recently proposed a three-migration theory for native American people. I find their proposal so compelling that I will use it as the framework for explaining interior prehistory in this chapter. According to the three-migration theory, American Indians (excluding Athabaskans) entered the New World first, traveling from their homeland in north central Siberia. Their population expanded southward, and they eventually occupied all of North and South America before the glaciers melted. Among the last places they reached was northeastern Canada, following the ice melt there, as recently as 7,500 years ago in some places.

Ancestral Athabaskans entered Alaska much later than the other American

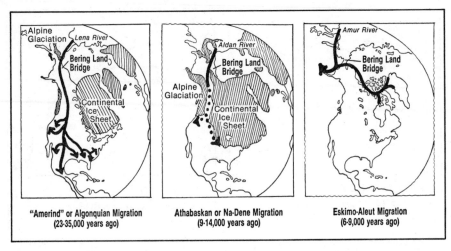

"Amerind" or Algonquian Migration
(23-35,000 years ago)

Athabaskan or Na-Dene Migration
(9-14,000 years ago)

Eskimo-Aleut Migration
(6-9,000 years ago)

*The sequence of three migrations to America from Siberia began about 23,000 to 35,000 years ago when the land bridge was fairly narrow but ice was not a barrier into Canada and the Lower 48 for ancestors of American Indians. The land bridge was broad but rapidly drowning about 9,000 to 14,000 years ago as major continental glaciers melted. Athabaskan ancestors were probably bottlenecked in Alaska, but we know that in the last several millennia they have expanded into central Canada, the Pacific Coast and the American Southwest. Ancestors of Aleuts and Eskimos were latecomers to Alaska. Their longstanding familiarity with ocean travel and coastal living permitted them to expand rapidly along the Arctic Coast.*

Indians and they came from a different homeland in the northeast Asian interior. They first settled in east central Alaska and southwest Yukon Territory, then later spread more widely in Alaska and into central Canada and northern British Columbia. Further population movements within recent centuries established other Athabaskans far to the south, to the Pacific Northwest, Great Plains and American Southwest.

Finally the Eskimo-Aleut groups expanded into the New World Arctic from the northern Bering Sea coast of Asia. Avoiding the Interior (already occupied by Athabaskans) and superbly adapted to the rich coasts and near-shore seas, Eskimos and Aleuts came to control virtually all the coastline from southern Alaska and the Aleutian Islands northward across the Arctic to Greenland.

When were these three migrations? Using guess dates based on dental evaluation, Greenberg, Turner and Zegura put the earliest American Indian migration at 15,000 years, the Athabaskan Indian migration at 6,000 years and the Eskimo-Aleut migration at 4,000 years. Recent archaeological dating shows clearly that people with Eskimo and Aleut adaptations already controlled the coastline of southwestern Alaska before 6,000 years ago and probably 8,000 to 9,000 years ago at a minimum. If we adjust the other dates accordingly, Athabaskan migrants would have arrived in Alaska around 14,000 to 9,000 years ago and American Indian migrants should have been on the scene about 35,000 to 23,000 years ago. All of these dates fit remarkably well with archaeological finds made during the last 10 years in the New World.

The key points to keep in mind are that biological and linguistic data indicate that American Indians, Athabaskan Indians and Eskimo-Aleuts have separate

Asiatic origins. According to the three-migration theory, no one of the three native American groupings derives from another, either in America or in Asia. Readers should remember that other interpretations exist and that scientists still have not reached a consensus about how many migrations into the New World actually took place and when they occurred. We can only examine the evidence we have found thus far and try to draw the most reasonable conclusions.

*The First Americans.* When European explorers arrived in the New World, it is estimated that more than 15 million native Americans were hunting, fishing, gathering, and farming the lands of North and South America. While all these people shared some general biological traits that distinguish them from other Mongoloid people of Arctic America and Asia, there was so much diversity among them that they must have occupied the Americas for many thousands of years. Even more diverse were their languages, some of them so different from one another that only the slightest connection can be shown. This also indicates a long period of development from one or several original Asian groups. In the process of spreading to the ends of the Americas, these people developed widely divergent languages while they also became physically different from one another.

During early times, more than 30,000 years ago, northeast Asians had several possible ways to enter America. One sea route and two somewhat different overland routes were available, each with its own set of requirements for success. The sea route along the south coast of Beringia required adequate boats and boating skills, and a culture geared to hunting and fishing on the northern coast. Successful use of boats for ocean travel was undoubtedly early — the subtropical waters isolating Australia were crossed more than 35,000 years ago. But had people developed ways to voyage across northern waters this early? We may never know.

Alaska was somewhat bigger when lowered water levels exposed part of its coastal shelf earlier than 30,000 years ago. A land connection probably existed at Bering Strait, creating a continuous coastline between Asia and Alaska. Sea mammals, birds and fish were there in numbers. However, as we have already seen, sea level rose and fell during the last 30,000 years. Sites of any coastal communities would have been marooned inland when sea level lowered farther and then would have been drowned when the sea rose again. For example, any coastal sites that were inhabited 30,000 years ago are underwater today.

Since we cannot know if early people could have crossed to the New World by water, we should look closely at the land routes. The connection between northeast Asia and Alaska required people to live at a latitude of at least 60 degrees north if not higher. We think such an ability was developed by about 40,000 years ago. A trip across the high North, above 70 degrees, was less likely than hugging the southern rim of Beringia. The northern route was high-latitude tundra, lacking the stands of trees and open woodland found farther south.

The southern route would have provided far better land and water resources. The major rivers of Beringia contained salmon and other fish, and the lakes and marshes had various fish, waterfowl and small mammals. Mammoths, bison, horses and caribou were present, as were moose, musk-oxen, mountain sheep and Asiatic saiga (antelope). The same animals lived on the Bering Land

Bridge to at least 20,000 years ago, and in lower numbers later. So the early ancestors of American Indians saw different conditions on the Bering Land Bridge from those found in either Siberia or Alaska today.

*The Living World of Beringia.* The evidence of fossil pollen indicates that any people living in Beringia earlier than 30,000 years ago would have found a mixed landscape of grassland-tundra on the uplands, shrub thickets and open woodlands in lower areas and lines of trees along riverbanks and streams. The Yukon and Kuskokwin rivers held their present courses (and probably had seasonal salmon runs), but both ran far out across the exposed coastal shelf and the Kuskokwim's mouth was south of its present location. The people of Beringia could have occupied about 20 percent more land thanks to lowered sea level, and that land was considerably richer than any of Alaska's Interior today.

The major land mammals of Beringia were quite numerous and lived in herds. Like their modern elephant cousins, mammoths were matriarchal and traveled in nursery herds of six to eight cows and calves. As long as mammoths were in Beringia, we know there was enough fodder to support and fatten such nursery groups. Horses, bison, saiga antelope and caribou could range widely between areas with sufficient food, and they might not revisit a locality for several years.

People who depended on these animals for food would have needed a high degree of mobility and flexibility in their territories. We know that their material goods were portable; for example, they probably used tents during much of the year. Perhaps in winter they settled down in more substantial houses and had time for socializing on a larger scale, renewing equipment and making short trips to hunt and fish. We can imagine that some people found areas with good hunting and fishing, where they could establish themselves in a territory that supported them year-round, year after year. Their populations grew and they moved to new areas. Inevitably, some lived where the resources were poorer and more scattered. These people might have gradually traveled more widely looking for better territory. Perhaps it was groups like these who pressed south and eventually spread throughout North and South America.

By 30,000 years ago, the oral traditions of our interior Beringian people would have recorded changes in the landscape. The climate was turning colder; mountain glaciers grew and snow fell lower on the slopes. Those who traveled to the coasts from inland areas had farther to go. Sea level fell lower and lower, reaching a minimum 18,000 years ago. This exposed land made Alaska about 50 percent larger than it is today.

Remember that while a wide corridor of dry land connected Asia and America, growing ice covered large areas, including the Aleutians, southeastern Alaska and most of Canada. By about 25,000 years ago, Beringia was truly a peninsula of Asia, cut off from the rest of North America by forbidding walls of ice. North of modern Bering Strait was intensely cold tundra, stretching poleward to a perennially frozen Arctic Ocean.

In the period more recent than 30,000 years ago, the Interior presents a paradox: on the one hand, evidence points to the same large mammals roaming around; but on the other, it indicates a time of increased cold, wind and dryness, with fewer resources than before. Fossil pollen indicates that the severe climate led to a sparse plant cover over parts of the Interior. There were no longer trees this far north, so after 30,000 years ago Beringian people would have done without wood for fuel and construction. Perhaps they burned fat rendered from bones, as the Athabaskans did until recently. Or they might have used wood from the small shrub thickets that grew in moist areas. However poor this landscape was, fossil pollen indicates there were still small areas with enough fodder to support the same mammals as earlier. Probably there were fewer animals, in smaller groups than before, roaming throughout a far larger region. And people had to follow suit. If ever there was reason to head south it was after 30,000 years ago, when resources were fewer and farther between, and before 25,000 years ago when glacial ice barred the way. By the end of the period, some 14,000 years ago, it is clear that many of these animal populations had failed altogether.

*Remains of the First People.* As I interpret the available evidence, ancestors of the American Indians first came in small numbers from Asia before 25,000 years ago. Such small and mobile groups of people would leave little behind for the archaeologist. In fact, we probably have discovered remains of these early people but have been unable to date the age of the sites. This is a special problem in the Arctic and some other areas, where tools left on the ground do not become covered with protective layers of soil and where bone and wood quickly rot away. Still, there are several possible sites of great age in northwestern Yukon Territory. A number of other sites in the United States, Mexico and South America represent later developments of the first American Indian migrants. The fact that these sites were inhabited so early indicates that people had moved south before glaciers blocked the passage from Alaska to the mainland United States from about 25,000 to 14,000 years ago.

Contenders for the earliest remains of native Americans include altered bones found in the Old Crow Basin, Yukon Territory, in deposits at least 50,000 years old. Archaeologists argue not about the age of the bones but about whether they are tools. Were they chipped and polished by people, broken by animals or fragmented by ice or some other geological process? Also found along the Old Crow River are several bone tools and a number of altered bones which are about 30,000 years old. In fact, one obvious tool, a caribou bone flesher just like those used in recent times, has been dated between about 29,000 and 26,000 years old. The question is, was this bone already thousands of years old

*This splinter of mammoth ivory was excavated from sediments near the village of Old Crow in Yukon Territory. Some archaeologists suggest that remains like this are tools worked by early Americans more than 30,000 years ago. (From* Paleoecology of Beringia, *1982, page 363)*

when someone made it into a tool, or was the tool made when the bone was fresh?

Whether or not the Old Crow flesher is proof of American Indians just across the border from interior Alaska nearly 30,000 years ago, a number of North and South American sites dating 20,000 to 14,000 years ago certainly indicate that people were in Alaska much earlier. People lived over all of the United States and had even reached the tip of South America more than 13,000 years ago. Idaho, Pennsylvania, Washington, California, New York and Florida all have old sites. Mexico claims a 20,000-year-old site and Central and South America have a number of sites more than 15,000 years old. Most interesting among the newly discovered sites is 14,000-year-old Monte Verde in Chile, where a band of people built huts like those of modern local Indians, hunted extinct animals including elephant, ground plant food in wood mortars and kept warm by fireside. There is even a child's footprint in clay that was stockpiled for the oven, reminding us of the glee with which we immortalize our footprints in wet sidewalk cement.

Sites in the southwestern United States from 14,000 to 10,000 years old preserve fragile materials like rope, skin robes, and sandals, attesting to the richness of material culture that archaeologists seldom find in ancient sites. Diverse cultures and adaptations in the New World from such early times indicate that people must have already lived here for thousands of years, elaborating and perfecting their lifeways.

Thus, descendants of the first Americans developed a wide variety of well-honed cultures during the last 25,000 years, adapting to a whole range of environmental conditions. Population grew from less than a few thousand to millions. While some people continued to hunt animals like the mammoth, mastodon, bison, camel and caribou, others found different kinds of animals and whole new arrays of plant life.

In Alaska, far to the north, it is possible that remnant people from this early migration still remained despite the deteriorating climate, declining resources and loss of contact with southern relatives. But in my view, descendants of the first people who remained north were eventually overwhelmed and culturally influenced by another group of Asians traveling east sometime during the last 15,000 years. These were ancestors of the Athabaskan people.

## The Second People: Athabaskans out of Asia

Europeans and Americans began learning about northern Athabaskans only recently, compared to their much earlier experience with other native Americans. Familiarity with Athabaskan lifeways gradually emerged first with the developing interests of the Russians, and later with the arrival of the Americans. The first written accounts of some Athabaskan groups resulted from United States military exploration of interior Alaska in the late 1800s. Somewhat earlier, in the 1850s, a few curious westerners had begun wondering who the Athabaskans were and where they had come from.

Athabaskans were originally classified as a group of people related on the basis of language — they are all members of the Athabaskan or Na-Dene language family. And they are distinct in other ways as well. For example, physical anthropologists have noted certain dental traits and genetic characteristics that appear to set them apart. As you will recall, the three- migration theory suggests that ancestral Athabaskans entered Alaska later than the other American Indians but before the coastal Aleuts and Eskimos. My estimated time for this migration lies between 14,000 and 9,000 years ago, about when the land bridge came to an end.

Indeed, the rapidly changing climate about 14,000 years ago could have been the impetus for people to invade Alaska from Siberia — times were getting harder in the old country. Not only were the familiar climate and resources changing, but new people were moving up from China and southern Siberia, putting more pressure on groups already living in the Far North. With the drowning of the Bering Land Bridge, it is not surprising that people from Asia and the Beringian lowlands began to congregate on the Alaskan frontier. Some of their remains are preserved in archaeological sites dating from 15,000 to 12,000 years ago.

*The Scattered Fragments.* Archaeologists have been confronted with a great challenge just trying to find any of these early sites. In recent years they have turned to studies of modern people who still follow a subsistence lifeway, hoping to gain information that will be useful in this search. For example, they have learned about annual cycles of subsistence activities, favored kinds of places for hunting and fishing, and alternative places to find resources in times of shortage — information that may help to locate ancient sites. Archaeologists have learned that one person may hunt, fish, gather and trap in locations spread throughout thousands of square miles during the course of a lifetime. Furthermore, the core of the territory someone uses can shift, so he or she might focus on different areas at different times of life — childhood, adolescence, adulthood and old age.

An individual may use dozens of camps, activity spots and trails in any of these areas in a single year. During the period of one person's adulthood these locations might run into the hundreds. Each of these sites is a tiny window into the lives of the highly mobile people of the North. But of the literally thousands of potential sites used by a small band of people in just one generation, only a few will survive. The best chance an archaeologist has is to find a place where a group of hunters or a family camped for a couple of weeks, cut up and tossed out bone, made tools and repaired gear and lived in tents held down with boulders.

Northern archaeologists not only have the difficult task of first finding sites, they must then study them in ways that allow a glimpse of life in the past. If we combined all the sites we have discovered from the second Asian people, beginning about 14,000 years ago, we would have accumulated only a tiny fraction of the amount of material used by a single band during one generation. Still, we try to understand life millennia ago by putting together information from all known sites. But we have a record of only a few remains from the distant past: shelters at Bluefish Cave, Yukon Territory, and Trail Creek Cave, on the Seward Peninsula, used by people who hunted extinct bison, elk and perhaps horses; the camp of hunters who intercepted migrating caribou at Onion

Portage; a hearth at Healy Lake, where hunters ate waterfowl they had trapped; the tent camp at Owl Ridge; and the spot at Dry Creek where hunters of bison and grouse made and repaired their tools.

These sites provide glimpses into the lives of interior people thousands of years ago, at a time when the land and animals were much different from today. Nonetheless, we think these are remains of people who knew and used the land

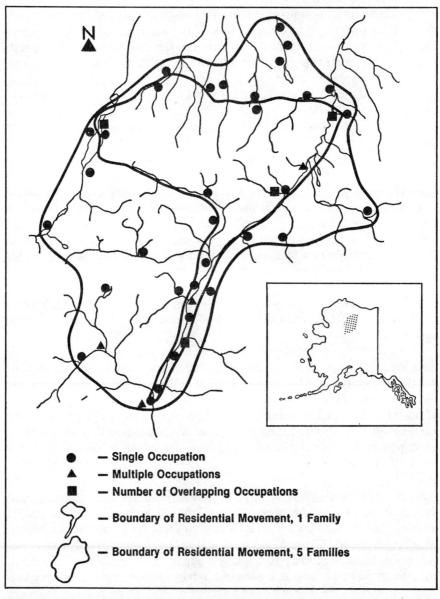

— ● — Single Occupation
— ▲ — Multiple Occupations
— ■ — Number of Overlapping Occupations
— Boundary of Residential Movement, 1 Family
— Boundary of Residential Movement, 5 Families

*Territories and annual movements of people of the Interior took in many miles. This reconstruction is based on actual moves undertaken by one family and by their band in Alaska. Many locations were visited and used for camping or short-term activities. Few traces are left behind for the archaeologist.*

much as the Athabaskans did later. And they were attracted to the same kinds of terrain — stone outcrops for toolmaking; lookouts for surveying the lowlands for game; game trails for awaiting animals during migrations; and lakesides for birds, fish and small animals.

*People of the Warm Time.* Great glaciers to the south made Alaska a peninsula of Siberia from about 24,000 years ago until about 14,000 years ago, after which melting ice opened a corridor to the rest of North America. During this long period of isolation from the south, people living in Alaska's Interior hunted large game animals like mammoths, bison, horses, caribou and saiga antelope. Small mammals surely were taken, as well as fish and birds. Small groups of people — perhaps 15 to 30 in all — traveled together most times during the year. Naturally they would communicate with other people; maintaining good social relations with others is necessary to finding marriage partners, for example. It is also important to have friends and relatives among neighboring territorial groups, in the event of poor seasons or years when families must split off and join other bands.

Whether they were old-timers from the early migration or newcomers from Siberia with a distinctive new technology that links western and eastern Beringian cultures, their tales must have dealt with rapid climatic warming, increasing rain and snow, dramatic loss of land under rising seas, and changing land animals. Increased warmth, rain and snow allowed growth of more vegetative cover, but not of the kind needed to counter the decline of large mammal populations. Mammoths, horses, camels and others became extinct shortly after 14,000 years ago. A fortunate few, including musk-oxen and caribou, survived by retreating far to the north; but only the caribou thrived.

During this period, interior people had access to moose for the first time in millennia. Sheep could still be hunted throughout a wide area, but they were never numerous. Caribou were the dominant large land mammal and would remain so. Their general migration routes might be known, but variation in their movements and cycles of low population strongly affected the stability, organization and numbers of interior people who depended on them. Moose remained in the lowlands, but sheep soon retreated to the high country and elk disappeared after a brief time at these latitudes.

More and more, a variety of fish, birds and small game became important resources for the increasingly dispersed bands of interior Alaskan people. As time passed, the new Alaskans approached even more closely a way of life resembling that of Athabaskans within the historic era. Seasonal caribou hunting, combined with fishing activities, provided the economic focus. These two resources were supplemented, by necessity, with other game, birds and plant foods.

From 14,000 to 8,500 years ago, Alaska's warmer climate underwent a few cooler fluctuations, but clearly heralded the steady warmth of the modern period. Glaciers continued to melt during this time and the sea rose to near modern levels. People of the Interior saw unfavorable changes in vegetation and animal resources after 10,000 years ago, as boggy ground developed, large game herds lost ground (literally, for Beringia was now entirely submerged) and solitary game animals accompanied the advance of forest into the Interior. As we will see, ancestors of the Athabaskans adjusted once again to changing interior landscapes after 8,500 years ago.

For evidence of the first Athabaskans, we should look for familiar material culture and strategies for living, beginning about 14,000 years ago. If the three-migration theory is correct, the earliest remains should be like those found across the Bering Strait, in Siberia.

*The Microblade Connection.* Although archaeologists are not sure what the tools used by the first New World people looked like, they are on much firmer footing when it comes to the second migrants, ancestors of the Athabaskans. Evidence reveals that their Asiatic predecessors lived on a landscape virtually identical to low-lying areas of the land bridge and Alaska. And we can show that some of the most important stone tools used by Asians and Alaskans were made in exactly the same way. Remains found in Siberia from this time period are called the Diuktai technology, and on the Alaskan side the similar remains are called Denali technology.

This is not to say that all Asians using the Diuktai technology were ancestors of Athabaskans. Undoubtedly a number of different ethnic groups learned about the Diuktai technology and its advantages. But the strong indication is that Athabaskans derived from some groups among these Asians. Further, Athabaskans seem to be the only living Alaskans who derived from the second migration, around 14,000 to 11,000 years ago. The nearly extinct Eyak of Prince

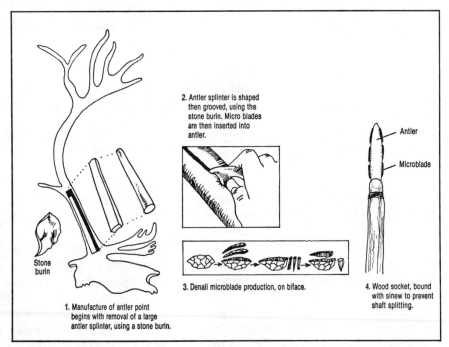

2. Antler splinter is shaped then grooved, using the stone burin. Micro blades are then inserted into antler.

Antler

Microblade

Stone burin

3. Denali microblade production, on biface.

4. Wood socket, bound with sinew to prevent shaft splitting.

1. Manufacture of antler point begins with removal of a large antler splinter, using a stone burin.

*Diuktai-Denali technology, perhaps giving us our first glimpse of Athabaskan ancestors, stressed composite weapons which inset stone microblades into caribou antler points. The antler points were shaped with scrapers and grooved with stone burins. Longevity and distribution of this technology suggests Athabaskans have been here for more than 10 millennia and had historic links to northeast Siberia.*

William Sound, relatives of the Athabaskans, remind us that many groups failed and have no living descendants.

Prominent among the tools found in Diuktai sites, from 18,000 to 10,000 years ago, are tiny, parallel-sided blades. These microblades were punched off small cores of material made from nodules, flakes or bifaces. The last objects are flaked on both faces and look to the untrained eye like knives or crude spear points. The technique for making one of these cores and detaching the microblades is well known. Microblades were apparently used to make effective points for hunting spears. They were inserted into grooves along the edge of bone or antler points, so they acted like razor blades, slicing into a struck animal.

Microblade technology appears in Japan, China and Siberia by 18,000 to 10,000 years ago, perhaps earlier; and it shows up in Alaska by about 12,000 years ago. This weapon system was widespread and successful, and some groups retained it for a long time, especially in Alaska. Recently discovered examples in the Tanana Valley may be less than 2,000 years old. Asian people, on the other hand, gave up the Diuktai microblade technology after 10,000 years ago.

The distribution of microlithic technology in northeastern Asia and in Alaska is an important line of evidence linking the regions historically. While all the modern evidence of human biology, historical linguistics and culture says that Athabaskan people are related ultimately to northeastern Asians, it is gratifying that there is archaeological confirmation of this link. And the excavated remains become older as we move farther to the west, just as we would have predicted.

A second aspect of Diuktai-Denali technology is the use of burinized tools. Most often, stone tools are shaped by removing tiny chips to create a sharp edge, like the typical Indian arrowhead. When a tool is burinized, part of the edge itself is removed as a long, pillar-shaped flake. Burinized edges are squared off like the side of a box, and the resulting tool is used for scraping skin, wood and bone. If two burin flakes are removed from intersecting edges, the result is a screwdriver-shaped end suitable to use for engraving. In the Denali technology sites of interior Alaska, many collections are about equally divided between burinized scraping and engraving tools.

A third feature of Diuktai-Denali technology is bifacial tools, chipped around all edges. These are different from early tools found along the Arctic and Subarctic coast, supporting the idea that the third migration — culturally ancestral to Eskimos and Aleuts — is distinct from that of the Athabaskans.

*Athabaskans and Microblades: Threads to the Past.* Of course, there is more to learn about interior prehistory than just describing the Denali microblade technology. Microblades do provide the Asian connection and allow us to follow the course of Athabaskan prehistory during the Holocene period, the last 10,000 years. But another important goal is to reconstruct what past life was like, and archaeologists working in Alaska's Interior approach this problem from several angles. Knowledge of traditional Athabaskan cultures suggests places to look and what to look for. Natural scientists help to reconstruct prehistoric environments and identify the meager bone remains from sites, to understand what resources people lived on. These studies add many important insights that would not be possible by focusing only on the visible one percent of the archaeological record — the stone tools.

Today the archaeologist tries to design research that will answer specific questions about prehistory, like describing land use patterns or discovering the nature of social groupings. The way a site is excavated can lead to important insights about the ways that ancient people lived. Finally comes the interpretation of archaeological information in temporal, spatial and cultural terms. This includes descriptions of similarities and differences among various sites and explanations of how these patterns came about. For example, do similarities in the tools or other remains found in different sites indicate that they are from the same people doing similar activities? Can sites with different remains be left by the same people, simply doing different activities that require a different set of tools? Or do they indicate an unrelated group of people with different styles of tools?

These questions are at the heart of archaeological controversies surrounding interior prehistory. By joining archaeological evidence with information from human biology and linguistics, I favor the idea that all remains from interior Alaska during Holocene (post-glacial) times are most likely those of Athabaskans. As we review the materials found so far, you will note that there are differences between some sites and areas. I will suggest ways of identifying these sites as Athabaskan despite their differences. While I could be wrong about certain details, I still think this reconstruction is the most logical one, given present knowledge and theories. Let me briefly explain why.

Archaeologists spend much time studying microblades because they link Alaska and Siberia at an early time. We have a good understanding of the age and distribution of microblades in northeastern Asia, and microblades are also the most distinctive objects in early sites throughout Alaska's Interior. We also know that Alaskan microblades were made and used the same way as in Asia. Even the ancient landscapes, vegetation and animals were alike in northeastern Asia, Beringia and Alaska. The connections, dating to some 14,000 years ago, are strong indeed.

Standard archaeological procedure would suggest that most long-term microblade users in the Interior were descendants of the migrants who brought microblades across the land bridge. These persistent stone tools have even been found in British Columbia, in Athabaskan houses said by some to be of historic age. They were used in the Tanana Valley and other parts of interior Alaska as recently as 1,500 to 1,000 years ago, while in southwestern Yukon Territory they were apparently given up much earlier, more than 4,000 years ago. There are changes in other technological elements, but microblades are extremely persistent. Perhaps the different items came through contact with other American Indians farther south. In any case, the long continuity of microblades, combined with other kinds of evidence about social and cultural adaptation, indicates to me an equally long continuity for the Athabaskan tradition. In all likelihood, the Athabaskans are a very ancient people.

## Camps of the Second People

What is the nature of archaeological evidence that supports the presence of Athabaskan people in the Interior for at least 14,000 to 9,000 years? Our finds indicate that most people in the region before 8,500 years ago were using a microblade technology. A few others either had no microblades or used them only at certain places or during certain parts of the year. Like Athabaskans in recent times, the early people were highly mobile, living in many different campsites throughout the seasons and years. Perhaps some groups needed microblade tools for their activities at one area or campsite, but not at another. So we must be careful that we don't mistakenly conclude that people who lived in camps without microblades never used them at all.

*Bluefish Caves: The First Stone Tools.* There is just a bit of archaeological evidence that ancestors of the Athabaskans crossed from Asia shortly before the Bering Land Bridge was drowned under rising seas. Some of these people followed the Porcupine River across the present Alaska-Yukon border and turned south to the Bluefish Basin. Along a limestone ridge in the Kekele Range, just above the Arctic Circle, are three caves that sheltered ancient hunters. Bones with scratches and cut marks were unearthed there, and radiocarbon dating placed their ages at approximately 15,500 to 12,900 years ago. (All radiocarbon dates have a slight range of error, and in these cases it is plus or minus 130 years and 100 years respectively.) Some archaeologists question whether these bones were marked by human activity or were remains from meals of lions or bears. More recent work in the caves by Jacques Cinq-Mars has revealed undisputed stone tools along with extinct animals in deposits which are apparently some 14,000 years old.

Animal bones from the Bluefish Caves include mammoth, elk, bison, horse, caribou and an extinct large cat, probably a lion. The stone tools include two microcores, several dozen microblades and flakes, and several worked flakes. This suggests the Diuktai/Denali technology. One of the cores comes from levels said to date nearly 14,000 years old. In another cave, small chips, found when the dirt was sieved through a fine screen, also came from 14,000-year levels; but the absence of formal tools led some to suggest they had filtered down from younger levels.

The importance of Bluefish Caves for recording early human occupation seems to be verified. Equally significant, these earliest stone tools from the northern Interior appear to be related to Siberian Diuktai microblade technology of the

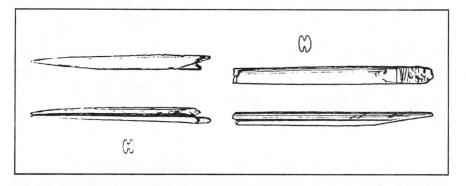

*These slotted arrow points made from caribou antler were excavated in the Trail Creek site. Similar points have been found in western Siberia with microblades still set into the grooves. Composite tools like these are featured in Diuktai assemblages of western Beringia and in Denali assemblages of eastern Beringia.*

same time period. In other words, these remains are what we would expect for people crossing from the northeast Asia interior sometime after 18,000 years ago. This must be the second overland migration to America.

*The Elk Bone Time Clock: Trail Creek Caves.* Other early remains have been found on the Seward Peninsula near the northwest Alaska coast. Here, complex deposits of soil and bone have been laid down beneath rock overhangs in limestone cliffs. Unfortunately, the deposits are not in nice, even layers but are quite wavy and mixed up. About 30 years ago, the late Danish archaeologist Helge Larsen excavated in these caves, unearthing bones from bison and horses that humans may have butchered. These bones were dated at 15,750 and 13,070 years old, with a possible error of several hundred years either way. Bona fide bone tools, including spears with inset microblades, were found at higher levels, so they must be younger. These tools resemble Diuktai remains from Siberia and Denali from Alaska. Can we suggest a basis for firmer dating of the earliest tool-bearing level of Trail Creek and Bluefish Caves? For a brief time after 14,000 years ago, elk were found in the North. Cut or hacked elk bones uncovered in the Bluefish and Trail Creek caves are good evidence that people occupied these sites 14,000 to 10,000 years ago. At Trail Creek Cave 2, bone which is probably elk comes from the same layer as a broken bone point, thought to be the oldest indisputable artifact found there. In somewhat later levels, probably 8,000 to 10,000 years old, there are bone arrowheads with edges grooved for microblades. They may be the earliest Alaskan remains of the actual bone tools which had microblade insets.

*Gizzard Stones and Glued Bones: Dry Creek Site.* The Dry Creek site is located on an old terrace in the Nenana River Valley, near the northern flank of the Alaska Range. It was discovered when Chuck Holmes, a young graduate from the University of Alaska, was taking his lunch break on a trip from Fairbanks to Anchorage, and noticed dark layers in an eroding loess bluff. As it turned out, the loess deposit dated back to around 30,000 years ago and continued into post-glacial times. In 1975, a full-scale excavation was carried out there, and because the research was of such high quality I will discuss the finds in some detail.

Dry Creek was a multidisciplinary project whose archaeological director was W. Roger Powers of the University of Alaska, Fairbanks. Dale Guthrie was the project's paleontologist. Of the four cultural levels found there, the earliest dates to more than 11,000 years ago. A small collection of 3,500 artifacts was unearthed from this early level, with some 40 tools made from stone cobbles and flakes, including thin knives and plain, triangular points, plus several thousand discarded and broken flakes. There are no microblades or microcores, indicating either that the Dry Creek camp lacked these tools, or that the small excavation simply missed any areas with microblades.

Buried just above this level is a large series of artifacts, nearly 20,000 of them, which date more than 10,000 years old. Separate activity areas have been identified, one without microblades and another with them. This occupation may be interpreted in two ways. Most likely it is the remains of one visit, with people doing different activities in separate places — just as we cook in one area and have our workshops in another. Less likely, it may contain materials left during separate visits by two cultural groups, both of whom exploited the same territory. One of these groups would have belonged to the Denali tradition, representing the newly arrived Athabaskans, and the other would have represented descendants of the first migrants. Because people often separate their activity areas, and because all the artifacts seem to be in one undisturbed layer, I am inclined to accept the first interpretation.

The work at Dry Creek included exact mapping of every object uncovered. Also, to collect information on past environments, student archaeologists developed a preservative glue to impregnate waterlogged and crumbling animal bones and teeth that otherwise could not be removed intact from the ground. This preservation of animal remains allowed Guthrie to identify the site as a camp of hunters who pursued bison, sheep, elk and perhaps birds. No bird bones were preserved, but collection of every single object led to the discovery of digestive stones from the gizzards of grouselike birds. Since the stones become more polished as the year passes, Guthrie has been able to tell that these birds died in the fall. Fossilized ground-squirrel nests from the same terrace add to our knowledge of the environment. Working like detectives to solve a 10,000-year-old mystery, the Dry Creek research team used bits of evidence like these to understand something about the lives of prehistoric Alaskans, possibly the earliest Athabaskans.

An important question has not been answered about the occupants of Dry Creek. Where was their main camp? A good bet would be along a river with a seasonal salmon run. Unfortunately, rivers cut their banks, change course and bury other banks. Although the remains of old riverside camps would be hard to find, they would be worth pursuing.

*Points and Microblades: The Healy Lake Controversy.* Just off the Alaska Highway between Fairbanks and the Canadian border is another important early site, at Healy Lake. This site contains an 11,000-year-old level with simple, triangular projectile points like those at early Dry Creek, along with a few crude microblades, plus other materials useful for making comparisons. John Cook, the archaeologist who worked there, showed evidence of both continuity and change during thousands of years of human occupation. Middle levels at the site contained microblades made just like those in Siberia and at Dry Creek. These are younger than 7,000 years, and they occur with bifacial pointed tools which have notches removed from their bases.

Cook presented detailed evidence that notched points and microblades occur together in interior sites. He suggested that these artifacts span most of the last 6,000 or 7,000 years, and eventually change into types and styles associated with historic Athabaskans. He also cited linguistic information that suggests Athabaskans were in the Healy Lake region some 3,000 years ago. This must mean that people still living there 2,000 years ago, using the Denali microblade technology and notched points, were Athabaskans. And since this same microblade technology is also found from 11,000 to perhaps 7,000 years ago, those much earlier groups must also be Athabaskan, Cook argued.

Critics have noted the compression of soil layers in the Healy Lake site, suggesting that this may explain the mixing of points and microblades. Some 11,000 years of deposits were crammed into only 18 inches of soil, and the thin, seasonally frozen earth showed movement of objects up and down. They argued that this may have moved some microblades almost to the surface, making them appear younger than they really are. But I think the association of microblades and notched projectile points throughout six inches of deposits is possibly valid, for the same combination occurs elsewhere. This is an important association to remember — Denali technology and notched (or stemmed) points — and is at the heart of an archaeological controversy.

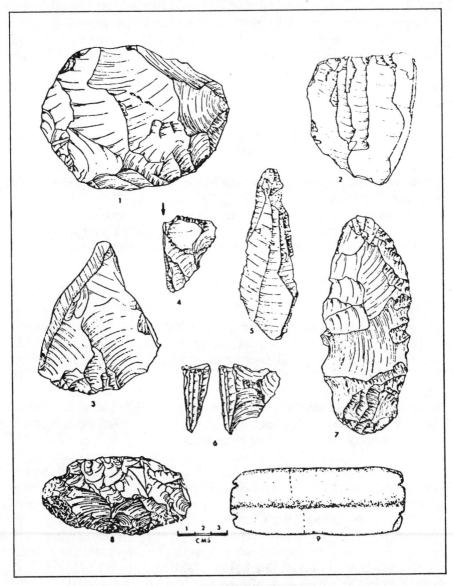

*These artifacts are from the Akmak site, a variant Denali assemblage at Onion Portage on the Kobuk River. The tools include large bifacial blades or knives (1,7), blade and microblade cores (2,3,6), unifacial blades or knives (5,8), burins (3,4) and whetstones for smoothing or sharpening spears (9).*

Whatever the connections between levels at the Healy Lake site, all seem to show a basic similarity in the season and type of use. Burned bones thought to come from hearths suggest that waterfowl hunting and perhaps other lake-shore activities in fall or spring were the mainstay there. The site was probably also as attractive for winter moose as it is now, and caribou calving grounds are only about a two-day walk away. The region surrounding Healy Lake changed during 11,000 years, but there was a stable combination of lake, shore and tundra-covered uplands that attracted birds and other game as well as people to the area.

*Caribou Hunters of Onion Portage.* On the Kobuk River, some 350 miles northwest of Fairbanks, is an important site called Onion Portage. This site shows evidence of occupations that probably span the past 10,000 years. Onion Portage is among the few deep sites in the Interior — gully wash has built up a thick layer-cake of soil with several separate levels of cultural inhabitation. For at least 8,000 years, and perhaps as long as 10,000 years, this was an important place to camp and intercept migrations of caribou crossing the river. The stratigraphy and sequence of main cultures at this site are illustrated near the beginning of this chapter.

The earliest remains there are clearly those of people who emphasized the Denali technology. Besides microblades and microblade cores, the site contains large bifacial tools that might have served as knives and bone-breaking implements, large retouched flakes probably used for cutting and scraping, and other tools used for making bone or wood implements. Among the latter are grooved sandstone objects for smoothing spear shafts that were inset with microblades. The bone and wood spears themselves are not preserved.

The Denali microblade technology links Onion Portage to Alaskan sites from the same time period, especially Dry Creek, and to Siberian sites containing Diuktai remains. The rest of the assemblage reflects unique activities that took place at Onion Portage, but activities that had to be part of the annual subsistence cycle of other interior Athabaskans. For example, the tools used to hunt and process caribou there look different from those at Healy Lake, which probably were intended for waterfowl. And they are somewhat different from Dry Creek, where bison and perhaps upland birds were important.

*Stories Written in Stone.* The material found in sites like these leads me to suggest that ancestry of the Athabaskan people can be traced back to early Denali technology and followed for the next 10,000 years. I am focusing on three kinds of information: first, the biological and linguistic relationships assumed by the three-migration theory require that Athabaskans derive from the interior of Asia, not America, and are separate from both earlier American Indian migrants and later Eskimos and Aleuts. Second, I am tracing the course of microblade technology in the Interior and suggesting that its long continuity results from one tradition being passed down from generation to generation. I will review the sites that support this idea in the next section. Third, I am taking the posi-tion that people move into an area, adjust and try to stay there even through times of change, rather than shift to an entirely new region and way of life.

Other interpretations have been proposed. For example, there is the idea that interior people, faced with changing climate and expanding forests, moved to the coasts to become Eskimos and Aleuts. Based on present knowledge, I think we can dismiss this view, because we can demonstrate that Denali technology persists in the Interior to recent millennia. We can also show that known coastal assemblages with blades and microblades are technologically unrelated to Denali. That is, there are many ways to produce blades and microblades, to burinize, and to make knives and other tools. The proposed coastal relatives of Denali about 9,000 to 7,000 years ago made their blades and microblades differently, used no bifaces at all, and had a different pattern of using burinized tools. Also, the stone technology in 4,000-year-old coastal Eskimo sites has counterparts in Asia but not in Alaska's Interior.

The next section begins to trace developments among descendants of the second migration to Alaska. We will see that during a time of marked environmental and landscape changes, interior populations grew, settled into Alaska and Yukon Territory, and expanded farther into northwest Canada. By this time the coastlines were already controlled by sophisticated Eskimo and Aleut descendants of the third migration. As the Interior filled up with people and their bands were crowded closer together, more regional traditions emerged. We begin to find evidence of conservatives and progressives, people who maintained the older Denali technology and others who adopted new forms of tools.

## Growth of the Athabaskan Tradition

After about 8,500 years ago Alaska's climate became warmer and most of the big game from earlier times vanished. People were forced to shift their subsistence from hunting large game year-round to focusing on a few concentrated resources like salmon and migrating caribou. Other solitary animals like sheep, moose, birds and fish were seasonal alternatives, often found in widely separated areas on the landscape. The modern Athabaskan subsistence pattern developed during this period, although many aspects of it dated back to Beringian times.

*A New Diversity.* It is not surprising that we have a fuller picture of people at this time than earlier. There are more sites, reflecting more people squeezed into a small area than before. They filled up Alaska's Interior and spilled over into western Canada. The best areas were probably taken earliest — good salmon streams with nearby caribou migration routes, favorite areas for moose, lakes and ponds attractive to migratory waterfowl, and mountains with sheep within reasonable walking distance. When too many people occupied an area, families budded off into somewhat less favorable areas. If they worked their way out toward the coastal tundra they would encounter Eskimos, and the fact that Athabaskan and Eskimo languages have few words in common shows that the two groups stayed well separated. Areas more likely for expansion were the forests of northwestern Canada.

Athabaskan people with distinctive languages and technology emerged. Archaeological remains seem to show different groups developed preferences for certain styles of tools by 6,000 years ago. There seem to have been pockets of technological conservatives still adhering to the old Denali technology. But elsewhere, people began using different tools — new forms of bifacial knives and spears set into handles, points notched for lashing around the base and perhaps barbed bone spears that didn't need microblade insets. Still others practiced a middle-of-the-road approach, sticking with microblades but trying out the new bifacial tool styles as well.

The archaeological picture for each subregion is not clear at this time period — people were highly mobile, populations were growing and crowding more closely and the number of known sites is limited. Archaeologists argue whether absence of Denali technology means a new people moved in. My view is that we are seeing the growing pains of a population developing regional cultural and language styles. Some of these styles last for millennia, as seems to be the case in the Tanana Valley. Others are short-lived and appear to change abruptly. I don't see this as evidence for new kinds of people arriving in the Interior. Rather, it could mean that a regional group has either failed or combined with some of its neighbors. The history of Athabaskan languages suggests a similar pattern of regional successes and failures, reflected by the appearance and disappearance of distinctive dialects and languages. But overall, Athabaskan languages show a long period of development.

People living in Alaska after 8,500 years ago found the environment much as it is today. The cold meadows and sedges of earlier times had given way to black spruce bogs, birch and white spruce forest. Thickets of alder also confounded movements across the land. Caribou were seasonally available, moose went on their annual moves around the high brush zones and sheep lived only in the uplands. Fish were found wherever there were streams, rivers and lakes. The various animal and plant resources were often located far apart, so each family had to make many moves and encampments during the year. At most, twice a year all the band members gathered together. Although the population and movements of game changed along with shifts in the climate and forest cover, the same general life pattern continued with little change for 8,500 years.

The time from 8,500 to about 4,000 years ago was slightly warmer than now, and during the past 4,000 years there have been only minor changes in temperature with little effect on the Interior. These short-term temperature fluctuations are not well enough known to link them to culture changes in the Interior, and possibly had little overall significance for people living here.

*The Athabaskan Lifeway.* Knowing about the ways traditional Athabaskan people lived in the recent past is important to archaeologists trying to interpret the remains they discover in ancient campsites. By looking at patterns of resources and the ways they have been used in recent times, we can infer many things about prehistoric subsistence and settlement. And by understanding the important differences between Athabaskan groups in the historic period — in customs, resources and details of lifeway — we can appreciate the probable diversity of groups in the past. This makes us extremely careful about generalizing from one site or area to any others.

All traditional Athabaskan groups used a variety of subsistence resources, the importance of each varying from one area to another. Fishing was important almost everywhere, and most productive in areas where summer salmon runs provided seasonal abundance of a fairly reliable sort. Other important species included whitefish, northern pike, Arctic char, blackfish and grayling.

Most groups situated themselves along caribou migration routes or maintained access to such places through cooperative relations with neighboring bands. Migrations of caribou, in spring and especially fall, offered the potential for abundant food. However, caribou populations may fluctuate in a region, and they do not always use the same routes from year to year. A missed year could spell disaster for an Athabaskan band.

To fill the in-between times, Athabaskans selected from a number of animals available seasonally or year-round, though again populations of any species might fluctuate from year to year. These resources included moose, mountain sheep, bear, muskrat, hare, beaver, grouse, ptarmigan, geese, ducks and ground squirrels. During each year, band members decided how to use the resources of their territory, scheduling their activities seasonally and considering which areas were most likely to provide the best returns of food for the work involved. Sometimes, perhaps frequently, miscalculations caused a band to disappear tragically, because some members starved and others joined neighboring groups not so hard hit.

There were some major differences in the subsistence economics of interior Alaskan groups. For example, people who lived along the lower Yukon and Kuskokwim rivers had access to unusually rich salmon fisheries, and so they gathered into larger, more settled groups. By contrast, some bands in the Tanana Valley made do without salmon, fishing instead for whitefish and grayling, and hunting caribou. As a result, they had smaller, less permanent groups and settlements. Some Canadian Athabaskans had fewer fish still, and lived even more precariously by hunting land animals. They were forced to move from site to site more often than the Tanana Valley people, who, in turn, used more sites during the year and throughout their lifetimes than did Athabaskans living along the great rivers. The major resources offered by a particular region also influenced what assortment of tools would be used by the people of that region, and this determined the kind of remains left behind for archaeologists.

During the winter, Athabaskans usually gathered in encampments where they had time to socialize, make new clothing and tools and repair old equipment. Often this encampment was located near water where men and women could fish through the ice. Men would also make occasional hunting trips, despite the usual low return in winter. Spring saw many groups move to fish camps along the rivers, where salmon would run later on. In the better areas these camps would be near the winter village; in others they were a distance away. Fish were caught with dip nets, traps, pole and hook, and spears, often to be stored for later use. In some areas, people also used fish skins for making bags and even waterproof garments.

Fall was the time when many Athabaskans aimed to stock up on moose and caribou meat. Along the major caribou migration trails, bands might build corrals for herding caribou together where they could be snared, speared, or shot with arrows. Another method was to drive the animals into lakes or streams for killing there. In caribou, the Athabaskan people had an all-purpose resource: the meat could be cached at strategic places in the territory for later use; skins were needed to make important items like clothing, boots and tent covers; bone was used for making tools like fish hooks, spears, fleshers, scrapers, knives and ornaments; and even the dried tendons were used to make sinew for sewing.

Each Athabaskan group used a large territory, and so people traveled widely in boats, on snowshoes and on foot. At the margins of their territories and at pre-arranged places, they met other Athabaskans to trade for certain important goods. For example, obsidian — a glassy volcanic rock ideal for making razor-sharp tools — was traded around Alaska for more than 10,000 years. People followed long-established overland trails for travel within their own territories and for trade throughout wider regions.

Individual Athabaskans belonged to small, local bands of a few families. These in turn were loosely joined into larger territorial groups, most of whom were friends and relatives, and most of whom spoke the same language. From this group men and women would choose their spouses. Bands living along the margins of the larger territories might have social arrangements with bands from neighboring territories. The boundaries and affiliations of bands could change throughout time, and this caused a constant shifting of territorial groups.

*Tributaries Of The Stream.* Tracing the lines connecting early sites to those of the last few thousand years reveals some interesting variations within and between regions. The highly mobile lifestyle of interior Athabaskans suggests that many individual language areas and the groups within them have not been stable for long periods of time. It also indicates that archaeological remains are not likely to reveal much about the history of specific Athabaskan groups. The sites in a given area could be remnants from a group who spoke an extinct Athabaskan language or dialect, or just as easily, they might be evidence of an existing language group. Nonetheless, in several areas archaeologists can trace enough similarities through time, mainly in stone tool styles, to suggest that a major Athabaskan language group, or several related ones, may be represented. This has been true in southwestern Yukon Territory, for example.

Archaeologists working in some other areas, who are unable to find such similarity throughout time, have been reluctant to postulate that prehistoric remains are those of a group known historically. However, what we know of the similarities and differences among Athabaskan groups does allow us to infer that most interior sites are from this general family of people. Linguistic evidence clearly indicates that the major area for Athabaskan language history and diversification is in Alaska's eastern Interior. Interestingly, this is one area where people retained Denali technology for a long time.

Archaeological evidence shows that people occupied interior Alaska continuously after 8,500 years ago. A number of sites from this time contain strong representation of the microlithic industries typical of the earlier Interior. Included are the Fairbanks Campus site and a number of sites in southwestern Yukon Territory. Some sites in northwestern Alaska and the Yukon Territory contain notched projectile points but no microblades; others have both notched points and microblades. In some areas these technologies occur together within the last 1,500 to 6,500 years. These differences among sites during the past 8,500 years probably reflect the growing diversity among Athabaskan language and culture groups.

Some archaeologists have emphasized the distinctiveness of the non-microblade assemblages with notched points, even suggesting they reveal new people who came into the region from the south with the expansion of the forests. This overlooks the growing number of interior collections where notched points and microblades are found together, and it contradicts the

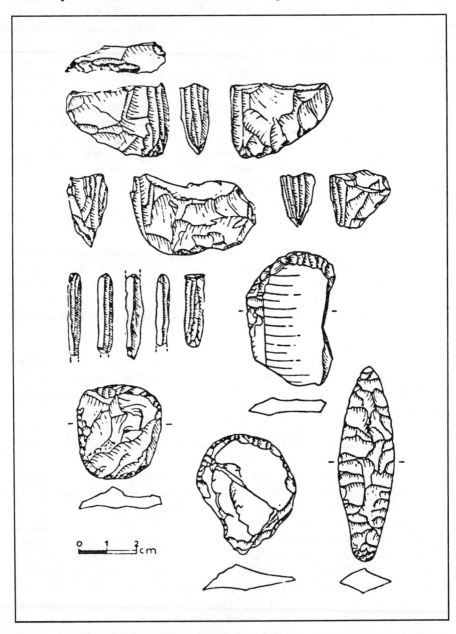

*Campus site remains include typical Diuktai-Denali microcores on bifaces and microblades for setting into grooved/slotted antler points. Several forms of points or knives are also found, including a corner notched specimen. Though precise dating is lacking, geological and Carbon 14 evidence suggests a middle Holocene age. Thus, we could call these late Denali materials on the basis of the microblade production system and later age, and not the apparent association with several types of bifacial projectile.*

evidence from language and human biology. Thus, after 8,500 years ago the archaeological picture shows cultural continuity in way of life, and regional differentiation in stone tool technology. I will now discuss some sites dating between 8,500 and 1,500 years ago that offer insights into the Athabaskan way of life.

*Tuktu: The Summer Campsite.* In the late 1950s a campsite named Tuktu was discovered at Anaktuvuk Pass, on the northern edge of interior Alaska. Unearthed along with distinctive microblades were many specialized stone tools such as leaf-shaped and notched points, knives, scraping tools, large blades, choppers and notched sinkers, as well as debris from tool manufacture. The site, like Healy Lake, directly links Denali technology with that of notched stone spear tips and knives.

The Tuktu site consisted of five distinct clusters located on a well-drained glacial terrace above the nearby wet lowlands. Apparently it was an attractive place for travelers to set up camp. One of the clusters was clearly the remains of an old tent or brush structure that was outlined by cobbles. A smudge fire was built in the entry and a warming fire inside. This suggested to John Campbell, the archaeologist who recovered the materials, that a family had lived in the structure during summer.

Campbell interpreted the site as the remains of five summer dwellings. Each cluster of tools was in an area of soil colored differently from the surrounding ground. People who came later would scrounge the boulders from earlier tents and use them to hold down the edges of their own; this was simpler than trekking down into the river valley for new ones. In each tent, residents had prepared food, made tools, worked on skins, stored fish from the river and nearby lakes and used parts of game they had butchered elsewhere. From radiocarbon dating, Campbell showed that one of these families had visited Anaktuvuk Pass up to 6,500 years ago. Obsidian tools in the Tuktu site revealed that people who stayed there had connections with the Koyukuk region to the south.

*The Livengood Hunters.* Good stone for toolmaking was a precious resource in early times. This is why a series of chert outcrops 10 miles south of the Yukon River near Livengood attracted interior people through much of the prehistoric period. In one unusual spot there, a student archaeologist named David Derry discovered a layering of three separate visitations on a ridge crest. Near the surface he found remains from a group of hunters who had scanned for game. Interestingly, their tools were made of rock different from the chert which was so near their waiting place. The tools included small flattish cores that look more like the ones from Tuktu than the Denali wedge-shaped type, as well as side-notched and lanceolate points and several forms of scrapers. Evidence indicates that these materials were left sometime after 5,000 years ago, but just how long remains unknown.

Below these remains, a level dating 6,000 to 5,500 years ago produced typical Denali microblade cores, some burins, and notched points. Lower and earlier still, Derry found more microblades, parts of large bifaces, and apparently straight-sided points. While the collections from the three separate visits are small, they represent people who used weapons with microblade insets along with projectile points or stone spear heads.

*Return To Onion Portage.* At the same time as the Tuktu summer camps in Anaktuvuk Pass, people who did not use microblades occupied Onion Portage. The earlier Denali remains there are followed after a millennium or so by assemblages 6,000 years old, whose distinctive tool is a simply flaked, notched point. There are also flaked knives, scrapers, notched stone sinkers, large oval bifaces and several large choppers. During the 1,500 years covered by these materials, the notched points seem to have gone out of vogue as people developed a preference for other styles with stemmed and straight bases. Although there were no microblades there after 6,000 years ago, the sinkers, choppers and points show direct links to places like Anaktuvuk and Livengood, where microblades were in use.

*Canada Heard From.* Far from Onion Portage, in southwestern Yukon Territory, Denali technology went out of vogue 4,500 years ago, about the same time assemblages with notched points show up. From then up to the time of contact, archaeologists think they see evidence of the ancestors of Kutchin, Tutchone and Han Athabaskans. Long after microblades ceased to be important in southwestern Yukon Territory, Tanana Valley people continued to use them. Did the idea to drop microblades come from the development of barbed spear points that did not require stone insets? Archaeologists won't know until old sites with preserved bone are discovered.

*Looking Backward.* The many sites known from the Interior for the past 8,500 years offer glimpses into prehistoric people and their lifeways. But these are not enough to reconstruct the whole picture for any time period or region. We can only piece together our reconstructions and compare materials from different areas, knowing that the record is incomplete. So far, our site discoveries have been heavily biased toward short-term camps, especially those used by a few members of a band — usually a hunting party of men or occasionally a family. We have found few early fish camps or winter villages, if any at all. This means that we have uncovered little evidence of the most important and stable kinds of settlements. We know that Athabaskan people usually recount their personal and band histories in terms of winter villages and fish camps, yet somehow the remains of such places have eluded us.

Furthermore, the highly mobile lifestyle that was successful in the Interior provides few sites with deeply stratified evidence of repeated use throughout time. Although it is hard to interpret small bits of information from the vast Interior, we have found consistent patterns of adaptation for much of the time humans have lived here. There is also evidence that people made adjustments to major climatic shifts beginning 14,000 years ago and again about 8,500 years ago.

We can show that some elements of culture persisted for many millennia, especially the Denali technology, which can be traced back to 12,000 years ago. In some areas this microblade tradition becomes mixed with a newer technology which can be traced for several thousand years. But in other areas we cannot make these connections for long time periods, though we can infer less direct relationships by comparing tool styles from neighboring groups.

In my opinion, microblade technology is demonstrably part of the long-standing tradition which is likely to be that of Athabaskans. This conforms to the model of Athabaskan origins which emerges from biological and linguistic evidence. Together they indicate that a single Asian migration 14,000 to 9,000 years ago accounts for the origin of the subsequent Athabaskan people. The Athabaskans developed or borrowed ideas about equipment throughout the millennia — notched points and several associated tools are the conspicuous examples. Some dropped microblade technology from their cultural repertoire; others retained it.

# People of the Legends:
# Tracing the Modern Athabaskans

Archaeological sites in northwestern Canada provide us with tangible evidence of a connection between ancient people and several modern Athabaskan groups. In Alaska, however, inadequate archaeological research and the apparent shifting around of prehistoric people prevents us from showing such specific links between past and present groups until a more recent time. In most of the Interior, historic Athabaskan people become visible archaeologically about 1,500 years ago. We can identify them from their principal winter villages and fish camps, and from features of their technology that persisted to the time of European contact. Several important archaeological examples are found in the Tanana River Valley and the Copper River drainage. I will use the site of Dixthada and several Ahtna sites to illustrate the kind of materials which more fully document historic Athabaskans and their prehistoric ancestors.

*Dixthada: A Question Of Ancestry.* A number of old sites are known by Athabaskan villagers of the upper Tanana River Valley, but only a few have been excavated. Among the important sites that have been studied is an ancient settlement called Dixthada, located along a clear stream that flows from Mansfield Lake into the Tanana River near the village of Tanacross. Pioneer Alaskan archaeologist Froelich Rainey, a professor at the University of Alaska, did major excavations there in the 1930s and early 1940s.

Dixthada is important because it was a fish-camp site and probably a winter village, one of the first to be excavated. It is also older than any other fish camp and winter village site that archaeologists have studied. So it is both an important kind of Athabaskan site and one that is not well represented prehistorically. Apparently most early remains of this sort have been either eroded away or buried under river and lake deposits.

Dixthada was used many times by Upper Tanana Athabaskans during more than 1,000 years. The last time people lived there was just after 1885, when inhabitants of the site moved to Mansfield Village. Shallow rectangular house pits are still visible in the ground there. A typical site of this kind might have only one to three such houses, but Dixthada has nine well-defined house pits, numerous fish storage pits and eleven tent rings.

Besides these features, Rainey also identified a refuse mound associated with each house depression. Digging into these mounds, he found boulder spall scrapers, a kind of tool known from thousands of years earlier at the Dry Creek and Tuktu sites. Along with these were typical Athabaskan stone, bone and native copper tools. He also found microblades, but were they of the same age

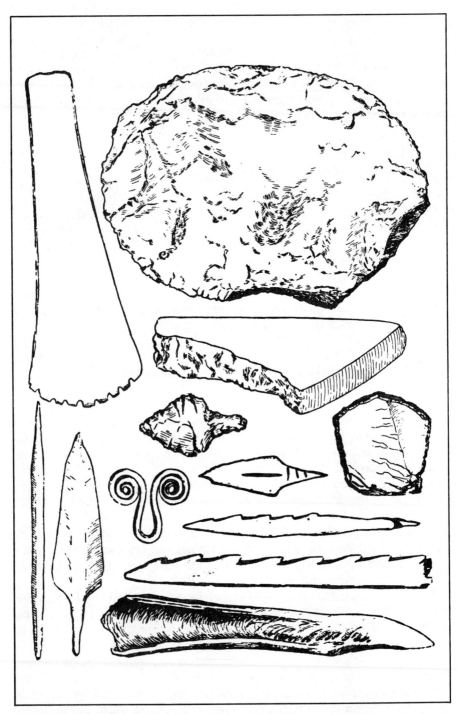

*Sites which are linked to historic Athabaskan groups, like Dixthada, suggest that for the past 1,500 years barbed bone points and copper replaced early stone-and-antler and stone counterparts in some areas. Stone is not common for tools although small stemmed points, honing stones and boulder spall scrapers are still present.*

as the identifiably Athabaskan tools? Rainey knew that interior microblades were pretty old, and his Athabaskan helpers had never seen or heard about stone tools of this kind. This suggested to him that the microblades were remains of an earlier culture, with refuse left by the later Athabaskans overlying them.

Rainey dug through six of the refuse mounds, removing the debris in arbitrary layers about nine inches thick. Since the mounds were 35 feet across and nearly three feet deep in places, he dug up a lot of dirt, ash, charcoal, wood chips, birchbark, burned stone, bits of shell, and bones from all sorts of fish, birds and mammals. Much was discarded that would be saved by archaeologists today, especially the food refuse that could give information about the subsistence lives of early Dixthada people.

From the items he uncovered in the mounds — including European and American trade goods — Rainey knew that some of the houses were occupied during the 1800s. Some mounds could be shown to date just about the time trade objects first came into the Tanana Valley, but others from earlier periods contained no trade items. Rainey was particularly impressed, however, by the objects hammered from native copper which probably originated on the Nabesna River. These included awls, needles, small stemmed points, facial ornaments, moosehide scrapers and metal scraps.

Local Athabaskan legend held that the migration into the upper Tanana was recent and that another group had lived there before. In the oldest mounds, presumably below the known Athabaskan refuse, were the microblades and other stone tools of Denali technology. Thus, Rainey had found some archaeological evidence to confirm the legends. It appeared that in the Tanana Valley microlithic technology persisted quite late but did not last to historic times. His late materials looked like Athabaskan tools found in southwestern Yukon Territory, especially the copper and small stemmed points. And later on, more similar materials showed up in Athabaskan fish camps at Cadzow Lake and Klo'kut near Old Crow, in northwestern Yukon Territory, and in southern Alaska along the Copper River at Dakah De'nin's Village.

In the 1970s, Anne Shinkwin led a University of Alaska team that re-excavated Dixthada and studied the earlier Rainey collections as well. In levels dating about 700 years old, she found an array of tools resembling those of historic Athabaskans. Among the stone tools were some points similar to recent Athabaskan points from Yukon Territory and others like the early points from Onion Portage and Tuktu; and there were cores, microblades and burins representing the Denali technology. These microlithic tools were mainly confined to early levels, dated about 2,400 years ago. Other microlithic elements found in later levels were explained as a result of mixing, as were more recent styles of tools that Shinkwin found in the early levels.

Interior archaeologists have often found remains of microlithic technology apparently associated with Athabaskan materials dating to the last thousand years or so. For a number of reasons, these associations are still discounted, even when there is no clear evidence that mixing has occurred. How would this mixing happen? People might dig house pits into earlier cultural levels; or dirt removed from house pit construction, containing earlier remains, might be used on the house roof which later collapses. People could also trample their refuse down into their house floors, mixing it with earlier remains underneath. Or house pit walls containing early materials could slump in, so they would lie on top of later material deposited beneath the floor. Mixing can also occur in other ways, but these are the most obvious and commonly cited ones. Often, of course, we must take the archaeologist's word that artifacts of seemingly different ages are found together because of mixing processes.

Thus, as we presently understand it, the Dixthada site shows that people using Denali technology, along with notched knives and points and other objects (found earlier in Tuktu, Healy Lake and Livengood), persisted in the Tanana Valley until 2,400 years ago. Later levels at this site, dating from 700 years ago, are the remains of people clearly related to the Upper Tanana Athabaskans of historic times. But it remains an open question whether the later inhabitants of this site were direct descendants of those represented in the earlier levels.

*Early Lifeways of The Copper River People.* Like the Upper Tanana Athabaskans, Ahtna people told Rainey that their ancestors had come into an area where others were already living. According to this story, they entered the Copper River country and largely destroyed the indigenous people who lived there. The archaeological record of historic Athabaskans in this area is about 1,000 years old, and again the relationship to earlier archaeological remains awaits clarification. Did Ahtna Athabaskans only move into the Copper River Valley during the last millennium or so? This is a possibility because we know that in recent centuries other Athabaskans invaded parts of the Great Plains, American Southwest and Pacific Northwest, displacing people who were already there. Perhaps similar movements occurred in Alaska.

Ahtna prehistory can be divided into three or four periods. First, there is the historic period after 1850, when European goods and influences became dominant. Second, from about 1770 to 1850, European trade goods first entered Ahtna life and the culture probably was being affected by the fur trade. Nevertheless, traditional material culture and ideas were still dominant at this time. Third, prehistoric Ahtna culture is visible in the archaeology record for at least 700 years before the advent of European goods. The period of Ahtna culture in the Copper River drainage goes back at least 1,000 years. Fourth, before 1,000 years ago the evidence of archaeology is too skimpy to talk about Ahtna or any other Athabaskan group, although the region was suited for occupation for about 9,000 years.

From the first period, archaeologists excavated Taral, a summer fish camp and winter village above Wood Canyon, in the Copper River Valley. Here they found trade beads, nails, china, pipe bowls, cartridge cases, stove parts and even an 1878 quarter. Traditional items included barbed antler points and iron knives made after the style of native copper knives. House pits found near Taral produced similar materials, along with food caches and evidence of an attached sweat bath.

In the Susitna Valley, archaeologists found wood, copper and other metal objects, and several aboveground coffin burials, one of which was associated with a Russian style cross. Near Batzulnetas, in the Copper River Valley, the archaeologist Rainey tested refuse deposits in a village, finding glass trade beads, house depressions and sweat house pits as well. You will note that rather than the typical camps and overlook sites of earlier archaeology, the recent centuries preserve the more heavily used band villages and fish camps, fish caches, cremation burials and sweat houses.

Rich remains of a similar sort are also present in the second period from 1770 to 1850. Dakah De'nin's Village, along the Copper River near Chitina, is the

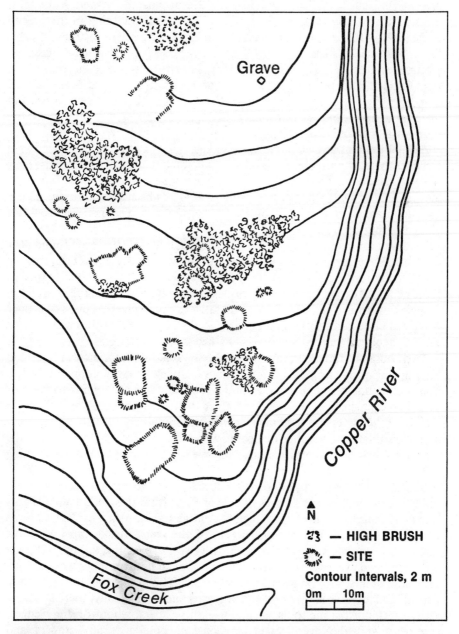

*This is an archaeologist's map of Dakah De'nin's village before beginning the excavation. The structures of the village represent houses, sweat houses, graves and other activity areas. These do not preserve well and most traces may be lost in a matter of generations.*

best known site, consisting of a number of cache pits, refuse deposits and house pits with attached sweat baths. The houses produced evidence of at least three different visits, but the tools left behind were similar each time. Native copper arrowheads, awls, needles, women's knives, men's knives, beads and copper scraps were outstanding artifacts found there. A few items of iron were also present, indicating indirect contact with Europeans. Bone and ivory tools included arrowheads and pendants. There was almost nothing in the way of stone tools — barbed bone points and metal tools had been substituted by this time. The crude stone tools still made included boulder spall scrapers, whetstones, hammers and grinding stones. The site even preserved some of the fine wooden and birchbark objects that must always have been part of Athabaskan culture. The two excavated houses were quite different in size and material items — one was probably the house of the leading family and the other of less prominent relatives.

Animal remains at Dakah De'nin's Village tell us about the main economic activities there. Most remains are those of salmon (an unusual find because their skeletons seldom preserve well), and there are bones from grayling, snowshoe hare, Arctic ground squirrel and porcupine. The absence of caribou, moose and mountain sheep remains highlights the importance of salmon fishing at this village during summer.

Evidence for another part of the Ahtna economic cycle has been found near Gulkana. Here, archaeologists studied a camp where people had been snaring snowshoe hares, probably just for a day or two in late winter or early spring. Little remained except the fireplace with its ash and burned rocks, the hare bones, a single iron knife (but in the fashion of native copper knives), a piece of copper wire, two bone point tips and a boulder spall scraper. Pretty slim pickings for the archaeologist but informative nonetheless.

Two house pits found not far away at Paxson Lake are associated with caribou hunting and processing. Tools left behind included fleshers, copper knives, a bone point, boulder spall scrapers and a few trade items. The preservation of bone in recent sites like this helps greatly in interpreting people's activities. We can count the bones and determine how many animals are actually represented, and so estimate the number of people who could be fed, how successful the stopover was, who was present and so on. We can also see the variety of hunting weapons that were used.

Remains for the third period, from 1,000 years ago to 1770, are less well-known than more recent sites. A couple of finds from this period add insights into early Ahtna activities in the region. A large site identified as GUL 077 was partially excavated during construction of the trans-Alaska pipeline. Most materials found there were associated with two large camps, although the site also contained other remains. In later times, much native copper was used for projectile points, knives, awls and ornaments. This is one link to the historic period, and another is the bone and antler technology. Finally, there is a large series of chipped stone tools, including skin scrapers, woodworking wedges, engravers and the ever-present Athabaskan boulder spall scrapers and whetstones. An archaeological bonus was the recovery there of preserved birchbark basketry.

Of considerable interest for archaeologists is evidence that chipped stone tools decreased in importance after 1,000 years ago. The growing use of copper tools, and perhaps new styles of bone points, reduced the number of stone tools to a few rather crude and heavy types. We may have clues there of the kinds of cultural shifts that led groups away from earlier microblade technology.

At GUL 077, archaeologists also excavated a number of substantial cache pits apparently used for storing salmon. Some of these were interconnected (up to nine in one case) and others were large single holes. Each one had a lid and was lined with poles and bark. Most of them had been left empty, so we know they had served their purpose before being abandoned. Dates for several of these pits range to at least 800 years ago.

While houses have not been identified at GUL 077, archaeologists have found campfires that were the focal points for people staying there intermittently throughout a period of 500 years. A number of artifacts were unearthed around these hearths. Shelters at the site probably consisted of simple brush lean-tos; their post holes are indicated by dark stains in lighter surrounding earth. Sweat baths and several cremations were also found there, although they relate to visits different from those of the campfires.

Some animal bones have been uncovered at GUL 077, mainly the remnants of hare and beaver, as well as moose, caribou and red squirrel. Unfortunately, few salmon bones have been preserved there. The animal remains were from several different camps and various times of the year. For example, the hearths are from winter and early spring hunting camps, while fish caches were used in different seasons. All in all, GUL 077 preserves many past visits and provides information on prehistoric Ahtna culture, including use of simple brush lean-tos, construction of large and elaborate underground caches, cremation of the dead, and trade for stone, shell and metal with coastal people.

Another important body of information comes from a site called MS 23-0 on the Copper River near Gulkana. Several house pits were identified, and in one burned house the archaeologists found inlaid spruce-wood bowls, fragments of an intricately woven container and remains of fish that had been stored in the rafters. Outside the house there were a few objects of copper, bone and stone. Excavations of the house pits suggested that they had plank floors, outdoor hearths and associated cache pits. The outdoor hearths and presence of fish and bear bones indicate a summer occupation. The site dates from sometime around 1300 A.D.

Clearly, the challenge for archaeologists will be to find fish camps, winter villages and other seasonal camps that are more than 1,000 years old. We have unearthed hunting camps and stopover sites for earlier periods, but they have revealed limited information about structures, tools and activities. These sites give us little to compare with the much fuller evidence about the entire annual cycle which has been preserved in younger sites.

Meanwhile, 1,000 years of Ahtna occupation are well-attested in the Copper River drainage. Summer fishing stations and winter camps are present, as are winter villages which have houses and attached sweat baths. Large cache pits seem related to the salmon which were the focus of the local people. The caches are in out-of-the-way places where raiders wouldn't have found them, a pattern that extended to the historic period. So at least 1,000 years ago we can infer that raiding neighbors and competition were part of the Athabaskan way of life. Additionally, trade with coast people is indicated by the presence of items not available in the Interior.

Comparisons show that some features of early Ahtna material culture — including a number of specific tool types and styles — are similar to those of the Upper Tanana people at Dixthada, the Kutchin people at Klo'kut on the Porcupine River and possibly ancestral Tutchone people of Yukon Territory. The ancestry of all these late prehistoric Athabaskan groups and culture traditions is not equally clear in the record. For example, the long period represented by sites in southwestern Yukon Territory contrasts with the shorter history known for the Tanana Valley. Perhaps the development of groups the anthropologists call Upper Tanana is more recent than the development of other Athabaskans like the Tutchone. If so, then it suggests a process of group formation and reformation which is probably ancient.

## The Long Journey

This chapter has explored the origins and long prehistory of interior Alaska's native people. It has emphasized a theory that ancestors of the Athabaskans migrated across the Bering Land Bridge from Asia, and that other American Indians and Eskimo-Aleuts came into the New World separately. This three-migration theory is based on information from linguistics, biology and archaeology, and it differs from the long-accepted view that Athabaskan Indians are an offshoot of the larger American Indian group. Throughout the chapter I have tried to show that modern Athabaskans may be the direct descendants of these ancient migrants and that their cultures have evolved in Alaska and adjacent areas of Canada.

The first migrants to the New World came from northeastern Asia's interior, possibly sometime between 35,000 and 25,000 years ago. They were adapted to the extreme cold of northeastern Asia, the connecting Bering Land Bridge and unglaciated Alaska. They were expert hunters and fishermen, taking even such large animals as mammoths and bison, and such swift ones as horses and antelope. They must have moved far south before glaciers barred the way through western Canada during the period of extreme cold following 25,000 years ago. In the long period when Alaska and Asia were separated, from around 25,000 to 14,000 years ago, ancestral Indians spread to the woodlands, coasts, tropical forests, deserts and mountains of North and South America.

Evidence of the early migration is scanty in the North, where archaeological sites do not preserve well and where landscape changes have been extreme. Hints of these people do exist, however, as in the caribou bone flesher from Old Crow, possibly 26,000 to 29,000 years old. Even older evidence is claimed but it is more controversial. The most useful information comes from the United States, Mexico and South America, where many sites from 20,000 to 13,000 years old have been excavated.

A better-recorded migration is the third one, the coastal expansion of Asiatic people who were the cultural ancestors of Eskimos and Aleuts. Their movements brought them to America at least 9,000 to 6,000 years ago, and the remains of both groups have been found along Alaskan coasts, revealing much about their traditional lifestyles. Expansion of these groups continued until all coastlines from southwestern Alaska to Greenland were under Eskimo and Aleut control more than 4,000 years ago.

The migration of these coastal people came after that of the Athabaskans, and so ancestral Athabaskans must have arrived in Alaska about 14,000 to 9,000 years ago. Initially, these interior groups continued with the cultural adaptations they had brought with them from Asia. Their prominent microblade technology was extensively present in Siberia from 18,000 to 10,000 years ago. It appeared in Alaska by 12,000 years ago, with remains of its forerunners submerged beneath waters covering the Bering Land Bridge.

The Siberian people using Diuktai technology and the Alaskan offshoots using Denali technology had originally developed economies geared to the large game herds and other resources of the Bering Land Bridge and adjacent areas on either side. These migrants spread throughout hundreds of thousands of square miles on the cold northern grasslands — first pursuing mammoths, bison and horses, then shifting to caribou and other game as the earlier animals vanished. The warming climate that caused these changes also raised sea levels, and the land bridge shrank away.

Some groups in Alaska kept on adjusting throughout the long period of climatic change leading to modern conditions shortly after 8,500 years ago. Because they retained the Denali technology, we can infer that major elements of the old culture continued to work even as forests spread across the open country. Undoubtedly these changes brought disaster and extinction to some bands, but enough survived to gradually develop fine-tuned adjustments to the Interior. This period was one of readaptation, then population growth, then expansion into marginal areas even at the expense of others. Eskimo and Aleut control of the coasts confined Athabaskan populations to the Interior, so they expanded most successfully into environments they knew best — the boreal forests of Alaska and Canada. This northern expansion took place especially during the last several millennia, as Athabaskans moved into the Northwest Territories of Canada and the Pacific Northwest. In the last 300 to 600 years they also made some amazing and successful incursions into new regions: the American Great Plains and the Southwest. At least some of their successes required hard fighting.

We would know more about these early Athabaskans if landscape changes had not destroyed the major winter and summer sites that I believe they used. Archaeologists must make do with camps and short-term hunting sites almost entirely. Even so, we can see elements of later Athabaskan culture from the beginning: male hunting camps, family camps, kill sites, spring camps for scrounging during the leanest season and tents held down with stones.

That group affiliations, languages and culture boundaries were constantly shifting is indicated by changes in tool types and styles used throughout the millennia. The original Denali technology persisted for a long time in some areas but was given up fairly early in others, apparently in favor of notched stone points and bone points. Some conservatives kept on using microblades at the same time they developed or accepted new kinds of chipped stone and bone tools. Formation of new groups was fairly typical in Athabaskan prehistory.

During the last 1,000 years or so we have our richest archaeological record of Athabaskans, because their main winter villages and fish-camp sites are preserved. Although the material remains are hard to identify, we can develop the theory that the ancestors of historic Athabaskan people were among the inhabitants of the many interior sites that span the last 10,000 to 12,000 years. We can use several lines of evidence to help toward a real understanding of Athabaskan culture history, ways of life and emerging historic groups. Only further archaeological research will allow us to trace the connections between prehistoric groups, to understand when modern Athabaskans came into existence, and to learn how these people emerged. Many mysteries still surround these ancient inhabitants of Alaska's Interior, but each summer archaeologists return to unearth more remains that may help to fill the blank spaces in this fascinating puzzle.

# On the Back Slough

## Ethnohistory of Interior Alaska

### By William Samuel Schneider

*Editor's note: An anthropologist by training, William S. Schneider is curator of oral history at the Alaska and Polar Regions Department, Elmer Rasmuson Library, University of Alaska, Fairbanks.*

## Recounting the Past

In the heart of Alaska's Interior, the Yukon River flows through a great level stretch of land called the Yukon Flats. It encompasses the area from Circle to Stevens Village, roughly 300 miles long and up to 100 miles wide, where the river wanders among old channels, sloughs, islands and sandbars. You can travel on that section of the Yukon again and again, following a different channel each time. From the air, it all looks similar — meandering streams with myriad ponds dotting the low relief. But from the water, a rich variety of terrain waits to be explored.

This chapter is a bit like that part of the river, a series of interwoven themes all related to the main current of Alaskan history. Certain themes like trade, communication, education and landownership flow together and form the main current. Each theme is composed of many smaller themes, adding to the flow and diverging — only to reappear a few pages later in a somewhat different context.

On the back sloughs, where a small part of the flow is diverted across the broad expanse, the current slows and the immensity of the main river gives way to the intimacy of each bend. Here we meet the old-timers whose stories, like the back slough itself, add detail and perspective to a broad and complex historical narrative. They speak of the places, the people and the events that have characterized and influenced their lives. These stories enrich our travel and remind us that there are many different ways to learn about the past — each gives us a somewhat different emphasis or point of view.

What follows is a series of episodes, moving between the firsthand knowledge of local people and the historical accounts or overviews drawn from books and manuscripts. People's stories are woven into the narrative and juxtaposed against analysis and summary, giving various differences in perspective. The chapter focuses on the Athabaskan people, but in the context of the many others who came into the Interior during the past two centuries. It captures a bit of the exciting drama that developed in this part of the world.

Included here are the dreams, desires and disappointments that some of interior Alaska's people have revealed in their words or writings. They are recorded here by one who has experienced a small part of the drama himself, read about a bit more, and been lucky enough to hear some of the personal accounts that old-timers wished to share.

As you travel down the river of interior history, you may read the water differently or choose another channel; there are many other ways to go. This

147

chapter runs through some of the deep main channel water, but it also explores some of the more interesting back sloughs, where local knowledge and memory add personal meaning to the story. For those who might wish to do some exploring on their own, a number of references and resource people are listed for this chapter . . . and fortunately there are still old-timers in Alaska who enjoy sharing their personal experiences over a cup of coffee in town or out in the woods at their trapping cabins and fish camps.

## The Traders

Long before explorers and fur traders made their way to the Alaskan coast, the goods of their world were arriving across Bering Strait. The Chukchi and Eskimo people of Siberia traded regularly with northwestern Alaskan Eskimos, who then made exchanges with Athabaskans of the Interior. Iron, copper, tobacco and reindeer skins enriched the traditional trade between these people. A famous trade fair occurred each summer at Sisualik Spit, across from Kotzebue, and other fairs were held at Point Spencer, Stebbins and Pastolik. The trade fairs were an exciting time for many people to get together to trade, feast, dance and visit. The gatherings were held at places rich in resources like fish and sea mammals, so there was enough food to support the large encampment.

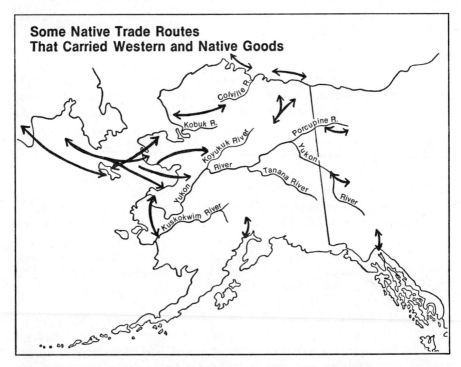

**Some Native Trade Routes That Carried Western and Native Goods**

*Long before Europeans entered Alaska, native groups carried out regular long distance trade with one another, following natural corridors such as rivers and mountain passes. Besides allowing cultural and economic exchange between different peoples, the trade networks brought European goods into Alaska from Siberia well ahead of the first white explorers.*

It is hard to tell how long ago this trade began, but it seems that once the Chukchi traders could obtain enough European goods these items quickly entered the exchange and appeared in Alaska. James VanStone has suggested that shortly after 1750 Russian trade goods were being acquired by the Ingalik Athabaskans of the lower Yukon River. In return, the Indians provided wooden utensils and furs of beaver, otter, marten, wolf, wolverine and fox. The trade goods were brought into the Interior through several well-known routes.

Some of the goods traded at Sisualik were then carried along the Kobuk and Noatak rivers to the Colville River, an ancient highway across the Arctic foothills. Where the mouth of this river enters the Beaufort Sea there was more trading, sometimes with Canadian Eskimos who would bring their goods and in turn would carry the new items farther east.

The Athabaskans also traveled to the Arctic Coast for trade, but probably not at these trade fairs. A popular trade route led from the Arctic Village area, on the south flanks of the Brooks Range, north through the mountains to the coast near Barter Island and Demarcation Point. Athabaskans approached trips into Eskimo country with a fair degree of caution. There was a long history of hostilities between the Indians and Eskimos, and both groups had heard stories graphically depicting the dangers. When they came to trade with each other, it was often at a prearranged time and place.

From the coast around Unalakleet, the Eskimos traveled across low divides into tributaries of the Yukon to trade with Athabaskans. One route led from Unalakleet to Kaltag, another from the coast to the Kateel River, which flows into the Koyukuk, a major branch of the Yukon.

For the Athabaskans who lived on the lower Yukon there were obvious advantages to maintaining trade relations with the Eskimos. They provided valuable coastal goods like sea mammal meat, strong bearded-seal rope, mukluk soles and the prized seal and whale oil. These products were important in their own right, before and after Russian goods entered the trade.

Frederica DeLaguna — one of the earliest anthropologists to investigate historic sites of the lower Yukon and collect oral traditions of the interior Athabaskans — was shown a site on the Kateel River, where coastal Eskimos portaged across to meet and trade with the interior Athabaskans. The Indians had built a ceremonial house for their coastal visitors. But, indicative of the fragile relations between the two groups, a few years later they also built a fort to protect themselves from these same neighbors.

DeLaguna's guide to this site was Johnny Dayton, an Athabaskan Indian. Years later his son, Roger Dayton, told what he had learned about this site from his father:

> One time in the fall of 1935 my old man and me were going up the Koyukuk River. A fellow by the name of Wilfred Evans was taking us up because we had no boat of our own at the time. My old man mentioned this old bunker that people used to have for protection against any enemies. He explained how villages used to fight quite a bit among themselves.
>
> Wilfred wanted to see this bunker so we stopped there and went up the bank. Maybe about a couple of hundred yards back in the

woods we came to the place of this underground bunker made of logs. I'd say it was just above the mouth of the Kateel River.

The lower Koyukuk, on the border between groups and near easy transportation corridors to the coast, was a likely location for social and economic conflicts. But it was also an area of opportunity and the neighboring people learned to live together. Trading partners played a key role in keeping up the communication and contact between groups. In *On the Edge of Nowhere,* one of the most amazing accounts written about this area, Jimmy Huntington tells the story of his own mother — an Athabaskan woman from the Koyukuk country — traveling to Nome to testify against the man who murdered her husband. After the trial his killer was released, and the discouraged, homesick woman started out on foot for her home. The trip took her many months and led through Eskimo country, and there were many who thought she wouldn't make it. But her father's trading partner, an Eskimo from the Kobuk River, was watching for her and ready to help. When he finally found her he said, "I saw your father not two moons ago. He had had word that you left Nome on foot. He asked me to watch for you. Each day my son has come down the river to wait. And now you are safe."

How many times before had partners called upon each other for such favors? The partnerships provided a means for Indians and Eskimos to peacefully meet and trade, and the relationships they developed were the basis for mutual assistance and exchange of goods across cultural boundaries. Through many years and lifetimes, they provided a familiar continuity among separate people and created a means for introducing new trade goods.

As European items came in increasing quantities, the Indians' way of life changed. Even though it was many years before they actually met the Russians, the demand for the Indians' furs and expansion of the influence of foreign traders affected traditional trade patterns on which the Natives depended. Eskimo trade with Siberian Natives continued after Russian expansion to Alaska, and when Russians entered the Interior, Eskimos actively thwarted their progress to guard their prized position as middlemen.

Lt. Laurenti Zagoskin, Russian observer for the Russian-American Company, remarked several times about the shrewdness of the Eskimos and how they jealously guarded their trading position with the interior people. In one case he illustrates this point by noting that the Eskimos guided the Russians into the Interior but were able to disguise their route of travel until:

> Finally an inexperienced boy betrayed the location of the real portage to [Russian explorer Vasilii] Malakhov in 1838, but even then the Natives did not change their two-faced policy. They kept up trade relations with the fort and family ties with the company employees, while following after our transports and undercutting our prices with trade goods.

While the Russians penetrated the Interior from the west, the Hudson's Bay Company was making its entree from the east. That grand old English institution, dating back to 1670, had by the early 1800s extended a string of fur trading posts across northern Canada from Hudson's Bay. Their presence, like the Russians', was felt years before they actually arrived. Trading posts

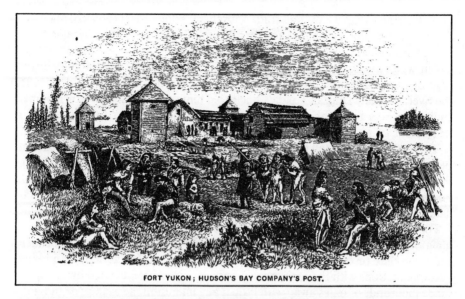

FORT YUKON; HUDSON'S BAY COMPANY'S POST.

*Fort Yukon, westernmost establishment of the Hudson's Bay Company, was built at the confluence of the Yukon and Porcupine rivers in 1847. When Alexander Murray selected this site he knew it was on territory of the Russian-American Company, but deemed the risk worthwhile to trade for the abundant furs available here. Fort Yukon is an important interior community today, but all that remains of the original settlement is the Hudson's Bay Company graveyard. (From* Territory of Alaska *(1869) by Frederick Whymper; courtesy of University of Alaska, Fairbanks)*

on the Mackenzie River drainages and the upper Yukon provided a sporadic flow of western goods into the heartland of the Athabaskans. Their posts were supplied through an extensive network of stations stretching back across Canada and connected by rivers, lakes and overland portages. Virtually all supplies came by this long and arduous route. At its farthest extent, some 4,000 miles from Hudson Bay, was Fort Yukon, located at the junction of the Yukon and the Porcupine rivers, only a few hundred miles upriver from the newly built Russian post at Nulato.

Establishment of these far flung posts meant that for the first time, some Athabaskan groups had to accommodate representatives of foreign nations doing business in their homeland. This was not true for all. Some groups, such as the Upper Kuskokwim, the Upper Copper River Ahtna and the Upper Tanana had a prolonged period of indirect contact, and they dealt through middlemen or traveled outside their territory to trade. Native and non-native traders competed for their furs, and they became conscious of the value of trade goods.

This point is made in the story of Diqelas Tukda, a 19th century Tanaina Indian from Cook Inlet who was famous for his trading trips inland to the Upper Kuskokwim people. They tolerated his trading until they determined that they weren't getting enough for their furs. Then they made it very clear that he must leave. The story is told by Shem Pete, a Tanaina elder distinguished for his knowledge:

> Long ago, when the Russians came, Diqelas Tukda would carry around a Russian gun. With his maternal uncle he would go to the

interior Athabaskans and trade with them, selling them tobacco, tea and matches in exchange for furs. From this Diqelas Tukda became a rich man.

But when the Upper Kuskokwim people realized that he was taking advantage of them they said, "He took too much from us . . . let's throw him in the river." Finally Diqelas Tukda's uncle told him that they should return home. Indicating how poor their reception had been, the uncle used to say, "Until he got out of arrow range . . . his back felt hot. . . . "

This is the last reported trading trip by the Tanaina to the Upper Kuskokwim people, who by then had more favorable options. Perhaps they were trading downriver at the seasonal Russian post at Vinasale or maybe they were trading north on the Yukon. In either case, they didn't have to put up with Diqelas Tukda any more.

For even the most remote Athabaskan groups, the fur trade eventually became a major economic focus and they were aware that their livelihood now depended on a complex mix of traditional relations with neighbors as well as making accommodations with the foreigners, whose concerns were dictated by decisions made thousands of miles away with little if any interest in the welfare of Indians.

## Fur Trade and the Far-Flung Companies

There were two great firms in the fur trade — the Russian-American Company and the Hudson's Bay Company, representing Russia and Great Britain. Each extended for thousands of miles in opposite directions around the globe, until they finally met on the middle reaches of the Yukon River. There they competed for the native people's trading allegiance and for the choice furs that the Natives could provide. Soon after arriving at the confluence of the Yukon and the Porcupine rivers, the Hudson's Bay trader Alexander Murray was introduced to the challenges his company would face:

> Blankets, axes, knives, powder horns and files went off readily enough, but it was hard to dispose of the clothing, as they consider their own dresses much superior to ours both in beauty and durability, and they are pretty right, although I endeavoured to persuade them to the contrary. I could not give them the reason for bringing so few goods, that we had brought only a few on trial, but more would be sent next year, which was the only way to prevent them from disposing of their furs elsewhere.

The company men had a difficult job. Communication with their superiors sometimes took years. Decisions about supply and trading policies were often held up so long that important opportunities were missed, and more than once the traders lamented their problems of supply. Hudson's Bay Company goods were transported by boat and pack along an interconnected river and portage route stretching clear across the subarctic. From Fort McPherson, the "end of the water" on the Mackenzie system, the outfit of trade goods from the east had to be packed or sledded across 60 miles of treeless uplands to the first water of the Porcupine drainage. Here, the hefty loads were exchanged for 90-pound bales of fur that had arrived after a tedious 400-mile boat trip from Fort Yukon. Once the transfer was completed, the York boats headed back to Fort Yukon.

These three- to four-week trips were made twice each summer. Some elders today, like Moses Cruikshank, recall stories from their grandparents who worked for the company, handling the boats and packing supplies across the portages.

> My grandfather worked for them, for the Hudson's Bay. . . . You know they had a big boat, big poling boat, loaded down with freight and they got men in there to line and pole and row, and one man, he was the captain or pilot. That was my grandpa's job. He was the pilot. A lot of those old-timers in Fort Yukon used to work for the Hudson's Bay that way too — like David Wallis when he was a young man. I understand he was a captain for the Hudson's Bay on the boat. When you're captain on a boat like that, you're the boss. What you say goes.

Acquiring enough food was often a problem for the traders. The Russian-American Company had some meat brought in by Natives and creoles in their employ, but they also depended on shipments of grain and other supplies to keep their posts stocked. In some places, fresh game such as seal, bear and water-fowl were acquired by the employees but conditions differed by region and despite their best efforts, the Russian-American Company constantly faced problems of supply.

Hudson's Bay Company employees bartered for caribou meat from the

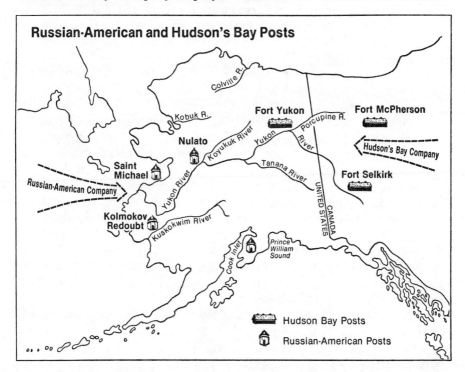

*The two great firms in the fur trade — the Russian-American Company and the Hudson's Bay Company — extended their activities in opposite directions clear around the globe until they met in Alaska's Interior during the late 1840s. Eventually the Hudson's Bay Company was forced back across the border into Canada, but not before establishing trade for furs as a basic part of Athabaskan life in the eastern Interior.*

Chandalar Kutchin at a meat trading post and apparently did some fishing themselves at old Birch Creek Village, 30 or 40 miles from their post at Fort Yukon. Game was also brought to the post and exchanged for trade goods although the company wanted to conserve these items for fur trading.

Attracting Natives to trade and holding their allegiance was a concern for both the Russian-American and Hudson's Bay companies. The employees had to be careful not to take sides in local disputes lest they offend factions, and they were constantly reminded of their delicate position with respect to the Native's traditional trade relations. This point was illustrated to Robert Campbell of the Hudson's Bay Company, when he was the trader in Fort Selkirk, at the junction of the Pelly and Yukon rivers. In 1852, the Chilkat Tlingits destroyed the post, defying Campbell's intrusion into their trade with the Tutchone Athabaskans. Campbell sought the help of his Tutchone companions to retaliate against the Tlingits. But they refused him, claiming that while they didn't particularly like to deal with the Tlingits, they had to maintain their allegiance since Tlingit people were their most reliable source of goods.

The importance of this event was revealed to anthropologist Catherine McClellan, who was trying to determine how native people perceived early white traders in the upper Yukon. To get this information she went directly to the people, and found that:

> For several years the Selkirk Indians simply melted into the bush whenever the Chilkat arrived. Finally the Chilkat became so desperate for furs that they made peace with the despised Tutchone on the latter's own terms.

> If this story is correct, the threat of Campbell's competition so soon after the renewal of inter-native trade must have made the Chilkat doubly edgy. On the other hand, one reason which the Tutchone gave for their ancestors' refusal to hunt down the Chilkat who destroyed the Fort was that they could not afford to break again with those who had so recently demonstrated eagerness to maintain trade relationships and who, though so unpleasant, remained the surest source of white men's goods. Campbell was, after all, a newcomer, and for reasons beyond his control, he had been short of goods throughout his stay. In his journals he complained bitterly of his dearth of trade goods, but he did not mention the intricacies of the inter-native trade described by my informants.

The irony of this situation is that the Tlingits had better access to company goods than Campbell, whose post was the most difficult to supply of all the Hudson's Bay Company stations.

Both the Russians and British did their trading with chiefs or their close kin rather than with individual hunters. For the most part these were traditional leaders, men who were influential in every sphere of life and whose positions were enhanced by the companies who wooed their support. The trading chiefs conducted business with the company by piling up the furs, meat and other provisions their group had brought in. After the transactions were completed, they distributed the knives, beads and cloth that the company had given in exchange.

The Athabaskan chief and his band traveled widely — hunting, fishing, trapping, visiting and, at times, making war. Shahnyaati was a Kutchin leader during this period. He and his band traveled throughout the Yukon Flats, eastward up the Porcupine River and northward into the Brooks Range. This chief's life spanned the later years of the Hudson's Bay Company and the early years of the American period. He died near Circle, around the time when prospectors were first coming into the country. One of his descendants, Sophie Paul of Fort Yukon, told about his death. He predicted when he was going to die, and after that a rainbow appeared which some people believe marked the spot where he should be buried. The chief's influence was so strong that after he died people continued to show him respect by firing their rifles whenever they passed his grave on the river. Even the steamboat captains would sound the whistle when they went by that spot to honor the old chief.

The chiefs were men who could attract many followers, lead the band's hunters and provide for themselves as well as others. They are recalled for their ability to take in widows or orphans, and still find enough resources to support several wives plus their children. Many of the stories surrounding these men also tell about their intense personal pride which could even lead to ruthlessness:

> Shahnyaati was packing a caribou and he just threw it off his shoulder like a little rabbit, threw down his gun, walked toward his wife and said, "What are you singing?" (He suspected that she had been with another man.) He grabbed her and killed her with his knife. When the first minister came, he had to tell him. That was the only time that he did wrong. He took care of a lot of people and sometimes when families broke up he took care of them.

The chiefs held great power and were expected to be decisive. They, in turn, required allegiance from others, whether they be wives or warriors.

The traders knew that the chiefs were powerful, but it is questionable whether they realized how their presence influenced the chiefs' actions. Company traders who attempted to take over the traditional native middleman position created conflict for themselves and others because they interrupted the balance of power that existed between groups. This put them in a position where conflict was likely. An event that occurred at Nulato in 1851 graphically illustrates this point.

On this occasion, a Koyukon chief and his followers attacked the Russian post and then went on to an Ingalik Athabaskan camp at Nulato and killed many of the inhabitants. At the Russian post they murdered the company manager, and mortally wounded an Englishman and another company employee. These two suffered on long enough to tell the story before they finally died. There has been considerable historical interest in this event, mostly because the causes of the attack defy simple explanation; even the details differ according to the teller. Lydia Black and Father Louis Renner, S.J., scholars of Alaskan history, studied the event in detail. Black led me to a journal prepared by Edward Adams, an Englishman stationed at St. Michael at the time of the Nulato affair. The journal provides some detail on the events surrounding the attack — from the standpoint of the British. On February 24, 1851, Adams received a note, from Lt. John Barnard, written as the Englishman lay dying from wounds sustained in the attack.

Dear Adams

I am dreadfully wounded in the abdomen. My entrails are hanging out. I don't suppose I shall live long enough to see you. The Koyukuk natives made the attack while we were in our beds. Bosky is badly wounded and Darabin dead. I think my wounds would have been trifling, had I medical advice. I am in great pain. Nearly all the natives of the village are murdered. Set out for here with all haste.

[signed] John Barnard

As quickly as he could, Adams left for Nulato. On the way he met Ingalik Athabaskan Indians who were mourning for their kin who had been slain in the massacre. By the time he reached Nulato, he found Barnard dead and the survivors fearful of yet another attack.

Petr Aleksandrovich Tikhmenev, a historian of the Russian-American Company, says that the attack occurred because the Russians were providing protection for the Nulato Natives (presumably the Ingalik people camped there) with whom the Koyukuk River people were feuding. Unfortunately, he does not discuss the nature of their disputes, although we can surmise that it may have centered on trade. A few years after the incident, William Dall, an American stationed on the Yukon for the Western Union Telegraph, had a chance to talk with a number of local people and his interpretation is quite different. He relates that the Englishman, Barnard, had been too forward in summoning a powerful Koyukuk River chief to the post to speak with him. Dall suggests that when rumor of the request reached the chief, he was angered enough to call a war council and then to mount an attack.

It is hard to know whether the chief was insulted by the brusqueness of the British naval officer or whether the conflict was primarily one of poor relations between the native groups who were vying for a trading edge over each other. Included in the later consideration would be the Eskimos, who were not pleased at all by the Russian post that had interfered with their trading advantage over people from the Interior. And there are probably other factors which will be disclosed after more research. But, whatever the cause or causes, three things are certain: trade competition was keen, the stakes were high up and down the river and foreigners sometimes ended up right in the middle of conflicts.

The business of the trading companies was further complicated by their rivalry with each other. An uneasy peace existed between the Russian-American Company at Nulato and the Hudson's Bay Company at Fort Yukon. They certainly knew about each other and they both knew that Russia had claim to Alaska. But the Russians had not been far enough upriver to reach their boundary or to determine exactly where the British were. On the other hand, Alexander Murray, the Hudson's Bay Company trader, was led to write in his 1847-1848 journal: "We are over the edge, and that by a long chalk, which I call six degrees of longitude across the Russian boundary."

The British therefore had the advantage, but as they became bold and expansive in their trading efforts, the likelihood of inciting Russian interest in their activities increased. The Russians began to suspect British interference in their trade and made plans to find out more about the British activities. So the Company sent a Creole employee named Ivan Semeonovich Lukin upriver to investigate. Lukin was a loyal company man who could be trusted with the assignment. He had served for many years on the Kuskokwim and was then transferred to St. Michael. Lukin's orders, excerpted below, were written in August 1860; but it was 1862 before he finally made the trip.

> Since the manager of Kolmakov Redoubt, Lukin, by my order of May of this year, is attached to the redoubt entrusted to you for reconnaissances, I instruct you to order Lukin to ascend the Kvikhpak [Yukon] River and positively locate the place where a settlement of Englishmen is believed to be located. After finding that redoubt or settlement of Europeans, Lukin should ascertain very accurately their trade relations with the natives, i.e. what exactly they sell, what the prices are on the chief articles of their trade, and what quantity of furs they obtain from the natives. . . .

When Lukin reached Fort Yukon, he presented himself as a deserter from Russian service. The Hudson's Bay Company employees apparently did not question his motives, for he had a chance to observe the fort and company activities. Then, one night, he left the post and paddled downriver to tell what he had learned. Lukin's trip confirmed the presence of a British post, Fort

*Trappers relax at Rampart House, a Hudson's Bay Company post on the Porcupine River, about 1910. Just after the beginning of this century, following the decline of the gold rush, a fully developed trapping economy emerged in Alaska's Interior. Many of today's Athabaskan elders were born at this time and spent their childhood years living in trapline cabins, learning to catch and prepare fur and traveling to trade centers during the summer months. (Fabian Carey Collection, University of Alaska, Fairbanks)*

Yukon, located on the same river as the Russian post of Nulato. His findings also made it fairly certain that the British post was in Russian territory.

Lukin's bold actions rivaled those of the cavalier Hudson's Bay Company employees who took the liberty of proceeding downriver to trade with the Natives in the spring. British traders took advantage of the fact that the ice always went out first upriver, so they could retreat up the Yukon before the Russians could make their way up to trade at the mouth of the Tanana.

Competition was keen, the two companies were stretched to their limits and they both faced similar challenges: inter-ethnic relations, the supply of trade goods and the difficulty of acquiring enough food for their own needs. Despite the similarities, there were many contrasts too. Russian traders since the previous generation had intermarried with local people. Their offspring, the Creoles, grew up in two worlds — the Russian and the native Alaskan. Under Russian law, the Creoles had a special status equal in rank to the townsmen (burghers) of Russia. Creole children like Lukin often received a good education. They were sent to schools at Sitka or back to St. Petersburg. Some of the Creoles had a good command of one or more native languages, they often knew how to survive on the land and they had native relatives they could call on for assistance. Loyal to the company, these people made possible its explorations in unknown lands; they often acted as translators and saw to the day-to-day operation of the posts. But most of all, as James VanStone points out, they were adaptable to the various conditions that exploration and fur trading presented.

In contrast to the Russians, Hudson's Bay Company employees as a rule maintained some distance from the local people. There were few intermarriages and the employees did not make much effort to integrate themselves into the population. The relations between the British and the Athabaskans remained rather formal.

These differences in approach by members of the two companies have left a lasting mark on Alaska's people. Elements of Russian heritage are present in the Russian Orthodox Church and its elaborate ceremonial life. Russian family names still identify the descendants of this period, and local stories about Russian ancestors are a familiar reminder of the era. There are also many Russian place names scattered all over Alaska. On the other hand, regional stories about the Hudson's Bay Company tend to focus on trading practices and employment. They tell about the amount of fur required to get a gun, or about grandfathers and other relatives who worked for the Company. The Anglican priests who followed the company trails are in some ways an exception to this pattern since they left a lasting impression on Athabaskan life. The work of the Anglicans was reinforced by the ecumenically similar Episcopal churchmen who took over their duties in Alaska — but that came later.

This episode of interior history concludes with the transfer of legal authority for Alaska from Russia to the United States. For the Athabaskans, the early movements of westerners into their homeland meant readjustment of traditional trading patterns. Company practices had strengthened the position of traditional chiefs, although this was soon to change under the Americans. And finally, a segment of interior Alaska's population now had mixed heritage, tracing part of their background to native traditions and part to distant lands of Europe.

# Commercial Interests Along the Yukon

The formal transfer of Alaska from Russian to American jurisdiction took place in 1867 at Sitka, which remained the capital for many years afterward. In general, the United States government took little interest in the new territory and the presence of officials was limited, for the most part, to southeastern Alaska and the coast.

However, on one occasion, a group of fur traders managed to entice the government into the Interior. Soon after the Russian-American Company vacated their holdings on the lower Yukon, Americans began moving in to do business. A party of traders went to the old rendezvous spot at the mouth of the Tanana River, and wintered over. Their presence was not known to Hudson's Bay Company employees until the next year, when they came downriver on their customary trading trip and met the Americans face-to-face. Their rights to operate in American territory were fiercely contested. The Americans took their complaint to the government, and in 1869 Captain Charles P. Raymond of the United States Engineer Corps was ordered to accompany a party of traders up the Yukon River to Fort Yukon to determine whether the Hudson's Bay Company was operating on American soil.

The Raymond party had a smooth trip, and they were received cordially by John Wilson, the company factor at Fort Yukon. The confirmation of position was officially made and the Hudson's Bay Company employees agreed to vacate their holdings. The trip is noteworthy not so much for the determination that Fort Yukon was indeed on American soil, but because it was made by steamboat and thereby demonstrated that the Yukon was navigable by such a craft. That fact opened up enormous new possibilities for supplying traders along the river, and it led to new economic opportunities for local people.

In the years to follow, there was a steady increase in steamboat activity on the Yukon, and Alaska Natives played a key role because they knew the river and could safely navigate the large, shallow-draft vessels along the uncharted waterways. Edwin Simon, in his biography, put it this way:

> Well, the last of the sternwheelers we had around here is the *Idler*. George Black. That Black Navigation. He had a sternwheeler. I used to be pilot on that. I started working the boat as deckhand. Then I take the wheel. I read the river pretty good. I was born [on] the river. So I should know. Any Indian. All the pilots is Indian. Because they know what is the river. They know when creek comes out there is few rocks and stuff through the river. You have to keep away from that. And they know when there's two cut bank on both sides of the river, bar is in the middle. All them things pilot have to know.

Other native elders, like Frank Tobuk, speak proudly of their relatives who wore the pilot's uniform and distinguished themselves in the wheelhouse:

> In the summer, I was always on the boats. Make a few dollars. Enough to buy flour and a little sugar. With the little meat we got, that was all right. I never got big money on the boat. I should have got a lot of money when I was all alone running the steamboat, no other pilot. They had to bring my meals up to the pilot house.

Native deckhands hauled and stacked cords of green spruce that fueled the boilers, and they pushed freight up and down the gangplank that led to shore. John Honea remembers the hard work and long hours:

> I just got through working ten hours longshoring and got on the boat. Started downriver. We got down the river about twenty-five miles below here and had to load on some wood. I didn't even have a chance to lay down to have sleep or nothing and have to load on about fifteen cords of wood. Pack it on the boat and put it on the barge. Go on downriver and stop at Koyukuk. Not even rest yet and they want me to work unloading freight there again.

Despite the tough routine, these trips gave native people a chance to see new areas, mix with different groups and experience a type of mobility that was never possible before. Some villagers traveled all the way from St. Michael to Whitehorse. Age-old barriers yielded to the new technology. The boats also created work for people who set up camps along the river and cut the cordwood needed for fuel.

It is unlikely that Raymond and the American traders who made that first trip were thinking about the possibilities of native employment on steamboats. The traders' concerns were getting supplies in, attracting native trappers and transporting furs out. As for the Hudson's Bay Company, after Raymond made his border determination, they left their holdings and retreated a modest distance up the Porcupine River. Reluctant to leave the fur-rich drainages of the Yukon, they clung for many years to the hope of maintaining a hold on what had been their most lucrative trade west of the Rockies.

A recounting of interior history would be incomplete without mention of three enterprising men who gave more than a bit of themselves to the country — Arthur Harper, Alfred Mayo and Leroy "Jack" McQuesten. They came from the Mackenzie side and followed roughly the same well-worn Hudson's Bay Company route. McQuesten reached Fort Yukon in 1873, and there met the trader, Moses Mercier. In his written account, McQuesten tells how Mercier was low on flour but gave him a 50-pound sack to share with his companions. That was to last them a whole year.

These men blended into the country; their first love was prospecting, but they knew how to live off the land and they knew how to trade. They set up posts along the Yukon to supply the growing number of white prospectors who were entering the Yukon Valley, and they served the needs of native trappers and prospectors as well. All three men married native women, and some of their grandchildren and great grandchildren are still here.

While the letters of Harper and McQuesten attracted some attention among prospectors, successive gold strikes in British Columbia and Yukon Territory were gradually enticing prospectors north. Until 1880, the main summer routes to the Interior were the old Hudson's Bay Company portage trails through northern Canada, or by boat up the Yukon. Coastal passes through the Chilkat-Chilkoot region were tightly controlled by the Chilkat Tlingits who zealously guarded their trade monopolies with the Interior. Eventually, through the diplomacy of Commander Beardslee of the United States Navy and the efforts of several native policemen in his employ, an agreement was worked out which

*Men work on the "face" in an interior Alaska placer mine. Thousands of men were attracted to Alaska around the turn of the century, seeking the elusive pay streak. Most left within a few years of coming, but some stayed to form the nucleus of permanent white settlement in the Interior. Only a handful ever struck it rich, but even today prospectors continue to search the hills for gold. (Vide Bartlett Collection, University of Alaska, Fairbanks)*

provided safe passage over the coastal passes for prospectors and other travelers bound for the upper Yukon region.

After this, Dyea and Skagway became the ports of entry for gold seekers, who made their way inland over Chilkat and Chilkoot passes to the headwaters of the Yukon, and thence downstream to the diggings at Dawson, Fortymile, Circle, Rampart and beyond. All had dreams of staking a rich claim; most left disillusioned. A few turned to trapping, trading and cutting wood for steamboats, and a very few found gold and got rich. Many Natives felt that the white men were foolish to spend their time searching for gold. But there were Natives who got gold fever themselves and found ways to get in on the activity.

For most Athabaskans, the chance to stake a claim and strike it rich wasn't even a dream. The general attitude among white prospectors was that Natives were not responsible enough to hold claims. Harold Goodrich, a geologist with the United States Geological Survey, who was reporting on the Yukon Gold District in 1897, put it this way:

> Mynook Creek is the only one in the country upon which Indian labor is employed, for it is the general experience that the Indian is not worth much as a miner or prospector. He lacks the perseverance and steadfastness of purpose which sustain the white man under difficulties and reverses; even when successful he has not

the necessary ambition; and however willing he may be, as soon as he gets a little money he will stop work and spend his entire fortune, with no thought of tomorrow. . . . On Mynook Creek an Indian staked out a claim last spring, but was not allowed to hold it, on the ground that it is illegal for a native to own mining land. As far as we were able to observe, the Indians bore no ill will toward the usurpers, but rather took it as a matter of course that the white man should take possession.

Mynook Creek was named after John Mynook, a Creole of Russian and Eskimo descent, who discovered gold there in 1893. But his rights to hold a claim and enjoy the other benefits of citizenship were questioned, and he found it necessary to bring the issue before the court of law. In what for a layman seems like a lengthy and detailed judgment, Judge Wickersham traced the question of citizenship back to Article III of the Treaty of Cession in which the government of Russia transferred legal jurisdiction for Alaska to the United States government.

Article III of this treaty attempted to provide for the rights of the native population by distinguishing between "inhabitants" and "uncivilized" tribes. The former were to be given the rights of citizenship; the latter were to be subject to the special provisions and laws such as the United States government might develop in their behalf.

In one sense, the treaty was designed to accommodate the Russian Creole trading communities on the coast and the lower reaches of the Kuskokwim and Yukon rivers. These were probably among the "inhabitants" entitled to citizenship; but even that wasn't clear, particularly where valuable land was concerned as in the case of Mynook. Wickersham concluded that Mynook was a citizen on two counts: first, by virtue of his status as an "inhabitant" of the territory, that is, one whom the Russians had recognized as a citizen. Second, Wickersham made special note of the fact that he had " . . . voluntarily taken up his residence separate and apart from any tribe of Indians therein, and has adopted the habits of civilized life."

From Wickersham's brief, it appears that residence apart from the tribes and assuming the habits of civilized life were the significant qualifications for judging citizenship, particularly in those cases where citizenship under the Russians had not been determined. Most of the native population was, therefore, labeled as "uncivilized." At one level, this meant that they were simply not known to the government. At another level, however, the label reflected a judgment that these people's ways were so different from the "inhabitants" that they could not be easily accommodated by the western legal system. Also, as Goodrich reported, there was a widespread attitude that they were not entitled to the rights of citizenship.

In most cases, Alaska Natives were denied the rights of citizenship until Congress passed the Citizenship Act in 1924, 20 years after Wickersham heard Mynook's case. Nevertheless, issues of land rights and the need to find means to protect personal interests came up much earlier. So the role of most Athabaskans in the gold rush was limited to supplying wild game to the camps, freighting goods for the miners and in some cases working for them as laborers.

An exception to this pattern was Old Adam, an Athabaskan Indian from the Yukon who took a liking to a young prospector who stopped at his fish camp. Old Adam took him up the river and showed him gold; then, they entered into a special pact to keep its location a secret forever. Each fall, the young fellow took the steamboat out for the winter, and when he returned the next summer they would go to their special place and mine the gold. Then finally he stopped coming, but according to Moses Cruikshank, until the day he died, Old Adam never disclosed the location of that gold, not even to his children.

Other Natives grew up amid the bright lights of gold rush towns like Rampart, Ruby and Circle. These places provided lots of surprises — coffee shops, new foods, fancy clothing and big horse-drawn freight wagons coming and going from the creeks where the prospectors worked. John Honea, in his biography, describes growing up around Ruby, celebrating special holidays like the 17th of March:

> That was a big holiday here, Irish Day. There was a dog race and boxing and things like that. Lot of people would go to Ruby from all over. All the miners came in, lot of Irishmen and Swedes. All hard workers. All nice people in those days. Native people from Kokrines and about four or five miles upriver would go too.

## The Military Responds

There was another side to the gold rush — the thousands of people who made their way into the Interior with little, if any, thought of how they were going to survive. These were the cheechakos. The responsibility for their well-being fell on the military.

Capt. P.H. Ray of the United States Army, who was stationed on the Yukon, witnessed the problems of supply and placed blame on the transportation companies.

> This failure on the part of the transportation companies to put into the mining districts a sufficient supply of food has not only given a serious check to the mining interest and caused great suffering, but has destroyed all confidence among the people here in their ability to supply the demand by this route. The people here are now afraid that the failure of the river route for travel will cause the construction of a railroad through British North America to the Yukon River above the boundary, and that the mining districts of Alaska will be dependent for supplies on a route through a foreign country with all that means in the way of discrimination in favor of the British merchants.

Ray ended his letter with a call for the government to survey a railroad route from Prince William Sound or Cook Inlet to the mouth of the Tanana River, which would alleviate the problems of supply.

In theory people and supplies came to the Interior along the same three routes: the old Hudson's Bay Company river and portage trail through northern Canada; the newly negotiated Chilkat/Chilkoot trails into the upper Yukon; or the ocean steamer route to St. Michael and then by river steamer up the

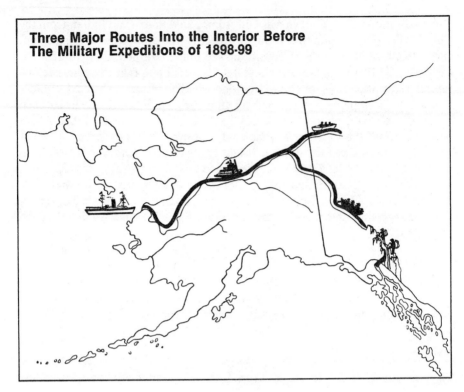

*Before the military expeditions of 1898 and 1899 there were three major routes to interior Alaska. The first, established by the Russians, came by sea to St. Michael and then up the Yukon River. The second, across the Mackenzie River portage to the Porcupine and Yukon rivers, was used by Hudson's Bay Company men from Canada. And the third, the American and Canadian gold rush trail, crossed Chilkoot Pass from Skagway and went downstream from the Yukon River headwaters.*

Yukon. The first two involved entering Canada for at least part of the way and led to concern that the Canadians might set up regulations limiting access. Also, these routes were not practical for transporting the amount of provisions needed to support the increased population. The route upriver was feasible only during the summer when the ocean passage to St. Michael and the Yukon River were free of ice. On the Yukon, there was always the problem of shallow water that could force even the best riverboat captain to offload supplies miles downstream from his destination.

The Army began actively to investigate possible routes from Prince William Sound and Cook Inlet. The goal was to find an all-American route from a northern ice-free port to the Interior and the diggings on the Yukon, a route which would some day support a wagon trail or even a railroad.

Pioneering explorations by W. R. Abercrombie, Henry Allen and Patrick Lowe, lieutenants in the U. S. Army, provided valuable information that eventually led to construction of a wagon road from tidewater at Valdez to Eagle on the Yukon. Later, when gold was found in the Tanana Valley and commercial interests developed there, the road was extended to Fairbanks. From Cook Inlet, Army expeditions also ascended the Susitna and Matanuska valleys, blazing the trails followed in part by today's Alaska Railroad and the George Parks Highway.

Leaders of the Army expeditions hoped to arrange with local Natives for guides and for hunters to supply food as their supplies got low. Although the formal arrangements were not very successful, on several occasions Natives from the remote unexplored regions gave assistance to the soldiers. For example, in 1885, Lt. Henry Allen was hosted by Chief Nikolai on the Copper River and, despite the meager provisions of the season, Chief Nikolai managed to provide for the soldiers in a manner befitting an Ahtna chief.

In 1898, Lt. Joseph C. Castner and his men were destitute near the mouth of the Volkmar River, not far from present day Delta. They were taken in by Upper Tanana Indians and guided down the Tanana River. Castner's report vividly recounts their dire condition and rescue:

> Each morning found us weaker, our clothes more torn and burned, and our sores more painful. We had little to look forward to if nothing was to be found at the deserted Indian cabin at the mouth of the Volkmar. As my men often said, it would be impossible to make others understand what we suffered those days. No tongue or pen could do the case justice. On the 25th of September, when within a half mile of the mouth of the Volkmar, we heard the sound of an ax. . . . The first one to see us was a squaw fixing a birch-bark canoe on the bank of the Volkmar. She aroused the village by her shouts. . . . We were shown to a big house. Bear skins were stretched upon the floor to sit on. . . . They needed no words to make them understand what we needed most. One buck spoke a few words of English, which he had learned at Circle City. We ate caribou, moose, and salmon, and drank plenty of tea. Two hours afterwards we ate again, and ate at intervals of two hours during the night, experiencing no discomfort therefrom. We spent the next day eating, resting, and trying to obtain information from the Indians. I succeeded in engaging three of them to go down the river in birch-bark canoes to the Indian camp 100 miles below.

The remainder of the trip down to Tanana was made without incident.

The most remarkable example of native assistance to a military expedition was the rescue of Lt. Joseph Herron and his men on the upper reaches of the Kuskokwim River. They left from Cook Inlet in late summer 1899, ascended the Susitna River to the Yentna, thence to the Kichatna, across Simpson Pass in the Alaska Range and onto the upper Kuskokwim River. Like Castner, Herron hoped to find a practical all-American route to the Yukon, but the party was terribly overloaded and depended on horses, which were totally inappropriate for the brushy terrain and swift stream crossings. With 15 horses and eight men, they carried 3,300 pounds of gear and supplies, including 600 pounds of bacon and 1,000 pounds of flour. Finally they became bogged down in the upper Kuskokwim lowlands, so they abandoned the horses and cached many of their supplies, including some bacon.

Lost, and with the season rapidly advancing, they were in a desperate situation. Fortunately they hadn't gone far when a bear broke into the cache and ate the bacon. Unbeknown to Herron, Chief Sesui and the other Telida Indians were hunting in the area and happened to kill the same bear that had found the soldiers' bacon. When they butchered the animal, Sesui recognized the white man's food in its stomach and knew there must be strangers nearby. He backtracked the bear's trail to Herron's cache, then followed the distinctive horseshoe and white man's boot tracks until he reached them.

*Carl Sesui, who was widely known as a dog team freight hauler, is shown with his wife in camp near Telida on the upper Kuskokwim drainage in 1919. His father, Chief Sesui, is credited with saving the lives of Lieutenant Herron and his men, who were near starvation in this area during late summer, 1899. (Stephen Foster Collection, University of Alaska, Fairbanks)*

Other versions of the story emphasize horse tracks and horse droppings. One of these was told to Charlene LeFebre by Chief Sesui's son Carl, who was a small boy at the time of the rescue.

> My father went down with a canoe and he took me down below my place. We see on other bank some kind of track there. He says horse. That summer he been to Tanana and he see white man and horse. That what he know. And he talk me that is white man and I don't believe it because I don't see that kind of track . . . nails and funny thing stick out behind . . . heel. . . . Go down 4-5 mile and see horse and my father told me we see horse. Still alive. And few miles farther father find men.

In each version of the story Chief Sesui identified the signs with white men, searched them out, took them to Telida and equipped them with mitts, caps, moccasins and snowshoes for a trip to the Yukon. After a couple of months, when there was enough snow for traveling, the Indians guided the soldiers via the Cosna River trail to Tanana Village on the Yukon.

The Army expeditions are particularly significant because they entered remote areas which had not been previously described. Often their descriptions are remarkable because they indicate that, even in the most remote places, western goods were to be found and the Natives demonstrated an astonishing familiarity with the white man's ways. The goods and knowledge were gained either through experiences at trading posts or through trade with other Natives who had direct contact with the posts.

Athabaskans living in remote areas, such as the upper Copper, Tanana and Kuskokwim rivers, had fairly easy access to western goods while their remote locations gave them a high level of control over their own way of life. That's the picture which emerges from the military expeditions. But in the years to come the picture would quickly change.

## Gold Discoveries on the Tributaries

Finally, like water from a full rain barrel, prospectors began to spill over into the Koyukuk drainage, up the Tanana, the Kantishna and into the upper Kuskokwim. There no longer were remote areas.

Wiseman, on the upper Koyukuk, was a multi-ethnic community where Kobuk Eskimos and Athabaskan Indians worked alongside a variety of nationalities. Telling of early days on the Koyukuk, Tishu Ulen, an Eskimo woman, recounts:

> I grew up hearing languages and accents of people from all over the world. We had a sampling of Yugoslavians, Germans, Irish, French-Canadians, Poles, Greeks, Swedes, Japanese, and Welsh. There was also a mixture of Eskimos from the Arctic Coast and Kobuk country and a very few Indians. A few of the miners had families waiting for them at home, but most were bachelors. Only a few hardy white women followed their men out to the creeks. Some of the miners took Eskimo wives, so the children in the area were full or part Eskimo. The miners really enjoyed the children.

Where the gold rush extended back off the major rivers and supply problems increased, the Natives came to play a larger role as operators of river scows, dog team mail drivers and suppliers of fresh game to the miners and roadhouses. In certain places, such as on the Nenana-to-McGrath trail, Natives owned some of the roadhouses.

Paying quantities of gold were found in the Fairbanks area in 1902 by the legendary Felix Pedro. In almost no time the town founder, E. T. Barnette, abandoned his plans for a trading post at Tanana Crossing and settled in to make a bundle of money off the prospectors. For once, the shallow water which plagued river transport on the Tanana above Fairbanks turned out to be a blessing . . . at least for Barnette.

Commercial river transportation included steamboats on the major rivers and horse-drawn river scows on smaller and shallower streams. To service the new mining areas, the Alaska Road Commission built roads and trails. Margaret Murie, who first came to Fairbanks as a young girl in 1911, describes her experiences growing up in the town. Each spring she waited eagerly to see the little white plume of smoke that meant the first steamboat of the season was coming up the river. That first boat brought supplies, old and new faces and helped to break the isolation of the long winter for those who came North to make their homes.

For Athabaskans of the Tanana Valley, the early years of this century brought massive changes into their lives and new pressures on the land that must have made them wish for a bit more isolation. In a few years, they saw many of their trails traveled by hundreds of others. The long period of indirect contact — when they had some white man's goods but still controlled their own homeland — was over. Now they had to find means to protect their land and lifeway while also benefiting from the new developments.

By 1915, the Tanana Valley was being scoured by prospectors and the native way of life was seriously threatened. In this year, a meeting of the Tanana Chiefs was held to talk about ways to protect native interests. The conference was initiated by Judge James Wickersham and the Reverend Guy Madara of the Episcopal Church, but it was called because of concerns being expressed by the chiefs in the Tanana Valley.

Practical, reasoned and experienced in the ways of the law, Judge Wickersham and Thomas Riggs, a member of the Alaska Engineering Commission, told the chiefs that more people would come and stressed that the Natives must find a legal way to protect their land. Wickersham suggested that they file for homesteads or ask that a reservation be established. In reply to this, Chief Ivan of Crossjacket [Cos Jacket, on the Tanana River southwest of Manley Hot Springs] eloquently presented the native position:

> We don't want to go on a reservation, but wish to stay perfectly free just as we are now, and go about just the same as now, and believe that a reservation will not be a benefit to us. We feel as if we had always gone as we pleased and the way they all feel is the same. We don't want to be put on a reservation. Now what we wish you to do is — as you are here as government officials and we know that you are the government's representatives — now, we wish you to give your word. You tell us that you will be our friends, and it

*Athabaskan leaders,* assembled for the Tanana Chiefs Conference in 1917, pose for a portrait. This was the first gathering of Interior Alaska native leaders intended to discuss protection of the Athabaskan homeland from whites, who were entering the country in large enough numbers to jeopardize the traditional way of life. Pictured (left to right) are Chief Alexander of Tolovana, Chief William of Tanana, Chief Thomas of Nenana, Paul Williams of Tanana, Chief Ivan of Coskaket, Chief Charlie of Minto and Chief Alexander William of Tanana. (Ben Mozee Collection, University of Alaska, Fairbanks)

*Chief Deaphon (fourth from the left)* poses with his band near Telida in March 1919. Whites did not enter the upper Kuskokwim country in numbers until the turn of the century, so these were among the last Athabaskan groups of interior Alaska to have prolonged direct contact with the outside world. (Stephen Foster Collection, University of Alaska, Fairbanks)

is for your people to promise us so that we will have your words in mind when we leave Fairbanks. The only news we hear are generally some rumors, which we hear from some young ones, not from the old middle-aged people, because they can not speak the English language, but these rumors we wish you to give us in writing so that we will know ourselves what you people are going to do for us.

The government's message was to settle down and show occupation of the land in a recognized western fashion. The native response was straightforward — to settle down would mean extinguishing their way of life, and that was unacceptable.

The problem of native land use was not decided at that Tanana Chiefs Conference, nor would it be resolved in later years. The issue re-emerges each time there are competing claims to the land and it strikes at basic cultural differences between Athabaskan and Euro-American concepts of land use and ownership. The Tanana Valley was the focal point of competing claims at this time, but such claims would resurface often around the Interior in later years. How ironic it must have seemed to the chiefs who in their youth had traveled many miles to get the foreigners' goods. Now, they were surrounded by strangers and they had to find ways to protect their way of life.

Family-based traplines became a feature of life in the Interior at this time. They developed as a response to new opportunities created by the traders but, in time, became a reflection of the Athabaskan people's growing concern over new pressures on the land. The powerful chiefs had depended on their ability to maintain special trading positions with the Hudson's Bay Company, and the Russian American Company. But after they left Alaska, there were many independent American traders eager to deal with anyone who had fur. So the chiefs lost influence and families began to identify with their own particular trapping areas. With the influx of prospectors there was a need to clarify who had rights to use certain areas and how those rights were transmitted to others. It became important to find new ways to maintain local control and the family-based traplines were a reflection of this need.

The large extended family group became the basic economic unit for trapping; each trapping area was recognized and identified with a family, and traplines were passed from generation to generation through that family. The picture that emerged toward the turn of the century was one of native families dispersed throughout the country trapping during the winter and fishing along the major rivers during summer. White trappers who married native women sometimes followed suit. In other cases they simply abandoned their lines when they left the country; and during later years they began selling them. This practice must have seemed foreign to the Athabaskans, who had never thought of land as having a financial value. But then, the elders had not expected to see such a large number of foreigners throughout their homeland — even up the remote tributaries. The gold rush had opened up their country.

## Missionaries and Social Service

In the trail of the traders came missionaries. Church of England or Anglican churchmen followed the Hudson's Bay Company and Russian Orthodox priests traveled in the footsteps of the Russian-American Company.

In contrast to the traders, who were looking for commercial control, the missionaries wanted to save souls, and they went to great extents to do so — traveling hundreds of miles, often alone, to visit with the people, make services and administer the sacraments. They are still remembered for their perseverance and dedication. The Upper Kuskokwim Athabaskans tell about the first priest who came upriver after the ice went out in spring, to visit with people gathered at the old Russian-American Company trading station at Vinasale, on the left bank of the Kuskokwim about 20 miles south of McGrath. The Natives would leave their camps and travel down the swift rivers to Vinasale to meet the priests, attend services and have their children baptized. As in the era before contact, people who joined these spring gatherings also spent time fishing and visiting one another.

Robert McDonald was one of the first Church of England priests to visit Alaska. He is sometimes credited with discovering gold on Preacher Creek but he distinguished himself for turning his back on the rich find in deference to his missionary responsibilities. McDonald was a fluent speaker of Kutchin Athabaskan and is credited with developing a written form of the language, and then translating the Bible, the Book of Common Prayer and a hymnal. His years of service to the people are not forgotten; a simple picture of McDonald hangs in the Fort Yukon museum and elders still remember his ministry among them.

Missionary efforts of the Russian Orthodox and Anglican churches continued after the United States purchased Alaska. V.C. Sims, an Anglican priest, worked with people of the upper Yukon and traveled extensively in Alaska. Finally, suffering from total exhaustion, he died in 1885 at Old Rampart House on the Porcupine River. When the Episcopal churchman Hudson Stuck visited the grave years later, he was touched to record:

> Let it be remembered to the honor of the Church of England that she had such sons and sent them into the wilderness long ago; upon whose labors we of the American church have tardily entered, in these more comfortable times, to reap, in some measure, the fruit.

In the latter years of the 19th century the Episcopal Church took over from the ecumenically similar Anglicans. On the lower Yukon River and the Kuskokwim, the Russian-Orthodox Church continued to serve. They were joined by the Roman Catholic Church, which established missions at Holy Cross and Nulato. As the gold rush gained momentum, churches expanded their activities to meet the needs of prospectors and Natives alike. Interior Alaska's hospitals and schools were mainly built and staffed by church people.

Following the activities as they shifted from the main rivers to the tributaries and overland trails, mission stations soon dotted the Interior. Archdeacon Hudson Stuck, perhaps the best known and most widely traveled of the Alaskan clergy, mushed the trails in winter and plied the rivers in summer, baptizing, marrying and preaching to a far-flung flock. The Rev. Sydney Chapman carefully recorded native stories and customs during a 44-year period beginning with his establishment of the mission at Anvik in 1887. Father Julius Jetté of the Catholic mission at Nulato meticulously documented Athabaskan languages and place names and distinguished himself among the native people for his ability and willingness to preach in Koyukon. Each of these churchmen, besides ministering to spiritual needs, also found time to publish descriptions of the people they served.

Their writings are not limited to the Natives. For instance, Stuck describes the Yanert brothers and their camp at Purgatory on the Yukon. William Yanert was a military man who came to Alaska during the search for an all-American route to the Yukon and did some of the pioneering exploration work in the Susitna drainage-Broad Pass region of the Interior. William retired with his brother Herman to live a quiet life on the Yukon.

Hudson Stuck used to stop at their camp and was fond of talking with the Yanerts. He writes that William and Herman devised a simple plan to protect themselves from the many undesirable characters who floated down the Yukon at the height of the gold rush. They killed a small Canada jay, commonly called camp robber, and buried the bird in a human-sized grave. The bird had been eating some of their bacon so they felt justified in placing on the headstone an inscription clear for all to see, "He Robbed my Camp and I Shot Him." There are many variations of this story, including one printed by a tourist company in their brochure designed to point out places of interest for passengers on the steamboat trip downriver. That version of the story states that a tourist, shocked by the grave, reported it to the U.S. Marshal of Tanana, who was then forced to investigate the case. The Yanerts got the last laugh while they watched the Marshal dig up the bird. Suffice it to say that the scholarly churchmen were careful observers and good recorders.

The Anglican Church, and the Episcopal Church that followed it, have always had a strong commitment to developing native clergy. Stuck put it well:

> The White men come and go, but the Natives remain. So far as
> the Interior is concerned, our permanent work, though not
> necessarily our most important work, is amongst the Natives.

In keeping with this philosophy, Bishop Peter Trimble Rowe appointed William Loola, a native student of McDonald's, to hold services at Fort Yukon. Loola served faithfully, ministering to congregations on the Yukon Flats and in the Chandalar country, and is often remembered as the first native preacher to serve his own people. His example was soon followed by others, including Albert Tritt, from the Arctic Village area. Tritt is credited with building a church and actively ministering to the Kutchin people along the Chandalar. Clara MacKenzie describes how Dr. Burke, a medical missionary, recalled the new Church at Arctic Village:

> Throughout the five-day visit, Albert Tritt, Chief Esaias, and the
> village elders took great pride in telling how they had built and
> furnished their church. Even the women and children had pitched
> in. The new chapel was carefully and solidly built, and furnished
> with benches, railing, altar, candle racks, glass for the windows, and
> a sturdy little wood stove. Everything had been hauled across the
> Flats and up the mountains by dog sled from Fort Yukon or made
> by hand on the spot.

Today, the legacies of William Loola and Albert Tritt are carried on by several native priests and lay leaders from Arctic Village and Venetie, as well as elsewhere in Alaska.

This was an era of public service, and the missions attended to people's health and education as well as their spiritual needs. The Catholic and Episcopal churches came to play a dominant role in shaping the lives of Athabaskans, particularly children. Many children were reared at the missions; orphans and those in need of medical assistance were brought up as part of the church family. If a mother or father died, the children might be taken to the mission; the family would make payments in cash or wild game foods such as they could provide.

Mission kids worked hard packing wood and water, tending the gardens and hauling in game from outlying camps. Moses Cruikshank, who grew up at the Nenana mission, recalls going out in spring on the old Kantishna trail, into the foothills of the Alaska Range. There he and the other mission boys would pick up fresh meat from native hunters who had gathered for spring hunting. Knight's Roadhouse was a familiar and welcome stop along the way, and there was usually a nice piece of fresh pie waiting for the boys when they stopped.

At the Catholic mission of Holy Cross on the lower Yukon, the sisters literally made their gardens by hand. Father Renner quoted from Sister Mary Joseph:

> . . . On our knees we tore up the sods with our hands, shook
> out the soil from the roots, and burrowed as deeply as we could until,
> little by little, slowly, very slowly, the garden patch grew to be twenty-
> two feet square. To the tender heart of Mother earth we confided
> the seeds. . . .

The children also helped in the gardens and, in time, the Holy Cross mission was able to meet its own fresh produce needs and even send some produce to other missions. Later on, during the war years, Renner reported that the mission also made sales to the U. S. Army at Galena.

At the Episcopal missions, children were given specific tasks that would prepare them for living in the country while also serving the needs of the mission. Moses Cruikshank was chosen to work with the dog teams, which meant that he was responsible for feeding them year-round and handling them out on the trail. He learned how to care for dogs from an old white prospector named Kobuk Dick who spent his summers in Nenana picking up a little wage work to support his prospecting.

In summer, Moses also worked on the *Pelican,* a church boat that plied up and down the rivers visiting mission stations, wood yards, mining camps and fish camps along the way. On one summer trip to Fairbanks he was in for a surprise. The *Pelican* had tied up along the banks of the Chena on Sunday morning and the churchmen had left for the service, leaving Moses to tidy the boat before he was to follow them. As he left the boat and started walking along the roadway, he came upon a strange bird in someone's yard. It was unlike any that he had seen before — this bird talked. The extraordinary animal captured his attention for so long that he forgot all about going to church.

The churchmen knew that mission children had to be able to live off the land, as well as learn skills of the white man's world. Hudson Stuck described the challenge:

Moreover, it is folly to fail to recognize that the apprenticeship of an Indian boy to the arts by which he must make a living, the arts of hunting and trapping, is more important than schooling, however important the latter may be, and that any talk — and there has been loud talk — of a compulsory education law which shall compel such boys to be in school at times when they should be off in the wilds with their parents, is worse than folly, and would, if carried out, be a fatal blunder. If such boys grow up incompetent to make a living out of the surrounding wilderness, whence shall their living come?

The church workers struggled to establish a balance between native and white survival skills, but in the area of cultural values and cross-cultural communication, they were less sensitive and more quick to judge based on their own standards. Most of the missionaries saw little of value in the Native's traditional religious beliefs, and whenever they could they discouraged practices like potlatching for the dead which they dismissed as wasteful. They also refused to accept practices of the medicine men. Even though they could do good or evil, the missionaries challenged their practices and spoke out against them whenever opportunities arose.

The missionaries' attitudes about these matters help to explain why they put such effort into developing native clergy and, in part, the emphasis they placed on native education. For native children, the church-run boarding schools meant years of separation from families and community members. In his biography, Roger Dayton of Koyukuk village talks about his own problems of readjusting to village life after being away at the Holy Cross mission school:

And people were so different. They were not religious. And we used to have a lot of fun down there at Holy Cross, laugh at every little thing. People weren't like that around here. Of course I didn't know any better so sometimes I'd laugh at somebody. I couldn't help it because I was down there for five years. I learned that from down there and when I came back up here, I started to behave the same way as when I was at Holy Cross. I was criticized for that.

Children from the Episcopal missions who showed outstanding academic promise were sent to the states for further schooling. The hope was that they would return to serve their people as doctors, teachers and ministers.

John Fredson was an example of the Episcopal Church's efforts. He joined the mission as a young boy after his mother died and his father, Old Fred, could not take care of all his children and still live out in the country. Of course, there was no steady wage work in those days so John was raised at the Fort Yukon and Nenana missions. When he could, Old Fred would come to the mission and take John out hunting or on trips back to the Chandalar country, where he and his relatives lived. Years later, John would write about these special times with his father and what they meant to him. Once after a long day's travel, he conjured up an excuse to get his father to stop, telling him that he smelled a wolf. Realizing the bluff, Old Fred named his son *Zhoh Gwatsan,* which means "wolf smeller," the native name which he bore the rest of his life.

John Fredson received his first formal education at the Fort Yukon and

Nenana missions. When the time came for high school he was sent to Mt. Hermon, a preparatory school in Massachusetts; then he went on to college at the University of the South at Sewanee, the same school from which his mentor, Hudson Stuck, had been graduated years before.

John Fredson finally finished college in 1930 and returned to Alaska. He served as the first school teacher at Venetie, a position which involved bridging the worlds of subsistence hunting and the ABC's. Sara Frank, who was rearing her own children then, recalls the struggle that she and the other parents faced to keep their children in school while still bringing in enough food for everyone. The village had seldom been occupied for long periods and people were used to traveling all the time, hunting from their traplines and fish camps. When the school started up they found it was hard to live in one place when they really needed to be out hunting.

As Sara tells the story, John Fredson knew both worlds, and he worked to keep the school open while he also struggled with the villagers to get enough food. He understood how difficult it was for people to live in one place, but he also knew the value of a formal education. The struggle was not unique to Venetie; in every part of rural Alaska parents were trying to decide how best to prepare their children for the future.

Schooling was a major problem. Children who went to the mission boarding schools suffered the strain of separation from their families. But village schools created a fixed population that could only be supported by increased supplements to the subsistence economy, and that took money, which few people had in those days.

The times were changing. Gradually the responsibility for many educational and health functions, first provided by the churches, were assumed by the territorial and federal governments. The transition to village-based schools was a reflection of this trend. In many areas there was a growing governmental presence, supported by new forms of transportation which helped link people together.

## The Growing Connection

In 1923, the Alaska Railroad was completed. Its route followed in large measure the course of William Yanert's exploration, up the Susitna and through Broad Pass to Cantwell. From there it went on to the bustling town of Fairbanks. But, at the time it was built, the railroad probably had its greatest impact on Nenana, 60 miles to the south. This is where the tracks crossed the Tanana River, and from here steamboats departed for the Yukon and Koyukuk rivers.

Nenana quickly became a hub of activity. The trains brought supplies up from Seward, to be loaded onto steamboats bound for villages which stood along the banks of the rivers, all the way up to the Canadian border and down to the lower Yukon. Nenana attracted men who wanted to make a little money working on the railroad or on the docks. Some were prospectors like Kobuk Dick, trying to get a grubstake so they could return to the creeks; others were Natives who supplemented their winter trapping with seasonal wage work.

Visitors could make a marvelous excursion through Alaska, beginning with

*The summer catch of salmon dries on racks along the Yukon River near Beaver. Dried fish were the staple food for dog teams, the major means of transportation for trappers, mail carriers and other Interior travelers throughout the early 1900s. (Fabian Carey Collection, University of Alaska, Fairbanks)*

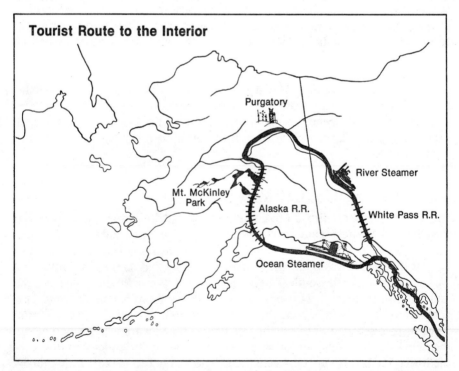

**Tourist Route to the Interior**

*During the early decades of this century tourists could visit Alaska in style during the summer months. After traveling north by steamer through the Inside Passage, they took the White Pass Railroad from Skagway to Whitehorse, then rode steamboats down the Yukon to the Tanana River. Disembarking at the town of Nenana, they boarded the Alaska Railroad for Fairbanks, Anchorage and finally Seward, where they caught another steamer for their return to Seattle.*

*Yukon River steamboats dock at Eagle around 1905. Stores along the major interior rivers depended on the steamboats for virtually all of their supplies. This made the shallow, treacherous rivers an essential lifeline for prospectors, trappers and Natives who were increasingly dependent on goods from the outside. Athabaskans also found work as pilots, deckhands and wood cutters during the steamboat era. (Bunnell Collection, University of Alaska, Fairbanks)*

the trip from Skagway to Whitehorse via the White Pass and Yukon Railroad, then a leisurely steamboat ride down the Yukon to Tanana, up the Tanana River to Nenana, and from there by rail to Seward. At Seward passengers boarded ocean steamers to cross the Gulf of Alaska and make the run south through the breathtaking Inside Passage.

Along the way there were unlimited scenic delights, not the least of which was Purgatory, the Yanerts' place on the bank of the Yukon, about halfway between Beaver and Stevens Village. At Purgatory, tourists were greeted by a life-sized devil with a pitchfork that popped up as the boat was tied alongside the bank.

> The devil on the bank is for tourists, who come by and stop a little once every two weeks on the boat from Dawson. The arms and lower jaw of the effigy are movable and attached to wires leading to the house. When the boat arrives one of the brothers from the house pulls the wires, the "devil" opens and closes its jaws and works up and down the hand with the pitchfork. All of which, with the real gruesomeness of the figure, must produce quite an impression.

Once ashore the visitors could peruse and perhaps buy some of the wood carvings made by William and his brother, Herman.

Another tourist attraction was Mount McKinley National Park, established in 1917 largely through the efforts of Charles Sheldon, a game hunter. Sheldon wintered over in a cabin on the Toklat River where he had a good chance to observe wildlife. As a sport hunter, he became concerned about the number of animals being taken to supply mining camps. He took his concerns all the way to Washington, D.C., and used his influence with Congress to have the park set aside.

Looking back at this episode, it is quite understandable that Charles Sheldon, himself a hunter, would take up the cause against hunting of game animals that were being depleted by commercial use. Years later hunting would again become an issue, when new additions were made to the park. Legislation in the 1970s would allow hunting in these additions, but would give preference in times of shortage to subsistence hunters over sport hunters.

In 1919, Indians living near the McKinley Park boundary on the lower Toklat River were stricken with a flu epidemic, perhaps the famous worldwide flu of 1918. Many died and were buried near Toklat Village; others made their way to Rex, a railroad camp, where they boarded a train bound for Nenana. Some of the survivors made their home in Nenana and found work on the boats and railroad. Years later, they still speak of their strong ties to the Toklat and the Indian heritage of McKinley Park. Some still hunt and trap in their traditional areas near the park boundaries.

For villagers located along the Tanana and the Yukon, the growth of the railroad and steamboat transportation meant that traders were well-provided with supplies. One old-timer remarked that the stores were better stocked back in those days than they are today, and there were a lot more settlements scattered along the riverbanks then. That was before airplanes took over carrying the mail. Airplanes really changed things.

Miska Deaphon, from the upper Kuskokwim, used to tell the story how in 1924, when he was hunting up by Telida he heard this "rumbling up in the sky by Fairbanks." Well, that turned out to be Ben Eielson and Ed Young on one of the first experimental mail delivery flights from Fairbanks to McGrath. Belle Herbert from the Kutchin village of Chalkyitsik described the first airplane this way:

> A lot of people who were sick went out with their blankets around them. I was among them, too.
>
> It was flying right around here, right back of the school. The plane looked like a big dragonfly.

At first, people didn't have much faith in airplanes and the early aviators had a tough time getting them to think of flying machines as capable of more than entertainment. That's not to say that there weren't some funny moments. According to research by James Greiner, one of Ben Eielson's first flights out of Fairbanks went to Nenana, but he got a little disoriented and almost missed the town. When he finally got there he put on a little air show and charged admission. In fact, he earned almost half the price of his new plane.

In time, it became clear that the age of aviation would revolutionize travel in the Interior. But the airplane's arrival wasn't celebrated by everyone; roadhouse keepers and dog-team mail carriers saw their livelihood being replaced by modern technology. Sam White told about the roadhouse keeper along the Nenana-McGrath trail who reflected his sentiments in a prominent sign which read: "Aviators trade not solicited here."

After the planes started getting mail contracts, the extensive trail systems that linked villages and other population centers gradually disappeared, and trappers could no longer depend on mail carriers to keep the main trails open. Percy Duyck, a trapper from the Kantishna area, describes going out to his trapline by boat in fall and returning to Nenana for Christmas, breaking trail ahead of the dogs in snow up to his waist.

But as Edwin Simon recalls, in times of medical emergencies, the airplane sure came in handy:

> One time in the spring around April, Richard Derendoff got sick. Young man not married yet. He got real sick and couldn't walk. . . . I talk to people. Sidney Huntington and lot of people. I said, "We can collect rats [muskrats] and send Richard to Tanana to the hospital." "Okay," they said. So I wrote to Dominic, send up plane. This spring when we come out we're going to collect rats and pay you up. . . . Three days later airplane come. Pick up Richard. Took him to hospital. They saved him.

Trapping and trading, that was the backbone of the rural economy and if a man worked hard at it he could make a decent living. Fur prices were good during the 1920s and there were many white trappers, men who settled in to the trapping way of life and made a good living at it. Some were legendary, men like Slim Carlson out at Lake Minchumina, Jimmy Carrol up on the Porcupine and the Swede brothers on the Beaver River. Fifteen or twenty years earlier these men might have been prospecting, but with fur prices high and a love for the country, they settled in to make a living on the trapline.

Advances in transportation also brought agencies and institutions of the

*Olaf Solvik stands beside his cache on the Yukon Flats in 1930, baling muskrats for shipment. In the early 1900s the trapping lifestyle was shared by whites and Natives throughout much of the Interior. Although many white trappers lived alone, some married Athabaskan women and became integrated into villages. The closeness of Natives and outsiders during this era promoted cultural exchange that went both ways and helped to create a lasting way of life in Alaska's Interior. (Fabian Carey Collection, University of Alaska, Fairbanks)*

outside world to remote villages and camps throughout the Interior. Provision of schools and health care, which had been provided by the missionaries, was gradually supplemented or replaced by the federal and territorial governments. There was even talk about a university so high school graduates wouldn't have to leave Alaska for advanced education.

Through the efforts of Judge Wickersham back in Washington, D.C., and territorial legislators Dan Sutherland and Andrew Nerland in Juneau, the university became a reality. Judge Charles E. Bunnell was appointed first president of the Alaska Agricultural College and School of Mines in 1921. Under Judge Bunnell's guidance, the university grew and attracted students from throughout the Territory. Bunnell always seemed to find time to meet and talk with people who stopped in from the rural areas. Turak Newman, an Eskimo from Beaver, and Frank Yasuda, the Japanese trader there, used to visit with him when they came to town. One of the students entering in 1934 was Frank Yasuda's daughter, Hana Kangas. When Hana made the trip to college that year, she traveled from Beaver to Circle City, and from there she rode Johnny's stagecoach overland to Fairbanks. That was before World War II, and it seemed that everybody knew one another. New forms of transportation and communication were linking people together.

## Defense of the Nation

The year was 1942 and in off the trapline for Christmas holiday, Moses Cruikshank learned he had been called to serve in the military. That meant abandoning his summer plans of prospecting and, instead, he began to count on four years of service with Uncle Sam. Like many other able bodied Alaskans, he proudly served, lending his native knowledge of hunting and cold weather survival to the job at hand. He demonstrated to the officers his Athabaskan canvas boots, which are ideally adapted to severe cold, and he showed how the canvas gun cases that his sister and the other women made were excellent for the northern conditions because they never froze stiff.

Meanwhile, at the Kutchin village of Old Crow in Canada, when they heard about war victims in London, they made a special contribution. They collected $393 to aid families who suffered in the London air strikes.

There were other victims too — the Japanese-Americans. Even in the remote Interior, the few Japanese people were forced to leave their homes and go to internment camps where they lived like prisoners until the end of the war. The extremes of this ruling are reflected in the following letter written by Alice Stuart, a concerned citizen, to the Governor of Alaska, Ernest H. Gruening.

> Sir:
>
> I am writing to you about one of the boys who lives in the "Arctic Village" which you visited with his former employer, the late Robert Marshall in the summer of 1938.
>
> Henry Hope is a half-breed Eskimo boy who was adopted as a small baby by Lutie and Sammy Hope. Lutie is Indian and Sammy Hope is an Eskimo. Henry has never seen his father, who was Japanese. His mother was Eskimo.

Henry has never been below the Arctic Circle until the other day when he was sent in to Fairbanks to register because he is of Japanese descent. He has never even seen a Jap, nor does he wish to.

He has spent all his life in the hills, or around Wiseman where he went to school and completed the seventh grade. He is a fine healthy seventeen year old boy who respects and helps his native parents. He accepts responsibility nicely and had enough get up and go to him to obtain a job freighting with the Schwaedsdall and Repo outfit who are mining at Myrtle Creek below Wiseman. He freighted in the winter of 1940-41, and during the summer of 1941, he operated a caterpillar tractor for the same mining company.

He loves the rivers and mountains of his native home and has no desire to leave it. He is the main support of his family and if he should have to stay away it will work an undue hardship on them as well as upon himself. His job at Myrtle Creek with the Schwaedsdall and Repo outfit is awaiting him. If you wish to get in touch with John Repo, his mail and telegraph address is Wiseman, Alaska.

Would it not perhaps be possible to find some way that he might return to the Arctic instead of being shipped out to California as I understand they plan to do with him next Monday?

The letter failed to do much good and Henry was shipped out as planned.

Frank Yasuda, the Japanese trader in Beaver, was separated from his Eskimo wife and children, who stayed behind and had to take care of themselves. There was, however, a small bit of humor in Frank's experience. His daughter Hana tells the story:

Before he left, he said to me, "You save this *shoyu,* Kikkoman syrup [soy sauce], these big cans." He said, "Save them for me. When I come back, I'll want them." And I was so happy to bring them out. We didn't use any of them you know. We brought them out for him; I think there were four big cans and he was so happy to get them. And when he tried them, he didn't like them.

In the camps they used Chun King brand (Chinese style soy sauce), and eventually Frank had gotten used to that kind.

For many Alaskans the war meant jobs, particularly at Fairbanks, Anchorage and the new military bases that were springing up. Construction jobs were filled not only by Alaskans but also by people who came from other parts of the United States to join in the boom. Many of these newcomers stayed to become permanent residents after the war ended in 1945.

During the war years, as Alaska became strategically important, the need for new supply lines became obvious. A great construction project was undertaken to meet this need, the Alaska Highway. It was 1,420 miles of rough going, but the end result was an overland supply link with the continental United States. The road brought in many workers and went right through the heart of the Tanana Valley, an area that had been fairly remote and inaccessible until that time. Before the road, this country was inhabited mainly by Athabaskan Indians who lived in widely scattered bands, made up of related kin. A picture of their life before the road is provided by Robert McKennan, a young anthropologist who visited the Upper Tanana Indians in 1929 and spent nine months traveling to their camps.

> ...[I traveled] first on foot accompanied by pack horse, later by dog team, and finally by small boat. In the course of this journey I visited all the Indian camps in the Upper Tanana territory except those of the small Scottie Creek band. . . . My usual procedure was to camp with a band of Indians for a month or two, living their life as far as possible. . . . When my observations and inquiries appeared to be approaching a point of diminishing returns from the standpoint of ethnology, I would employ one of my Upper Tanana friends to move me with his dog team to the next camp.

During the next 10 or so years things didn't change much but when the highway was built, life in the valley changed a great deal. Athabaskans found opportunities for wage work on the highway, and the road gave them nearly unlimited access to urban centers and other communities. Knut Peterson, an old-timer from Tok, has seen a lot of change with the road:

> Men came up here by the thousands, and no one thought they could build the road that fast. Then they came through later and put the blacktops through here. That's quite an improvement. One thing about it, you can really get around this country now.

There were also drawbacks to the road. In time, people noticed that their communities attracted outsiders who competed for the game they depended on. One native elder from Tanacross put it this way:

> They spoiled all the good hunting places, the hunting and trapping ground and blueberry ground. White men want to take everything away from Indian people. I can't see why.

Nevertheless, for many people in this area, the focus of settlement gravitated toward new communities along the highway and connecting roads. The village of Tanacross had little choice, since the highway went right by their community and the Air Force wanted access to their airstrip. Northway and Tok sprang up during the construction phase and attracted many Athabaskans from nearby areas and Dot Lake soon had a permanent population. The settlement of Tetlin remained a modest distance from the highway, people there choosing insulation from the highway traffic and sport hunters over the conveniences of road access.

The military buildup of World War II also involved amassing air support. Under a joint agreement, the United States provided military planes to Russia, and these planes were flown along the route of the new highway from the Canadian border to Fairbanks. The Tanacross airstrip became a strategic stop along the way. Robert McKennan, on a break from his academic duties back East, served as Commanding Officer of the Tanacross Air Force detachment — a position that provided him some time to add to his store of knowledge about the land and people.

To really take hold, aviation in Alaska had to have appropriate ground support. The federal government played a key role by establishing the Civil Aeronautics Authority, which eventually became the Federal Aviation Administration. Air-to-ground navigation aids were developed and navigation

The "Swede Boys," legendary trappers of the Yukon Flats, pose on the trail with their pack dogs around 1930. Before airplanes and roads came to the Interior, summer travel was done in boats along the rivers or on foot across the country. This kept much of the land inaccessible during the months when there was too little snow for travel by dog team. (Fabian Carey Collection, University of Alaska, Fairbanks)

Before World War II, trapping was the center of rural Alaska's cash economy. These furs, displayed at Tanana in 1915, were worth about $40,000 at the time. Fur prices dropped after the war and people turned to other sources of income as Alaska's population grew, the military presence continued and government became increasingly important even in remote communities. (Ben Mozee Collection, University of Alaska, Fairbanks)

stations were established throughout the Interior. Kenny Granroth, an old-timer from Lake Minchumina, came to the lake during the construction period and, like several other FAA employees, he liked the area well enough to stay. Maybe it was the spectacular views of Mount McKinley and the rural lifestyle that attracted them, but the other FAA stations at McGrath, Bettles and Galena were also attractive to federal employees who wanted to be assigned to rural sites.

In postwar years, the strategic military position of Alaska and declining relations with the Soviet Union prompted the federal government to develop better security against air attack from the north. They built Distant Early Warning (DEW Line) sites along Alaska's northern coast and the Aircraft Control and Warning (AC&W) System on the coast and in the Interior. Military bases in Anchorage, Fairbanks and Galena were upgraded. These measures were designed to give the necessary detection and interception capabilities to ward off attack. Satellites eventually made many of these systems obsolete, but from the mid-1950s through the 1970s, the AC&W's "golf ball" domes and the White Alice "billboard" antennas were a clear sign of Alaska's strategic importance to the nation's defense. Construction of these installations provided job opportunities and many skilled carpenters and construction workers from the Interior learned their trade at this time.

## Government in Rural Alaska

In addition to the military, other government branches played key roles in rural parts of the Interior during the 1950s and 1960s. The Territorial School System, Bureau of Indian Affairs and Indian Health Service became increasingly involved in rural Alaska during this period, along with many other territorial, state and federal agencies.

The rapid growth of regional centers like Fort Yukon, Tok, McGrath and Galena were a reflection of the increasing government activity. Services of the urban areas were making their way to the Bush. Unfortunately, they brought with them a regulatory structure developed hundreds of miles away in Juneau or Washington and often not appropriate for local conditions.

A common concern of villagers was fish and game regulations and their enforcement by territorial game wardens. Conflicts centered on the enforcement of game limits and setting of hunting and fishing seasons. Village people saw these limits and seasons as regulations designed for city hunters, for whom the season made little difference, not villagers living without electric freezers and dependent on the game.

Spring waterfowl hunting has been a particularly sensitive issue in rural areas. When the ducks and geese return each spring, villagers are short of fresh meat and cannot understand why they should deny themselves the resource. They see waterfowl coming north by the thousands to nest on the rivers and lakes, and find it hard to imagine continent-wide population declines or the competing interests of sport hunters in the Lower 48.

The game warden's job wasn't easy. Some men stayed long enough to learn about the people, recognize their particular circumstances and be accepted.

Others left after a year or two with little, if any, local savvy and plenty of local resentment toward them. Sidney Huntington describes how Sam White handled a difficult problem with beaver hunting on the Innoko River:

> The beaver is the other animal which was almost eliminated. I remember so clearly, in the early 1900s beaver pelts were selling at high prices, about $6 each. Heavy shooting with rifles was used to take the beaver. . . . The beaver was almost eliminated by 1922. At that time the law stepped in . . . the season for harvesting was closed — period. By 1926, it reopened only to have it closed again. The take was heavy as the price was up to $40 each. They opened the season again in 1929 for trapping only. Again, the expert subsistence user got his .22 rifle out and began crack shooting the beaver in the eye or the mouth leaving no bullet mark anywhere. . . . The local Game Warden at that time was Sam White whom many people respected. . . . He went from camp to camp or village and taught anyone interested how to trap beaver. That set is still being used today.

Sam White became a game warden in 1927, a post he held for many years. He was well-known by everyone in the Interior.

The presence of big government was also being felt in Alaska's cities, where discontent with the federal government created a growing clamor for statehood. People hoped that statehood would provide more economic and political opportunities and a degree of independence from federal control, especially where management of resources was concerned. A major concern was to have some voice back in Washington. In a Statehood Commission interview in 1981, the late Ada Wien described her experiences as a school girl in Nome, sitting in the classroom studying the Boston Tea Party while the old *Victoria* was being unloaded offshore. It occurred to her that territorial Alaska was like the colonies, with taxation but no representation. Years later, she was living in Fairbanks when the statehood issue was raised, and she stepped forward to help with the fight. She was joined by others like Les Nerland, whose father — pioneer Fairbanks merchant Andrew Nerland — had brought his business over the gold rush trail from Dawson, worked to get a university and staunchly supported statehood. The elder Nerland died on the day that delegates signed the statehood document, just a few minutes after reading his son's copy and saying how pleased he was by the work they had done.

As people had hoped, statehood brought political and economic opportunities to Alaska, although few predicted that the state would one day be wealthy. The Statehood Act certainly raised the political consciousness of all Alaskans, who felt for the first time that, with delegates seated in Washington, they had a chance to influence the course of federal policy in their new state.

The Statehood Act did not address native land claims, but starting in the 1960s, native leaders recognized that the political climate was becoming more and more conducive to addressing their claims. They had fought for their country in World War II and learned a great deal about how the military operates. They had worked with federal and territorial agencies and had been affected by their policies. They had worked on large construction projects, and they had followed the urban-based fight for statehood. In the coming years, when the timing was right, they would draw upon these experiences and work politically to resolve their claims to land and resources.

## The Growing Native Political Consciousness

In the early 1960s, plans were introduced for a dam across the Yukon River. The dam would be built by the U.S. Army Corps of Engineers between Rampart and Stevens Village, where the river narrows to a single channel called the Ramparts. While this dam would provide massive amounts of power for the state, it would also flood the entire Yukon Flats. This included thousands of square miles of wildlife habitat and the communities of Stevens Village, Beaver, Birch Creek, Venetie, Fort Yukon, Chalkyitsik and Circle. The prospect of villagers driven from their homeland and re-establishing a way of life elsewhere was overwhelming. It was entirely different from the usual Lower 48 scenario of moving from one town to another; learning to subsist in an entirely new and unfamiliar region — even if such a region was available — would impose great hardship on the people. Leaving the homeland and the myriad of personal associations with the terrain and animals would mean losing a sense of cultural association that had developed throughout many generations. One piece of land was simply not replaceable by another.

Native leaders also pointed out how the dam would affect the social aspects of their lives. For most of the community members their whole lives centered around the four or five communities where they grew up, had relatives and shared common experiences out on the land. Many of these people grew up knowing one another from childhood and the fear of losing those personal ties was unsettling. As the Rev. David Salmon said:

> I am against it because there would be no suitable place to move to. Further, that should the dam be built, all the young people would move to the dam site, and the old people and villages would fade away.

Native leaders began to realize how poorly their way of life was understood by other Alaskans, and how important it was to speak out. The Fairbanks *Daily News-Miner* for February 3, 1964, reported on the formation of a new native political organization:

> Representatives from villages throughout the immense Yukon Flats met in Fort Yukon this weekend and have formed a group on Rampart Dam.
>
> It will seek the services of an attorney to help it deal with problems concerning the proposed hydroelectric project.
>
> The dam would flood the 11,000 square miles in which the Natives of the Yukon Flats live.
>
> The new organization, named Gwitchya-Gwitchin-Ginkhye, The Yukon Flats People Speak, will not only deal with the dam but also other issues concerning the people of the flats. . . .
>
> Of prime concern to the villagers was the issue of land, whether the federal government has the right to take it, how it would pay

for it, who would select new village sites, and when would they pay for the land.

Responding not only to the threat of Rampart Dam, but also to fish and game laws that seemed to favor the sport hunter, native leaders throughout the Interior were beginning to organize. They decided to meet at the traditional spring gathering spot, Nuklukayet, where the Tanana and Yukon rivers come together. Villages on the Tanana, middle-Yukon and Koyukuk rivers were asked to send representatives there, to the traditional place where important matters were discussed. At the revival of the spring gathering were representatives not only from many interior villages but from the government as well. Whatever the lasting affects of these first meetings, it was clear that leaders were stepping forward and native organizations were addressing threats to their land and way of life. The Fairbanks Native Association, formed in 1963, was another early political organization for interior people.

Leaders like Richard Frank from Minto, Al and Delois Ketzler from Nenana and Chief Andrew Isaac from Dot Lake put their energies into the fight for native claims, and toward developing a regional network of leadership. They were joined by people from other sectors of the state and nation. The Fairbanks-based Alaska Conservation Society took up the issue and rallied national environmental groups in the successful fight against Rampart Dam. They also entered the fight over a state plan to build a road into the Minto Lakes, a popular place for sportsmen from Fairbanks but also the subsistence hunting grounds of Athabaskans from Minto village. The society brought the conflict to light when they called a meeting to discuss the proposed Minto Lakes Recreation Area. Mary Clay Berry reports:

> The meeting, attended by local sportsmen and conservationists, went along smoothly until the Society produced a surprise guest. He was Richard Frank, a 36-year-old Athabaskan Indian with a sixth-grade education. Frank was chief of the Minto Flats people, whose permanent village was Minto on the Tanana River below Fairbanks. . . . Frank told the sportsmen that the lakes belonged to his people, that this was their traditional hunting ground, and that without the use of the lakes, his children and his people's children would go hungry. There was absolute silence while Frank spoke.

Once again Alaska had faced an issue that revolved around who owned the land and who had the right to make decisions about it. Clearly, the matter of native claims had to be settled if the state was ever to proceed smoothly with plans related to land use and development.

This was the 1960s, and the federal government was putting large sums of money into fighting the war on poverty and funding a wide variety of social action programs. In Alaska, the Rural Community Action Program (RuralCAP) and Alaska Legal Services Corporation emerged as strong advocates for the villages and their way of life. Representatives of these groups and Volunteers in Service to America (VISTA) traveled or lived in the small communities and assisted villagers with paper work, helped with community projects and clarified their rights and opportunities under law.

The combination of threats to the land base, emergence of regional native leaders, economic and program resources from the federal government and educated guidance through service programs provided a natural context for action.

That was the setting in 1968, when a large oil find at Prudhoe Bay was announced. The state wanted to proceed with oil production and construction of a pipeline, but could not do so until the thorny issue of native land claims was finally addressed. The plan was to build a pipeline that would extend from Prudhoe Bay on the North Slope to Valdez in Prince William Sound. The project would cut clear across Alaska and would match the greatest construction efforts ever undertaken. It was also one of the most controversial, from the standpoint of engineering and the potential for environmental damage. Assuming that these problems could be overcome, there was still the question of native claims to the lands. The issue had been sidestepped many times before; but now the way had to be legally cleared, for here was a massive project that would mean huge profits to the state and would involve a great deal of land. The oil companies took their concerns to Washington, D.C., and lobbied for a final settlement of native land claims.

The growth of support and rising expectations were not overlooked by the native leaders, who knew there was little time to lose if they were going to take advantage of the political and economic climate. But how much land could they reasonably expect to get? How big a cash settlement was possible? And what would the act mean for their children?

Questions like these don't get settled overnight, and it was a long struggle that brought plenty of pressure with it. After all, the settlement had to satisfy many different constituents. Even within the native community there were disagreements as to whether it was right to divide up the land, and questions about what ownership would mean. In the Interior, Athabaskans recognized and respected each others trapping cabins, fishing camps, hunting areas and miles of traplines; they knew who had rights to use and inherit each of these places and which places were for everyone. But the idea of formal legal owner-ship went beyond traditional protection of rights to a kind of rigidity and formality quite foreign to most native traditions. Urban Natives often saw the settlement differently than their rural relatives, who were directly dependent on the land. Of course, the state had interests to be protected, too, and there was the United States Congress; all of this meant even more compromise.

Despite these hurdles, agreement was finally reached — the Alaska Native Claims Settlement Act (ANCSA) was passed by Congress, signed by President Nixon and became law on December 18, 1971. The act provided for a land and cash settlement, organization of profit-making corporations at the regional level and establishment of village corporations with the option of profit or non-profit status. The major regional corporation for interior Alaska was Doyon, Limited. Ahtna Corporation, one of the smaller regional corporations, was formed for the Copper River Valley. The regional corporations received surface and subsurface rights to lands they selected, and the village corporations received surface rights to their lands. A few villages like Arctic Village, Venetie and Tetlin had been able to establish Indian Reservations years before, and at the time of the native land claims they elected to take title to the reservation lands.

A major provision of ANCSA was section 17(d)(2) — now simply called D-2 — which set aside national interest lands that someday would be national wildlife refuges, forests, parks and monuments. If the state was going to be divided up, then the federal government felt that all Americans ought to have a share.

While the Natives geared up for their selections, the federal government began making plans for the national interest lands. Actually, the federal government still knew shockingly little about Alaska, so each agency sent a task force to study the areas that might eventually come under its jurisdiction. All were asked to develop draft management plans for Congress to consider.

After ANCSA was passed in 1971, there ensued a busy period in which regional and village corporations selected the lands they would eventually own. But there was a world of difference in the basis for their selection. Regional corporations were formed as profit-making entities and had to be concerned about gas and oil, minerals, timber and investment potential. That was different from the villages, where it was common for people like Uncle Art to go up to the map and point out his trapping cabin, or for others to point out a stretch of riverbank where they hunted moose, and say simply that it was important to keep on using those areas as they always had. Sometimes they pointed to places that were already labeled D-2 on the map and there were always lots of questions about use of those areas.

Some of the young leaders who went to the maps were also looking for resources like gravel and timber. They were thinking of the day when there would be taxes on the land, or of the revenue from gravel and timber that might bring needed income to the community. The young leaders debated about things like gravel. Before ANCSA they had never thought much about gravel, but now it made a big difference whether lawyers determined it was a surface or subsurface resource.

Meanwhile, back in the Doyon Regional Corporation offices, the staff was readying their land selections. They studied the most up-to-date information about the 200,000 plus square miles of land within their boundaries to make the difficult choices that could spell economic security or disaster.

The village corporations had the difficult job of coordinating their selections and making sure they were consistent with the regional selection patterns (compact and contiguous). There were lots of meetings and large commitments of time. For example, in the little community of Beaver, the corporation president was always being called into Fairbanks for meetings. Invariably when he got back and was ready to head out on his trapline, an intense cold spell set in and forced him to stay at home. He didn't make much money that year and the idea of working so hard to preserve a way of life, then not being able to live that way of life, must have seemed ironic to him. For other residents of Beaver — and I suspect most interior villages — it was all confusing, and people often wanted just to have someone "fix it up" right.

This was not just a difficult time for the native community. It was also a trying time for the white trappers living in the Interior. The native land claims provided some legal recognition of native rights, at least on village and regional corporation lands. But many of the white trappers had no legal claim to their traplines. Small in actual numbers, the few white trappers and their families were suddenly vulnerable. The land base was being divided up, and there was no organization or group looking out for their interest. There were, of course, cases where the native village corporations made verbal assurances to these people, and there was hope that the federal government would recognize their interests, but when they thought about the long term prospects, things were pretty bleak.

For the short term, there was pipeline construction work for Natives and whites; big wages made pipeline work attractive. Hiring took place out of the Fairbanks union halls, and villagers hoping to get on the line had to make their way through the city. And on the way back from the pipeline, Fairbanks became an easy place to get stuck.

The long term picture still wasn't clear. Despite the fact that it was a terribly busy time and many villagers were back and forth on pipeline work, the village corporations made their selections and braced for the future. The federal government's task forces from the Fish and Wildlife Service, National Park Service and Forest Service prepared their proposals for national interest lands. No one was sure what would happen with these proposals when Congress got around to them, but one thing was certain: the land was going to be divided up and future maps would show a mosaic of federal, state and private landowners. Local control was being lost to regional corporations and state and federal managers. Once more it seemed clear that the land was simply not large enough for everybody.

If the delegates to the first Tanana Chiefs Conference had been present 56 years later for the Alaska Native Claims Settlement Act, would they have been disappointed? Certainly their descendants were living a much more comfortable life. Now there were airstrips, regular flights to Fairbanks, schools in all the communities and health aides who could call daily to the hospital. And with pipeline earnings, useful new items like snow machines and high-powered outboard motors were more accessible.

Despite all these considerations, the delegates would almost certainly have wondered, like their children and grandchildren, how long they would be able to hunt, fish and trap in those big areas on the map marked D-2 — the national interest lands. Federal officials who came for hearings always assured people that they would be able to continue using their traditional lands . . . as long as they had need to. The last part of the statement always seemed to carry an unspoken message that obviously some day they wouldn't want to live off the land.

## D-2 and the Subsistence Issue

The native regional and village land selections provided under ANCSA were finished just in time. For outsiders looking in, the haste and pressure seemed like college term paper time and the mad rush to meet a deadline. Of course, in this situation the consequences were immeasurably more serious. Future anthropologists and social historians will look back at the land claims and describe the process as a case of willing but painful participation in legislated culture change. The settlement represented a fundamental shift in orientation toward the land, creating an array of new opportunities which ownership of land might provide and giving Alaska Natives a greater measure of legal control in land management decisions. But, the native leaders knew they could not achieve legal ownership of all the land that their people needed for subsistence. These needs would have to be negotiated with the state and federal government.

After native selections were made, the focus of attention shifted to the national interest lands, the D-2 question. Some people thought that the government was going to lock up Alaska in newly proposed national parks, monuments and wilderness preserves. Sport hunters and miners were outraged to see frontier areas that held great trophies and perhaps countless fortunes proposed as off limits to them. Others praised the management plans as the last great chance to preserve national treasures. The state was divided between people labeled developers and those called environmentalists. The Natives were not included under either label in the dispute, but with their subsistence interests at stake they stood to gain or lose as much as anyone.

Alaskans who had spent a number of years in the state found that the labels cast a strange set of pre-determined judgments on them. Few were comfortable being categorized, and most did not think of themselves as falling into one camp or the other. In fact, most people went out of their way to point out how much they favored reasonable development. People outspoken on the extremes aggravated the tendency to divide and categorize.

To rural Alaska Natives, these labels meant little, although the prospect of additional restrictions on activities like hunting for subsistence, trapping, cutting house logs, rebuilding cabins and using snow machines off the trails created deep concern. These were necessary activities that they had always taken for granted, but in the D-2 proposals such activities on certain national interest lands could be restricted or allowed only with special permission. Labels were of little consequence when such basic parts of their lives were going to be tightly controlled. They wondered why their activities, so inconsequential in terms of overall impact, would suddenly come under restriction.

When Congress failed to act on the D-2 legislation, then-Secretary of the Interior Cecil Andrus proposed establishing national monuments through executive order. In December 1978, President Carter signed the necessary proclamations establishing national monuments for 17 areas, encompassing 56 million acres throughout Alaska.

The regulations drawn up after these areas were established showed that the agencies had done some homework in rural Alaska; but there were still serious problems, like who would qualify as a subsistence user. Developers and sport hunters worried about losing access to mining, hunting and guiding areas. Rural Alaskans squirmed about new classifications that attempted to sort out who was qualified to carry out subsistence activities in the new monument lands. Were some villages more subsistence-oriented than others and therefore more qualified for subsistence resources? How long did you have to live in an area to qualify as a subsistence user? These were difficult issues that rural Alaskans had never considered before, and they reflected a shift away from local control to control by government agencies and private corporations.

When questions like these are asked, certain unsolvable complexities can emerge. A case in point was the elderly woman living in Nenana, who had grown up on the Kantishna and Toklat rivers and hunted in areas now classified within a national monument. When Park Service researchers questioned her about the area, she indicated that she had not been there in years, but she still felt strong ties to the area and could not understand why the park had taken over what she saw as her homeland. A similar situation presented itself to Park Service researchers working in Nikolai, on the northwest side of the Alaska Range. The elders talked about the foothills of the range as a traditional caribou and sheep hunting area. Although they hadn't used some of the area for subsistence in recent times, they considered it part of their land and they wanted the Park Service to know about their historic connections to it. After all, subsistence hunters survive by knowing about and using historically important places when the conditions are right. But how does a federal agency manage for the flexibility that is always a part of subsistence?

Game guides and miners also became concerned when they saw that they might be restricted from large areas where they had enjoyed free access before. For them, the issue was economic — they feared that their businesses would be ruined, and in some cases they were right.

More than anything else, opponents of the December 1978 proclamations resented the federal government for taking such strong action without a full congressional vote. The papers were full of editorials and articles on both sides of the issue. Denali (formerly McKinley) National Park was even the site of a demonstration, called the "Denali Trespass" because the demonstrators planned to enter the park and disobey some of the new regulations. The event generated strong interest in Cantwell but had little impact in Washington.

That isn't to say that the issue was settled once and for all with the proclamations. Congress continued to work on a legislated solution, and President Carter voiced support for its efforts, noting officially:

> Legislative action offers Congress the opportunity not only to designate the Federal lands in Alaska but also to provide for tailor-made management schemes which in some cases are more lenient than the current situation.

Finally, in 1980, the Alaska National Interest Lands Conservation Act (ANILCA) was passed by Congress and signed into law by the President. The act replaced the monuments with units of the Park Service: wildlife refuges, national forests, wild and scenic rivers, and wilderness preservation systems. Now the map of Alaska really had some color to it. A multi-shaded patchwork delineated the boundaries and areas of jurisdiction for the different federal land units. A batch of new regulations soon followed from each agency, and things got pretty complicated for the village people. A hunter or trapper might find himself crossing several boundaries every time he went out, each with slightly different management regulations that he was supposed to know and heed. Despite all this complexity, the regulatory structure was considerably more lenient than under the proclamations, and that took some of the heat off sport hunters and subsistence users — for a little while, anyway.

ANILCA addressed the question of subsistence directly, by stating that such uses were a value in their own right and in many of the new areas, subsistence

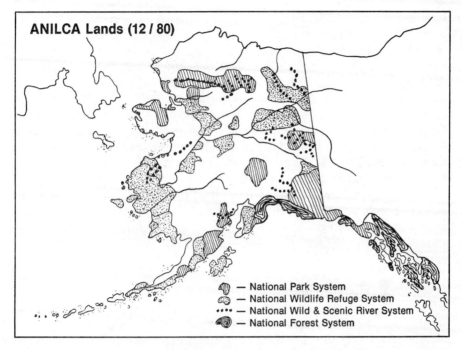

**ANILCA Lands (12 / 80)**

- National Park System
- National Wildlife Refuge System
- National Wild & Scenic River System
- National Forest System

*The Alaska National Interest Lands Conservation Act (ANILCA) of 1980 established a patchwork of federal land jurisdictions throughout the state. Management schemes being established for these parks, refuges, and national forests will have important effects on land and resource uses, especially subsistence activities carried out by rural Alaskans.*

rights were to be preserved and managed along with wildlife resources, scenic vistas and historic sites. Under ANILCA, subsistence regulations were to be established and enforced by the State of Alaska, which was to report to the federal government. If the state failed to manage subsistence, then the federal government could intervene.

The Alaska Department of Fish and Game was given responsibility for regulation of subsistence activities and harvests. For this it depended heavily on its Subsistence Section, which was later enlarged to a full departmental division. The Division of Subsistence was assigned the task of documenting subsistence land use and presenting information to the public, the department and the boards of Fish and Game. It would also assist the department and the boards in determining uses, users and methods of subsistence; and it would evaluate the impacts of regulations on subsisters and make recommendations to the boards. As if that wasn't enough, the subsistence division was also set up to work with other offices of Fish and Game on a range of management plans.

This was a large assignment, made even more difficult because the subsistence staff was part of the agency that many Alaskans equated with enforcement. Some villagers also questioned how the information they provided might be used: Would it be used against them? These questions gradually resolved themselves as individual staff members worked with local people and gained their trust. Another factor in overcoming problems of trust was a statewide move by urban-based sport hunters to have the subsistence law repealed. The division's staff saw their jobs on the line and the subsistence users felt that their way of life was being threatened.

Sport hunters and urban subsistence users challenged that the state had a mandate to make its natural resources available to all the citizens, and that the subsistence provisions were discriminating against their rights. People started to see the battle lines as drawn between rural and urban, even Native and white. Once again, it seemed that the land and resources could not support everyone.

The voters took the issue to the polls in November 1982 and voted to retain the subsistence law. Their support for the law meant they were willing to accept the fact that some people, sometimes, would have to be denied access to resources. The vote was an important bit of soul searching — it reflects the Alaskan people's growing appreciation for their state's diverse cultural traditions and a commitment to giving special consideration to these differing ways of life.

# Retrospect

Seventy years after their historic meeting with Judge Wickersham, and at a time when all Alaskans have celebrated 25 years of statehood, the Tanana Chiefs would surely see these events as an achievement worth cherishing. They would also be pleased by the way their people had organized to fight against the Rampart Dam and then gone on to help in formulating legislation that profoundly altered the course of Alaska's history.

Perhaps their most shocking observation would be that the hinterlands of the Tanana Valley are less populated by native people today than they were back in 1915. Chief Alexander of Tolovana would find his village deserted for much of the year, as would Chief Charlie of Old Minto and Chief Ivan of Coskaket (Cross Jacket or Cos Jacket). Disease took many, and the attractions of settled village life drew others into places like Nenana, Tanana and New Minto. But the old places are not forgotten, many of their people still hold close associations with traditional camps, with places imprinted on their lives through stories passed down from ancestors and with places whose meanings are enriched by new experiences as life on the land continues.

If the chiefs could see the country far north of Fairbanks, where the Dalton Highway (North Slope Haul Road) crosses the Yukon River, they might find some of their descendants gathered at the bank with boats ready to go upriver to Stevens Village or downriver to Rampart. They would see that new transportation patterns have reshaped the ways people get around and the places where they go. But they couldn't help but recognize the traditional fish camps, still situated on the main channels and back sloughs, in the special places where the schools of salmon congregate each summer, as they have for millennia. Development has brought great change to the descendants of the Tanana Chiefs, but it has not overwhelmed them. Life goes on and remains meaningful through the immense struggles and personal satisfactions which come from reconciling past ways with present opportunities.

# Raven's People

*Athabaskan Traditions in the Modern World*

By Richard K. Nelson

*Editor's note: Richard K. Nelson is an anthropologist and author of several books on the Athabaskans of interior Alaska.*

My uncle, John Shuman,
was not the first one.
Before that Nildhat Ti's father
settled there
so they say.
Before then, ever since the earth came to
be, throughout the years, people always
used to go and stay there.
And after everybody left, that's when we came.

That was my uncle,
Deetree John they called him;
it was his village
and so he stayed there too, and when we
got there it became our village.
And the same way, ever since the earth began. . . .
All the Indian people's settlements
are along the river up that way.

—Belle Herbert,
village of Chalkyitsik

## People of the Villages

Two centuries have passed since the earliest influences from a distant western world were felt by the Athabaskan people of interior Alaska. First came trickles of mysterious goods and rumors of foreign strangers, and then the strangers themselves appeared, moving gradually inward from the far boundaries of Athabaskan country. Before long there were newcomers everywhere, bringing with them a whole array of new goods and ideas. Change built upon change, as elements from European and American traditions slowly blended into the indigenous native cultures.

What has emerged from this intermingling of people on the northern frontier is a unique 20th century lifeway, carried on by the residents of villages scattered widely across the interior wildlands. In this chapter I will describe something of the modern village lifeway, its roots in Athabaskan tradition, and its place in the context of present-day Alaska. What I say here is based on my own learning and experiences as an anthropologist visiting these communities,

*Log houses, caches and drying racks of Beaver personify the charm of interior Alaskan villages. Beaver is located on the Yukon River about 100 miles north of Fairbanks and is reached only by airplane or riverboat. (Courtesy of Richard Nelson)*

on the writings of others who have worked and studied there and on the words of Athabaskan people writing or speaking about themselves.

*The Cabin Towns.* There are about 55 Athabaskan settlements in Alaska's Interior today, most of them situated along the major river systems: the Yukon, Tanana, Koyukuk, Copper and Kuskokwim. Their populations vary from less than 50 to more than 500 in a few cases, with most having between 150 and 300 residents. A few villages are accessible by road, but most can be reached only by air, snow machine, dog sled or by long boat journeys during summer months.

Travelers bound for a modern Athabaskan village are likely to start their journey from an urban airport like the one at Fairbanks. The small plane is tightly packed with passengers, luggage, mail bags and freight ranging from Pampers and snow-machine parts to sled dogs. For an hour or two after takeoff, the great expanse of mountains and forested valleys passes by underneath with few, if any, human imprints on the land. Then the plane banks above a small cluster of dwellings and touches down on a landing strip between closely bordering trees.

A small crowd of people usually gathers when any plane arrives; everyone is anxious to greet old friends and see who has come to visit. From the airfield, a path or road leads into the settlement and fingers out among the houses. Most Athabaskan villagers live in homes made from logs, which the surrounding forest supplies in abundance. Houses may be small one-room cabins with sod roofs or large double-storied buildings divided into many rooms. Like elsewhere in America, you can guess something about the owner's wealth or ambition by the size and condition of his home. In this case, however, he (or she) is almost certain to have built it himself with the help of relatives and neighbors.

Walking through an interior Alaskan village, the visitor will be struck by familiar and unfamiliar sights. Clothing much like that worn in places like rural Minnesota or North Dakota, likely bought through catalogue stores, hangs on outside lines. Even during winter it will freeze-dry in the arid cold. Small groups of children play on the paths or around the houses, while older brothers or sisters help with daily chores such as splitting firewood and feeding dogs. During summer and fall, strips of meat or fish hang in latticed smokehouses, curing for use through the long cold season. There may be a few cars or trucks, but people usually get around the village on foot, drive snow machines or ride motorized three-wheelers. In many communities people still keep dog teams, although they have declined in numbers and importance today. Modern teams are often kept more for the popular sport of dog sled racing than for hunting or trapping.

Even a casual visitor to an Athabaskan settlement will notice many signs that life here is changing, results of the steady growth of influences from the outside world. There is noise from a large generator that supplies electricity to all the houses. And there will be a number of public buildings where people's educational, health, social and economic needs are served.

The largest and most imposing structures in any settlement are almost certainly the school and nearby teachers' quarters. Sometimes they are situated right among the houses, but they often sit apart or up on a hill, protected from the threat of floodwaters. There will also be at least one church in the village, often a simple, lovely building made from logs. Schools and churches were first built in most Athabaskan communities around the turn of the century, though in some areas they came as late as the 1940s. They reflect the active interest of outside government and society in bringing elements of western culture to the native people in Alaska's remote northern communities.

Nearly all Athabaskan villages have several other kinds of public buildings. One of these is the general store, often, though not always, stocked with a wide selection of goods — tools, equipment, parts, clothing, bolts of cloth and assorted groceries. There is usually a small clinic where a trained local health aide tends to basic and emergency medical needs, and a community hall where people hold meetings and social gatherings. Most communities also have a village corporation building, where they run small businesses established with money and land granted through the Alaska Native Claims Settlement Act of 1971.

During the past century, villagers have faced a wide variety of new possibilities for change. In confronting these possibilities, they have decided which ones seemed good or bad, which might take them in promising directions or create problems and which would fit with their traditional values or violate them.

> Two or three people came to discuss the new laundry from the government and a lot of us were against it. I spoke against it. We did our own washing up in our own washtubs. After the laundry got built and after so long it would be turned over to us and we'd have to stand the cost of the operation. And we couldn't afford all the fuel for the generators and all that. That's what we thought and that's why we were against it.
>
> —Roger Dayton,
> village of Koyukuk

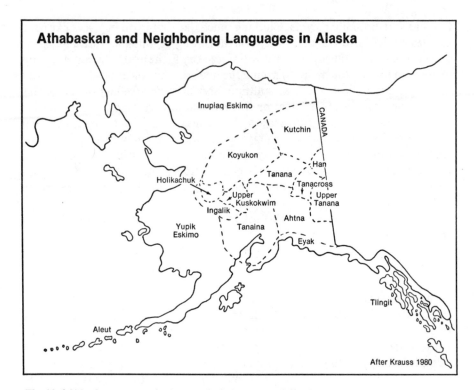

**Athabaskan and Neighboring Languages in Alaska**

Inupiaq Eskimo

Kutchin

CANADA

Koyukon

Han

Holikachuk

Tanana

Tanacross

Upper
Kuskokwim

Upper
Tanana

Ingalik

Ahtna

Yupik
Eskimo

Tanaina

Eyak

Tlingit

Aleut

After Krauss 1980

*The 11 Athabaskan groups who live in Alaska's Interior differ in language, cultural patterns and social ties. Distant relatives of the Athabaskans include the coastal Eyak and Tlingit, while Eskimos and Aleuts represent completely separate language and cultural traditions.*

*Life at Home.* Village people usually have a strong sense of pride in their community and feel it is important to show hospitality to visitors. Before long a newcomer is almost sure to be invited into someone's house to visit over a cup of tea or coffee. Most homes have a large main room dominated by a wood-burning stove, with a kitchen area, a table for work and eating, chairs and a couch, perhaps a bed. Smaller partitions are sometimes made by hanging cloth, or there may be separate bedrooms off to the side or upstairs. Some villages have running water and indoor plumbing; in others the people use outhouses and carry water from the river.

The main room is often a cluttered and busy place. A visitor might find a woman preparing hides or sewing in the light beside the window. Children run in and out during energetic rounds of play and visiting. Family members do many other projects in this room, such as making equipment or skinning fur-bearing animals brought in from the trapline. A newcomer is likely to attract curious neighbors who listen in or join the conversation. Cooked meat and homemade bread may be offered, since food is an important part of nearly all social occasions.

> The Natives were used to feeding one another all the time. They
> go in a neighbor's house and always eat. Or they go into another
> village where they're always welcome to eat no matter what house

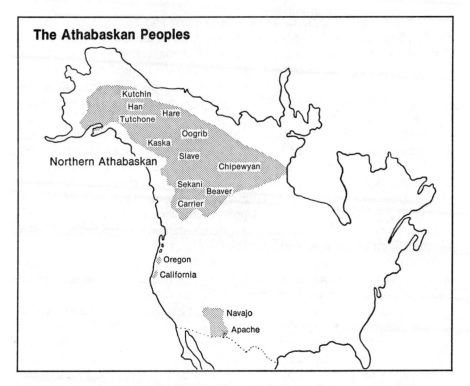

## The Athabaskan Peoples

Kutchin
Han
Tutchone    Hare
Oogrib
Kaska
Northern Athabaskan    Slave
Chipewyan
Sekani
Beaver
Carrier

Oregon
California

Navajo
Apache

*Athabaskan peoples inhabit a huge territory in northwestern Canada and interior Alaska. Other Athabaskans include the Navajo and Apache in the Southwest and several groups on the Pacific Coast who came from the northern homeland many centuries ago.*

they visit. Especially if they went to some other village they were watched so that they wouldn't go hungry. I guess this woman thought all white people was that way I guess. I don't know what she thought.

Anyway, first time she come to Ruby she was walking along the street, she see people going in and out of the Chinaman Wing's big restaurant. Walking closer, right through the window there she could see people eating and soon as they get through they go out.

I guess she was hungry and went in there, sat down. She didn't know how to speak English and this Chinaman don't speak very good English himself. Anyway, she eat. Soon as she got through eating she just went out. Down the street she went.

This Chinaman come out hollering and a hollering to beat the band. Sally Pilot didn't know what the heck he's hollering about. Later the other Natives told her that people supposed to pay when they eat in there. She didn't know. She was scared to go back there again. . . .

—John Honea,
village of Ruby

Hosts and newcomers are naturally shy, but they soon find common grounds for conversation — topics like village events, hunting or fishing activities and family history help people to become acquainted and feel at ease with one another. Someone who has spent time in other Athabaskan towns might be questioned about them, perhaps asked about friends or relatives who live there. Often today, people from one village will have acquaintances throughout the Interior, friendships developed through the years by traveling to social events, attending meetings in the larger towns or cities, or perhaps spending time in the hospital or at a boarding school.

*Inheritors of the Tradition.* Athabaskan villages like the one I've just described are found all across Alaska's Interior, from the lower Yukon River eastward to the Canadian border and from the Brooks Range south to Cook Inlet. There are about 7,000 Athabaskan people in the state today (1980 census), divided into 11 groups by differences in language and culture. These groups include the Ingalik, Holikachuk, Koyukon, Upper Kuskokwim, Tanaina, Ahtna, Upper Tanana, Tanacross, Han, Tanana and Kutchin. Distant relatives within Alaska are the Tlingit of the southeast coast and the Eyak of Prince William Sound.

All of the Athabaskan groups share a broadly similar cultural tradition and language, but they are completely distinct from the neighboring Eskimos. These two people have separate origins, their cultures are fundamentally different and their languages are no closer to each other than English is to Japanese. About 20 other Athabaskan groups, with a total population of more than 20,000 people, live in a broad stretch of Canada from central British Columbia to northern Yukon Territory and east to Hudson Bay. Ancient wanderings also established Athabaskans far to the south, in the Pacific Coast states and the Southwest. Best known of these groups are the Apache and Navajo. Taken together, there are more than 200,000 Athabaskans in North America today.

Until recent times, Alaskan villagers had no acquaintance with their far-flung relatives although neighboring groups often made contact with each other. Nowadays, people from widely separated areas have many chances to meet, talk about common concerns and recognize their ancestral bonds. At the same time, modern education, along with ease of travel and communication, have greatly broadened people's horizons. In this way, Athabaskans are developing a view of themselves as a related human community. Incidentally, the word "Athabaskan" comes from the Cree Indian name for a lake in Canada, gradually adopted by whites to designate people of the western subarctic forests. Canadian Athabaskans nowadays call themselves Dene, based on a word meaning "people" in certain of their languages.

I have mentioned that Athabaskans throughout interior Alaska share a common lifeway and a similar cultural tradition, but each of the 11 groups is also distinct from the others. There are even variations in dialect and culture between villages of a single group, such as the Kutchin or Koyukon. This chapter talks about Alaskan Athabaskans in general, focusing on broad traditions followed by most or all communities. I have illustrated each topic with examples from particular groups but you should keep in mind that each community expresses Athabaskan culture in its own way. Aside from visiting interior villages and talking with the people themselves, the best way to explore this diversity and richness is through books written by or about them. Some of these books are listed on page 255.

# A Snare in the Willows

Life in a remote Athabaskan village takes on a flavor and meaning of its own, clearly distinct from the world outside. Each community is fairly self-contained, and even a short-term visitor can easily forget how small it is — a tiny nucleus of humanity amid the encircling wildland. Yet however untrammeled and unchanged this wildland might appear, it has long provided the community's resources of food and essential materials. Trails thread outward from the houses into the forest and along the rivers, fingering through the infinitely varied terrain. They lead to traplines and fishing lakes, berry patches and moose thickets, camps and cabins.

In fact, the wildland and the village are inseparable, at least in human terms. From the forest and waterways, Athabaskan people have drawn their physical, cultural and spiritual sustenance for millennia. Their traditional lifeway has emerged and exists in concert with the force and stimulus of the surrounding environment, in an ancient process of adaptation that continues today. In the following pages, this creative relationship between people and nature will become more clear, as we explore the varying dimensions of Athabaskan culture.

Perhaps nowhere is the essential link between northern Athabaskans and their boreal forest environment more evident than in their ways of making a living. Since their ancient origins, they have been hunters, trappers, fishermen and gatherers — subsisting on the wild resources of a difficult and often sparse environment. If interior Alaska may be said to provide anything in abundance, it is the constant supply of challenges to human cleverness and perseverance. That Athabaskans have been equal to the challenge is evident in their very survival and in the ingenuity of the techniques they have devised to assure it.

> Grandpa have trap right down around the bend from the camp where we were. . . . He was strong but he go blind. We talking about the trap. He knew he got something, I guess.
>
> "Why don't you go with me?" he say. I was small. Maybe six or seven. . . . We went around the bend maybe two miles from our camp. Then we had to go off the bank there where he had trap. I see that trap. The animal move it, stick and all, over fifty feet. "Oh Grandpa! I see it over here!" But I forget the name of that animal. It was fox, you know. "What is in the trap?" he tell me.
>
> "I don't know." I forgot the name. He started to call out names.
> "Wolf?"
> I tell him, "No."
> "Wolverine?"
> "No."
> "Lynx?"
> "No."
> Pretty soon he say, "Fox?"
> "Oh, yeah." So I tell him over this way to get that fox.
>
> —Moses Henzie,
> village of Allakaket

The pattern of life in an Athabaskan community is set by the yearly cycle of seasons. Perhaps no climate in the world changes to such extremes as the boreal forest. For many months each winter the temperature hangs far below zero; the sun creeps over the horizon for a short time each day, if at all; and the entire landscape is shut tightly beneath snow and ice. On the other hand, summer temperatures can climb into the 90s, and sustained by almost continuous sunlight, the land bursts into a brief glory of green. All plants and animals respond to these changes, and so the Athabaskan people pattern their lives accordingly.

The annual cycle of subsistence activities is generally similar throughout interior Alaska, though each area has its own variations. For example, villagers along the major rivers have a strong focus on fishing, especially during the summer and fall salmon runs. Those located near major mountain ranges or tundra areas are likely to depend more on seasonal hunting for game animals such as migratory caribou. Some resources — like moose, black bear, water-fowl and snowshoe hare — are important almost everywhere in the Interior.

*Fall: Season of the Moose.* In a typical Athabaskan community, fall is the time of the richest and most intense harvesting activity. For many village people today, this season is almost synonymous with moose, the most important large game animal. Since ancestral times, Athabaskan people have studied the moose and developed an intimate knowledge of its behavior; this is the key to their great skill in hunting the animal.

Modern villagers wait until the September mating season, then travel long distances on the rivers in outboard-powered boats, hunting the moose that come out onto broad sandbars. The great bulls are heavy with fat, in prime condition, and expert hunters can tell the best animals at a glance. Sometimes a husband and wife will go out together, camping for several nights in promising areas while they search for moose. Many Athabaskan women are accomplished hunters capable of bringing in the year's meat supply on their own if necessary.

> Falltime is about the best time. I like to spend a night out. Make campfire and listen for moose. No mosquitoes to bother you. Nice and cool. Bulls hit their horn on a tree and make that dragging noise like. So my husband would make a horn out of bark and rub it on a tree to make the same noise. That moose would be sneaking towards our camp. Early in the morning, if we wanted, we could get him. . . .

> —Lorraine Honea,
> village of Ruby

Like all large game, moose are hunted with rifles nowadays; but modern technology has not displaced the need for traditional skills of tracking, calling and stalking. An expert Athabaskan hunter can read many things from a moose track — the animal's sex, its size and condition, what it was doing and how long ago it was there. By knowing the nearby landscape in detail, hunters often have an uncanny ability to predict the exact place to look for the animal.

After shooting a moose, hunters face the long, difficult task of skinning and butchering it. There are Athabaskan names and traditional uses for almost every part, so little goes to waste. Women usually prepare the meat — which can be roasted, boiled, fried, smoked or dried — following a variety of recipes that have been handed down for generations. Meat is often used for making stews with added vegetables, rice or noodles and condiments. Other recipes, such as boiled tongue, roasted nose and head cheese, are as tasty as they are unusual. Moosehead soup, a special delicacy saved for village feasts, is made from bits of head muscle and tissue painstakingly removed and then simmered for many hours. It takes long practice to master the many special ways Athabaskans have developed for using each game and fish species.

Villagers throughout the Interior also hunt black bear during the fall near freeze-up time. Fattened by feasting on berries, the animals are a prized source of meat and bear grease, which is eaten with other foods as a kind of butter. Some people, like the Koyukon, put much effort into hunting black bear after the first snows, when they have entered their hibernation dens. Nowadays they use rifles for this dangerous activity, but in earlier times men hunted these bears with only a bow and arrow or a spear. Even today a man's success can depend on his willingness to crawl part-way into a den and locate the bear inside.

Other animals hunted in the fall include grouse, ptarmigan, ducks, geese and snowshoe hare. In some areas, hunters climb to the high slopes for Dall sheep; and where migrating herds of caribou are found the people go out to intercept them. Snares are among the most ingenious traditional devices used by Athabaskans for catching caribou or almost any kind of game. In earlier times these were made of sinew or rawhide, strung at openings through drift fences or hung inconspicuously along game trails. Their deadly effectiveness was increased by making spring poles that would kill the animal quickly when triggered. Today, snares are used mainly for catching small game like snowshoe hares, ptarmigan and fur animals.

The fall harvest also includes late runs of salmon and whitefish, caught with nets set in the rivers or lakes. Fish and meat are either dried or frozen outdoors for storage; nowadays people also own freezers.

Besides bringing in supplies of food, villagers prepare for winter by cutting and splitting firewood well before cold weather arrives. Chain saws, steel axes and snow machines have made this far easier than in earlier times, but it is still a time-consuming and sometimes exhausting job.

*Winter: The Trapline Months.* Winter's early snows signal the year's longest and most challenging season. For Athabaskan people everywhere in the Interior, this is the time for trapping. Throughout the cold season they make periodic rounds of traplines that stretch across the broad flats, through the river valleys and up into the foothills. Their take of wolf, wolverine, lynx, otter, mink, marten, muskrat and beaver supplies hides and meat for home use. Pelts sold to fur buyers, who often fly from village to village in small planes, are an important source of cash income. Some people, like the Kutchin, have refined trapping to a high level of expertise and place great value on their identity as trappers. Many women also trap or have done so in the past.

> Last year [1977] we got little more than three hundred marten. The male, worth around forty-five dollars. Next year we should do better. We'll go farther, work harder. Trapping is a lot of work. You got to make trail, know what kind of place to set trap. I tell them boys how to do it. . . .

*Trapping dominates winter activities in most Athabaskan villages and provides furs for local use or commercial sale. Some furbearers, such as these large beavers, are also valued for their meat. Elman Pitka is shown here on the traditional trapline he inherited from his father, located about 60 miles from the Yukon River village of Beaver. (Courtesy of Richard Nelson)*

I tell them they got to watch animal, too. Got to learn the animal. Some of them animals is smart. Know better than you do. Wolf is the worst. Pretty smart, he can smell the trap from far away. Lots of time I watch where fox go around the trap. You got to keep moving it around, fool 'em.

I never use bait for smart animal. They know. When there's bait, smart one knows it's trap there. Snare is same thing, I have to trap them different. You just can't play around with it for nothing if you want to trap. When you work, when you make something, you got to use your head. . . .

—Joe Beetus,
village of Hughes

Most modern villagers now depend on snow machines to reach their distant traplines, which are often 50 miles or more from home. The line itself is a circuit 50 to 150 miles long, usually with a small cabin or tent for overnighting. Families used to stay in trapline cabins all winter long, going out each day on foot or by dog team to check their traps. Now that people have settled in villages and children go to school during the winter, men usually travel out to their lines alone and return within a few days. Because snow machines are faster and more powerful than dog teams, they are a great asset in shortening the time away from home.

Hunting activity wanes during the coldest months, especially when the temperature drops to minus 40 or 50 degrees and glittering frost crystals drift in the still air. It is hard to be outside for long, and game is difficult to approach because the snow creaks loudly underfoot. In some areas there are caribou only during the winter, so the men dress in their heaviest clothes and travel across wide areas on snow machines hunting for them. Young boys bundle up and walk out from the village carrying light rifles, looking for grouse or ptarmigan. Perhaps they also check a few traps they have set nearby for ermine or mink. The women put out snares for snowshoe hare or ptarmigan, usually in willow thickets within walking distance or a short snow-machine ride from home.

During the winter months, deep accumulations of powder snow make walking almost impossible without snowshoes, and Athabaskans have elevated snowshoe-making to a refined art. Men usually make the birch frames and women weave the intricate rawhide mesh. Most Athabaskans use two types of snowshoes: long and wide for deep untracked snow, shorter and narrower for walking on packed trails. Without snowshoes, ancestral Athabaskans probably would not have survived in the boreal forest, so it is small wonder they have developed such elegant designs and have mastered their use so well. Unfortunately, few younger Athabaskans are learning to make snowshoes and the art could vanish within a few decades.

Setting fishnets under the ice is another ingenious technique used by the Athabaskans. During early winter, villagers make good catches of whitefish and pike this way. The trick is to chop a series of holes through the ice, then tie a line onto a long pole and push it from one opening to the next until it can be pulled out through the farthest one. Then the line is tied onto one end of the net and pulled back, so the net ends up stretched beneath the ice. Later, the line is attached again so the net can be hauled out, checked and then pulled back under the ice. Removing the fish bare-handed, often in subzero weather, is cold work indeed. Sometimes it almost seems like the catch freezes solid in mid-flop.

Developing an effective technology and the skills to apply it has been the key to survival for Athabaskan people for millennia. Nowhere is this more important than in making clothes warm enough to be comfortable and allow activity in the deep cold of interior Alaska's winter. Before contact with whites, the Athabaskans made their clothing from animal hides, with the fur left on for winter or removed for summer. The usual wear included light fur underclothes, a long coat with separate hood or hat, mittens, and pants with attached moccasins. The most common materials were moosehide for durability, snowshoe hare for lightness and warmth and caribou for the greatest warmth of all. Clothing was sometimes beautifully decorated with fur or feather designs, leather fringes, dyed porcupine quills or dentalium shells.

Today's winter outfits are made mostly of cloth, and are ordered through catalogues, bought from stores or made at home. Athabaskan women sew colorful hooded parkas with ruffs and trim of wolf or wolverine fur. During cold weather people wear heavy snowpants. — often down-filled — and traditional-style boots of fur or canvas with moosehide soles. Women also make beautiful mittens, using tanned moosehide or furs such as wolf or otter; those meant only for special occasions are decorated with elaborate beadwork in lovely floral designs.

*In former times, caribou were driven into an enclosure where they were speared, snared or shot with arrows. This drawing by an early explorer shows Koyukon people using muzzle loaders to shoot animals corralled during their migration. (From* Travel and Adventure in the Territory of Alaska *[1864] by Frederick Whymper; courtesy of Archives, University of Alaska, Fairbanks)*

*Spring: The Lean Season.* Interior Alaska's winter fades all too gradually into spring; the change is marked first by longer days and then by easing cold. Although it might seem a paradox, spring can be the season of greatest scarcity for Athabaskan people, when stored food runs low and game is still scarce.

So
as I was walking along
I came upon big lynx tracks
from the night before,
and so I followed it along
and I came to the edge of a big lake and it
    had walked around the lake
and it was lying out on a point. . . .
So
I walked around it and
I stopped right behind it, but because it didn't
    even lift its head,
I whistled at it.
Then turning its head toward me, it lifted it,
and with my twenty-two
I shot it right between the eyes.
And it was really
a fat one.
And that was another time when we were out of food.

—Chief Henry,
village of Huslia

Before they had access to imported foods, people sometimes made it through a tough spring by catching blackfish if they could find a lake with a good supply. Using a small trap, shaped like a wicker basket with an inverted funnel entrance, they caught swarms of the minnow-sized fish at holes in the ice. Some village elders can also remember surviving a late spring cold snap by picking up songbirds that froze to death under the spruce trees.

Certain winter activities, like trapping, carry over into spring. From February until April men travel among the lakes finding beaver houses and setting under-water traps or snares near their entrances. Catching beaver is a skill that takes years to develop, especially learning how to take only the large ones while leaving the smaller ones for "seed." In the old days, Athabaskans made various kinds of complicated deadfalls to catch beavers in or near the water. They used other types of deadfalls for all kinds of animals, from squirrel-sized ermine up to full-grown bears. One of the outstanding technological achievements of traditional Athabaskan people was their invention of devices that could be left in the woods to trap animals "automatically."

Another important quarry for spring trappers is muskrat, which are sometimes abundant in lakes and sloughs. Both men and women set steel traps for these little animals inside their feeding houses or hunt them with light rifles later in the season as they sit on the ice or swim in the open water. Like beaver, muskrats are valuable not only for their hides but also for their rich, tasty meat. After the ice is gone, hunters travel the lakes and rivers in light canoes or boats hunting

*Hunting canoes exemplify the highly evolved Athabaskan technology; they are swift on the water, inconspicuous because of their low profile and light for easy carrying across portages. Modern versions, like this one being inspected by John Luke of Beaver, are made of spruce with a canvas covering rather than the traditional birch bark. (Courtesy of Richard Nelson)*

for muskrats. The canoes look like open-decked kayaks and are canvas covered today, replacing the birchbark of former times. These sleek, beautiful boats are gradually disappearing as villagers switch to fast, versatile motorized skiffs which they either make themselves or buy from stores in places like Fairbanks.

> We'd go out in the evening about six or seven o'clock. Then hunt all evening till about midnight when it get dark for about an hour. Then we stop and build a fire . . . and go out again until the sun is up pretty good about four or five o'clock. Usually a couple families camp together. There's always someone else back at camp so if you're too tired you just go to bed and they take care of skinning and stretching . . . we're not out there to kill all the muskrats or trying to get rich or anything like that. . . . We get everything we want to eat out there. We get all the fresh ducks that come in, fresh fish, and whatever. In the village we can't get that.
>
> —John Honea,
> village of Ruby

During long, bright days of early spring, people range widely around the villages hunting snowshoe hares and ptarmigan, which are often easy to find in this season. Caribou are also important spring game in certain areas, especially where large herds predictably migrate nearby. Caribou meat is cut into strips and hung outside to dry, making delicious jerky for summer travel and camping. Another springtime activity in some river villages is fishing through the ice for

*Salmon caught in gillnets during the summer are cut and hung on drying racks to cure for later use. Catching and preparing fish is often the responsibility of women in Athabaskan communities. (Courtesy of Richard Nelson)*

pike and ling cod (often called louche). Although people do not make large catches, the fresh fish is a welcome change after the long months of winter.

When the April thaw begins, some families move to temporary spring camps away from the village. Living in canvas tents, they enjoy the season's growing abundance and renew themselves in the country they have known since childhood. At the same time, their own children can learn outdoor skills and traditional knowledge. As meadows become bare and ice melts from the ponds, flocks of ducks and geese appear. These waterfowl have always been a prized source of springtime food, especially since they are hard to get in any other season. People hunt them with shotguns nowadays, but there may still be a few living elders who can remember watching canoe hunters take waterfowl with bows and arrows

Some of these old people can also recall living in traditional spring shelters instead of canvas tents. During warm weather they stayed in temporary lean-tos covered with moss or boughs, or they made rectangular houses with bark-covered walls and roofs. Sometimes a single family lived alone, or several families might have shared a larger house. Heat came from an open fire, with a smoke hole in the roof to keep the air reasonably clear inside. During the colder winter weather some Athabaskans — the Kutchin, Upper Tanana and Han — lived in domed shelters covered with moose or caribou hides. Others depended on log houses of various designs, often dug part-way into the ground and covered with moss.

*Summer: Time of the River.* Seasons change quickly in Alaska's Interior. During May the last snow vanishes and the rivers become free of ice. Suddenly the world is transformed and people are released from the harsh discipline imposed by cold weather. While the water is high, anyone wanting to build a house during the year ahead will cut logs beside the riverbank, fasten them together as large rafts and float them down to the village. Hauled up onto dry ground, they will cure in the summer sunshine and heat.

June's pleasant weather brings out the North Country's least welcome inhabitants — thick droves of mosquitoes. Athabaskan elders can remember taking refuge around smudges and inside bark houses before village stores sold modern repellents. When they were busy outdoors, they even carried little smudge pots everywhere they went, surrounding themselves with protective clouds of smoke. Summer must have come as a mixed blessing in those days.

Sometime during June and July, depending on the area, migrating runs of salmon show up in the rivers. People mend their nets and set them in favored eddies where fish gather out of the main current. Some families load their boats heavily with gear and move to fish camps for one to several months. Daily catches of salmon are specially filleted and hung on racks to dry, some for winter dog food and others for human use. Preferred fish like king and silver salmon are smoked in strips to make a rich, tasty delicacy prized by Natives and non-Natives alike.

Villagers do most of their summer fishing with gill nets, usually bought from stores but sometimes still made at home. In certain swift, muddy rivers — like the Yukon and Tanana — salmon are also caught with fish wheels. These clever devices, with their current-driven baskets that scoop fish from the water, were invented earlier in this century. Traditionally, the Athabaskans fished with nets made from willow bark, but even more important were various kinds of elaborate weirs or fish traps. In some areas, people were also skilled at spotting ripples made by approaching schools of salmon, then paddling out to the fish in canoes and catching them with oversized dip nets.

Fishing activities have always been dominated by Athabaskan women. In earlier times, men often went away on long hunting trips while the women and children stayed at riverside fishing camps. Many men still leave their villages or camps in summer, but now they go to find wage jobs such as forest fire fighting or construction work. Not surprisingly, Athabaskan women are self-sufficient and highly skilled in the outdoors. They have the main responsibility for setting and tending the nets, and for cutting the large numbers of fish they catch each day. Operating fish camps also means that the women must know a whole array of other skills for living out in the woods far from the conveniences that many of us consider necessary.

Runs of salmon and other fish carry on through August and into the fall. Late in the fishing season people turn their attention to berry picking, a favorite family activity. Adults and children crowd into boats and travel to favorite places, where in good years they find abundant harvests of blueberries, cranberries, raspberries, cloudberries and currants. Other edible plants such as wild rhubarb, fern roots and wild chives are occasionally used by modern villagers.

Summer passes all too quickly and the days shorten. Splashes of yellow appear

*Fish from interior Alaska's lakes and rivers provide one of the most reliable subsistence resources for Athabaskan villagers. Here James Gilbert of Arctic Village displays the whitefish and northern pike he has just removed from a gillnet fastened to the bank in the background. (Courtesy of Richard Nelson)*

in the willow thickets, frost whitens the muskeg sedges and before long the mountaintops are dusted by early snows. Village people anticipate the serious business of the fall harvest as the boreal forest year turns toward another beginning.

*The Forest of Spirits*. Looking back at the variety of resources available in the boreal forest throughout the year, it might seem that Athabaskan villagers have a reliable and secure economy. But in fact, this can be a meager place where human existence is frequently called into question. When the elders speak of times past, they are sure to bring up the hungry years and tales of near starvation.

Almost every kind of animal and edible plant species of Alaska's Interior is subject to constant change in abundance or availability. Some species — like salmon, ptarmigan or muskrats — can be common one year and scarce the next. Others have long-term population changes, such as the approximately 10-year cycles of snowshoe hares and the irregular ebb and flow of caribou herds. So there have been rich times when many resources were abundant and lean periods when people could find almost nothing. Traditional Athabaskans knew ways of using almost every edible thing in their environment, and at times this knowledge was their only means of survival.

> There is a story from the Telida people, about a man and wife who had a little baby. They were starving and could not make it through the winter. The man hunted but never got anything; he even looked for blackfish in the lakes.
>
> While he was going along he found an otter that kept coming up through a hole in the ice. He had only a knife, and by the time he managed to kill it his clothing got wet and froze. He was too weak to carry it all, so he took only its tail and tried to return home. But he got too tired and gave up.
>
> His wife became worried and went looking for him, but by the time she found him it was too late. The next morning she followed her husband's track and came across the rest of the otter where he had buried it under the snow. Although her husband had frozen to death, she and her baby survived by eating the otter.
>
> —Based on a narration by Miska Deaphon, village of Nikolai

Through the accumulated experience of their own lifetimes and the lessons passed along from earlier generations, Athabaskans have learned how closely their existence depends on nature and how important it is to protect their environment. On the one hand, they have developed sophisticated concepts of ecology, and from these have come practical methods for conserving resources. On the other hand, they have established a code of environmental ethics and beliefs about the spirituality of nature, which helps to assure that nature is benevolent toward humanity.

Villagers follow many practices designed to keep populations of subsistence resources healthy. Most important are self-regulation to prevent excessive use during any season or year and stringent prohibition against waste of anything from nature. For example, Kutchin trappers focus on catching each animal during the season when its fur is prime, to prevent waste and get the best return for their work. The Koyukon people avoid taking young animals or cutting small trees, preferring to let them grow and reproduce first. Elders often repeat the old warning that overuse or waste of game could mean scarcity sometime in the future. These rules and practices are identical to the basic principles of modern game management, but they were developed independently by generations of Athabaskans whose lives depended on nurturing their environment.

Aside from these practical concerns, Athabaskan traditions teach that everything in nature is fundamentally spiritual and must be treated with respect. This includes not only avoiding waste, but also following an elaborate code of morality toward plants, animals and the earth itself. For example, if an Upper Tanana man kills a wolf, he should never touch it until he formally apologizes and explains that his family needs it. Children are taught not to bother bird nests or eggs, because all living things are kin to people and must be shown proper respect. Upper Tanana hunters also learn that they should never brag about their success or ability to kill game. Anyone who ignores this may be killed by one of the animals he has offended.

Each living thing is believed to have a spirit of its own, just as Christians have a soul. Offenses against these living things can bring punishment — bad luck in the hunt, illness or even death. For traditional Athabaskans, nature is the source of great supernatural power and the sustainer of human life. People are only given resources if they make themselves worthy by showing reverence toward the omnipotent forces around them.

These beliefs are still taught by elders and followed in many Athabaskan villages today, alongside Christian beliefs adopted during the past century. As a middle-aged Koyukon woman explained: "Christianity works for all people everywhere on earth, including us. But the Indian way works for us, too, so I got to have both." There is considerable difference in commitment to the older beliefs from one area to another, and even individuals or families in the same community will vary when it comes to following religious traditions. But the general belief that respect must be shown toward nature is still followed widely among Alaska's Athabaskans.

> After a while, we were subsisting entirely on ground squirrels. The dogs ate nothing, and fell over at our sides. Once again they saw the land where there had been much game when they were young men, but there were not even any tracks there now. . . .
>
> Finally, we camped in a place, and our food was entirely exhausted. Early in the morning, near a prominent rock, we set a trap, hoping to eat again. In the morning he went to check the trap, but the dog had apparently eaten the ground squirrel that was caught in it. My father got very angry at the dog, and though it had done it out of hunger, he whipped it. "Stay near the trap on the chance that you might kill a squirrel," he told me; and putting his gun on his shoulder, he slowly disappeared in the direction we were traveling. . . . I stayed at our campsite until after noon, and then [I saw] my father coming from a long way off. I stared at him, for

he did not seem the same. He was wearing nothing but his trousers. He also seemed to be holding something in his hand. As he came nearer, I saw that he was holding something red. "My son, say thank you," he told me. "Yes, thank you!" I burst out.

He had walked up on a sleeping moose and shot it, so he told me. Where there had been no food, now bull-moose fat was skewered and roasting over the fire. . . . "

—John Fredson, Kutchin

*White Man Grub.* Although subsistence remains the keystone of Athabaskan life, the modern village economy is also based on wage earning and cash exchange. For example, a family wanting a new snow machine — the basic vehicle for winter travel, hunting and trapping — might use the wife's earnings from part-time work at the community school and the husband's income from last year's fur catch. So the cash economy and subsistence are completely mixed, just as a blending of modern and traditional elements pervades all aspects of village life today.

Sitting down for an evening meal, members of an Athabaskan family might find moose meat, bear grease and wild berries on the table along with store-bought soup, bread and butter, and canned fruit. Before eating, someone may give a Christian blessing; and then a young daughter might be told not to eat a certain food because it is tabooed for a woman her age. During the meal, the mother perhaps talks about her day's work as cook at the village school, and the father tells what he saw while out hunting or cutting firewood. A son may have spent his day in school, then walked out to check his traps in the woods nearby. And a daughter might be deciding whether to take a job at the village store or spend her time at home sewing, tanning hides and learning traditional ways of living.

Jobs are fairly scarce in rural Alaska today, although the number has increased in recent years. The main employers in a rural community are the school, store and village corporation, and there are jobs like postmaster and maintenance person for the village generator or water system. Other work is temporary and unpredictable, such as forest fire fighting, construction projects in the village or nearby communities and employment in areas like the North Slope oil fields. While people often have to leave their villages to find work, they feel that the income is important enough to make the sacrifice.

This mixture of cash and subsistence economies has brought a kind of stability to interior villages that never existed in the past. The specter of severe shortages and starvation is now gone because people can depend on imported foods if necessary. But Athabaskans are not satisfied with a steady diet of "white man grub" because they strongly prefer traditional foods and consider them more healthful. Villagers away from home complain of constant hunger, "You eat and eat, even expensive restaurant food, but you just can't get full when you don't have that wild meat you're used to."

Athabaskan people not only prefer to eat native foods, they have also made them a central part of their social lives through networks of sharing that bind families and neighbors to one another. Subsistence foods are an essential part of social and ceremonial events, such as potlatch feasts, which symbolize the

*Trimble Gilbert hurries home to Arctic Village after a successful fall moose hunt. Formerly paddled or poled, boats are now powered by outboard engines, sometimes provided with a lift attachment for negotiating shallow stretches. (Courtesy of Richard Nelson)*

intense connection between villagers and the wild resources they depend on. In the conclusion of his speech at a village feast, a Koyukon elder summarized this dependence by saying, "Food is the meaning of our lives."

What he left unspoken is that Athabaskan people find deep meaning in the process by which they obtain their food. For thousands of years they have wrested a living from the boreal forest, not just by skill and cleverness, but by ordering their entire culture around the quest for survival. Nearly everything in the Athabaskan tradition is somehow a reflection of the natural world, which not only sustains people physically but also gives them their highest source of satisfaction and fulfillment.

## Paths Between the Cabins

As I found out later
that day when they had gone back down to get
    the things they had cached
they had seen my tracks there

And there
the one I was named after had said,
    "This looks like him,
    that's the way he walks. . . ."

A long time ago
people used to recognize each other's tracks.

—Chief Henry,
village of Huslia

*Ties That Bind.* In a community so small that one person can know another from his tracks, people are inevitably knit by the close bonds of kinship and interdependence. The social network is so tightly bound that everyone in a village is likely to be related somehow to everyone else. These relationships are cemented by shared ancestry, the more immediate sharing of resources and a readiness to give help whenever there is a need. In this way, people can give extra comfort to others during the good times and perhaps spare them from serious distress when times are bad.

For Athabaskan people, even in the villages today, kinship is the key to understanding social and economic relationships. A community usually consists of several large extended families, each arising from one or two ancestors — often grandparents — who settled there when permanent villages began earlier in this century. But roots and relations are not traced in ways familiar to Euro-Americans; the kinship system is bewilderingly complex by those standards and is based on different principles.

Athabaskan kinship systems are generally similar throughout interior Alaska, though each group has its own variations and points of emphasis. Most groups stress the maternal line in tracing ancestry, in other words, relatives from your mother's side are considered closer than relatives from your father's side. There are two kinds of uncles and aunts: your mother's sisters and father's brothers (note the parallel sexes) are regarded much like your own parents, and their children are like your brothers and sisters. Your mother's brothers and father's sisters (note crossing of the sexes) are more distant kin, and their children — called cross cousins — were traditionally your preferred marriage partners. Modern villagers have become less concerned with these formal relationships, which in earlier times had a strong influence on the ways people organized their lives.

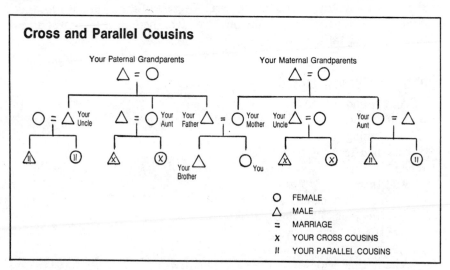

**Cross and Parallel Cousins**

Your Paternal Grandparents    Your Maternal Grandparents

Your Uncle    Your Aunt    Your Father    Your Mother    Your Uncle    Your Aunt

Your Brother    You

O    FEMALE
△    MALE
=    MARRIAGE
X    YOUR CROSS COUSINS
II    YOUR PARALLEL COUSINS

*Athabaskan people emphasize kinship as the basis for many social and economic ties. An important principle not present in western kin systems is the difference between cross and parallel relatives. For example, an Athabaskan may call his parallel cousins brother or sister, while his cross cousins are considered more distant relatives.*

In traditional Athabaskan societies each person would belong to a larger descent group or clan, inheriting membership through his or her mother. The usual number of clans is three; but some groups, like the Upper Tanana, have many clans which are then divided into two larger groups or moieties. In any case, the kinship system's geometry dictates that fellow clan members of your own age will be parallel cousins — called brothers and sisters — whom you are not supposed to marry. Members of the opposite clan are cross relatives, including the cross cousins with whom marriage is (or was) encouraged.

> My mother and father are almost same tribe [clan], not quite, but
> I belong to my mother's people. All children belong to mother's tribe.
> Young people must know these things to know who are his friends,
> who fight with him in war, who he must give meat when hunger
> come, and who he can marry.

> —David Paul,
> village of Tanacross

Each clan was fairly widespread during earlier times, so people could often find support and hospitality from clan-mates no matter where they traveled. Within your own group, the clan helped to organize people for events like funerals and potlatch feasts, and usually each band of people who lived and moved together was headed up by the leader of one clan. In some areas, such as the Upper Tanana villages, clans still have many social functions and are an important part of community life. In other areas, people know which clan they belong to, but groups like the village council have taken over the business of organizing community events and activities.

Although formal groups like the clan have weakened, people are still bound together by shared kinship, and traditionally defined relationships are an important part of their social lives. Villagers are sometimes bewildered by how little attention their non-native friends pay to relatives. They might point out the security and comfort that comes from having an extended family nearby — someone is always available to take care of children, lend a hand with large or small tasks, listen with understanding when things go wrong and give unfailing support that comes only from kindred.

> Ah! grandchild, really
> all
> winter
> I was poor,
> but
> my uncle treated me
> and when it got a little warmer,
> he took me back home.
>
> And just as I am now,
> even though I didn't see a doctor, I'm
>   this way. I was fine and I'm still
>   just like that. . . .
>
> So because of my grandmother

I am still alive; she didn't want to see
a child of her uncle's family suffer.

—Belle Herbert,
village of Chalkyitsik

Village life is filled with expressions of kindred. Related families often live close together within the community. Several brothers and sisters may build houses near their parents, for example. Their children form strong friendship bonds as they grow up together, learning by experience the special obligations shared by cousins and other kinsmen. Family members drop by to visit one another far more often than they visit non-relatives; brothers and sisters, grown children, cousins or other kin might come in the evening, perhaps just for a short chat, to bring some fresh-killed game or to ask a favor of some kind. Through these social relationships, solidified by emotional and economic interdependence, kinship takes its place as a dominant theme in the Athabaskan community.

*The Nomad Settlers.* Tradition runs deep in an interior Alaskan village, so deep that a casual visitor might forget how recently these communities came into existence. Among some Athabaskan groups, the elders can remember a time before there were villages at all.

Well, grandchild,
in the fall
was the only time
they stayed in one place, to make
    toboggans and snowshoes.

Then in winter
until the spring thaw, people moved around
    all the time.
All winter long until it got warm.

Ah!
grandchild,
they walked around all winter until it
    was time to camp for break-up and make canoes.
After they made the canoes, they canoed
    around until fall time.

. . . That's the way it was, but
today we live here on the point.
We just stay in one place and work for ourselves. . . .

—Belle Herbert,
village of Chalkyitsik

Before the great changes wrought by contact with whites, all Athabaskan groups were divided into small and widely scattered bands. Each band had two to five households, or from a dozen to about 75 people. If there were enough resources in one place the entire band would live together for a while; but usually smaller groups, a few families in each, dispersed into different parts of the band's territory. This territory was private in a sense, though members of another band could use it with permission, especially if food was scarce in their own area.

People like the lower Yukon Ingalik and Cook Inlet Tanaina, whose river and coastal environments were unusually rich, gathered into larger and more settled bands. As many as 200 people might live together in semipermanent communities. But for the other Athabaskans, food sources were too scattered and temporary — only by spreading out and moving freely could they be reasonably sure of making it through the tougher seasons.

When people recall the early days they nearly always speak of hardship, endurance and toughness. Before contact with whites they had no dog teams but might use one or two dogs for packing and hunting. Later on they had small teams with up to three dogs; there was too little food to support more. Not surprisingly, today's elders were great walkers, able to cover long distances with almost no food or sleep. There are tales of men walking 60 to 80 miles or more in a couple of days just to visit friends in other camps.

> I looked back down our trail in the direction of Arctic Village, and there was nothing but blue mountains. . . . All along the way it was nothing but rocks. We all wore moccasins. It hurt my feet very much, as if I were not wearing moccasins. . . . And all this time, as I said, I was packing around seven-month-old Bessie. For three months I packed her up there among the mountains.
>
> —Katherine Peter,
> village of Fort Yukon

Nomadic bands began a gradual process of settling after the first white people entered Athabaskan country. White traders set up permanent posts offering imported goods and food in exchange for furs. People from outlying areas were drawn to these posts and sometimes stayed for several months at a time. The newcomers also brought diseases for which the Indians had no immunity. Decimated by the epidemics that followed, people from different bands joined to form new groups and unite their territories. Not long afterward, Christian missions and schools were built along the rivers, and these became the most powerful anchoring forces of all. Throughout the first half of this century, Athabaskan people congregated more and more around these centers of white influence.

In the beginning, families would live in the settlements only during the warm months. When fall came, they left for distant traplines and stayed through winter, returning by boat after the river ice broke up in spring. But as time passed, the tents clustered around trading posts gave way to log cabins. More stable food supplies allowed people to keep larger dog teams, so men could leave their families for trips to the trapline while their children learned to read and write in one-room village schools.

Some interior Alaska communities existed well before the turn of the century, but others were established as late as the 1940s. In most areas, people of middle-age or older can remember living in scattered semi-nomadic family groups or bands for part of the year. Modern villages bring together members of different bands who no longer consider themselves separate but feel a strong sense of belonging to the same community. Lands surrounding the village, once divided into separate band territories, are now regarded as the special domain of all village residents. Traplines are owned privately by individuals, but this applies only to fur animals; hunted game found anywhere is available to everyone from the community.

*Stranger and Friends.* Although Alaskan villages were granted legal ownership of some nearby lands under the native claims settlement act, residents feel a strong connection to all lands surrounding their communities. Their sense of de facto ownership is based on a long tradition of use by ancestors, going back for generations beyond memory. People from a given village focus their hunting and other subsistence activities within a specific area, and vaguely defined boundaries separate this from the areas around neighboring settlements. Residents of one village usually avoid using their neighbors' territory, but this depends on how physically and socially close the settlements are.

Nevertheless, all villages in a given region or cultural area have a sense of common interest and separateness from everyone else. In recent years, many villages have felt the effects of people from urban areas hunting for major subsistence animals, especially moose and caribou. This has brought them together and led to a broader idea of territory, as groups of communities have united in efforts to limit access to their subsistence resources. The goal, of course, is to protect animal populations from overuse and keep village subsistence economies healthy.

Still, even neighboring settlements are distinct from one another, although their social distance depends on how much ancestry and tradition they share. This was also true in times past — the nomadic bands who lived closest to one another usually had many kinship links and were similar in language and culture. Differences between groups accumulated with distance, and the sense of having close ties gave way to unfamiliarity if not outright unfriendliness. In some areas there were abrupt changes from one cultural group to another, such as the boundary between Kutchin and Koyukon people. But in other areas there was no sharp change; for example, only gradual transitions of language and culture separated the groups now called Tanana, Upper Tanana and Tanacross.

In the old days, there were many occasions when people got together with neighbors — events like potlatch celebrations, trade gatherings or communal caribou hunts. Athabaskans were great travelers, and occasionally a person or small group would make a long journey to trade for exotic goods or just to visit. These goods included native copper, obsidian for stone tools, dentalium shells, seal oil and many other special items from faraway places in Alaska and Canada. Ingalik and Koyukon traders even obtained goods from Siberia through coastal Alaskan Eskimos.

> One morning they went out to work some on this beaver house. This uncle of mine happened to look down the lake and he seen two [Eskimo] guys coming towards him. . . . My grandfather recognized them right away, these two guys. Oh, they were happy to see each other. Then my grandfather invited them to their camp. Made a pot of soup, bear soup. Fed them everything. Dry fish. They talked all night and the way he tells it, they didn't sleep at all. And they'd sing for each other you know. They'd sing in their language and my

grandfather would sing for them. They never seen one another for quite a few years but that way they sort of got together again.

My grandfather and these two other guys never slept all night until about noontime. Then finally these two guys from the coast had to go. My grandfather gave them some meat, little grub, little dry fish. They'd exchange grub. Like the people from the coast would bring over seal oil and blubber. They become acquainted like that.

—Roger Dayton,
village of Koyukuk

Like all people, the Athabaskans had both good and bad relationships with their neighbors. Some groups were generally hostile to one another, others got along well and still others alternated between friendship and conflict. When strangers met somewhere out in the country, they approached one another with great caution, ever aware of the chance for sudden violence. Old stories tell of surprise raids on camps during the early morning twilight, men killed with knives or clubs, women and children taken away as captives. If they could identify the raiders, leaders or councils would organize for revenge, and in this way the hostilities carried on — a grievance satisfied led to a grievance in return.

Northern groups of the Kutchin, for example, had both peaceful and unfriendly encounters with Eskimos from the Arctic Coast. Although the hostilities ended at least a century ago, stories are still handed down on both sides:

While it was pitch dark [one] morning, they fell upon our people with shouts. The dogs were howling, the men, women, and children were screaming and crying, and the noise was fearful. While our people were asleep, the [Eskimos] did this, and though we defended ourselves with all our might, they soon slaughtered our people. They even killed off the dogs. When they were about to fall upon our people, one old man crawled under the snow, and he alone was not killed. He had only one child and someone killed him too. Now truly, he was in anguish. . . .

All summer, while there was a lot of game, he made long splinters of bones of all kinds. . . . When the ground froze in fall, around where he thought [the Eskimos] might be, he unhurriedly built a small sod house for himself. All around the house he stuck the splinters of bone in the ground. . . . As it was snowing a little in the fall, he suddenly heard some noise. As usual, in the morning, as it is said, he knew they would attack him. He felt a little fear, but not much, as he curled comfortably under his fur blanket. After it dawned . . . he slowly pushed aside the tent flap and slowly went outside. The [enemies] lay scattered all around there; he took in the sight. With his arrows he shot in the hearts of all those who had not already died, taking his time at it. "You are the very ones who killed my son." Indeed, not a single Eskimo left there alive. The old man set off walking back to his country.

—John Fredson, Kutchin

Relations between people from different Alaskan communities and cultures are friendly today, and villagers might even prefer not to tell these old stories of warfare. A strong feeling of unity has developed among Alaskan native people as they face new challenges together and recognize their cultural similarities against the larger backdrop of Western influences.

Easier travel and communication often brings people from neighboring and distant villages together these days. For example, there are social and ceremonial gatherings in every region each year — potlatches, dog team races, elders conferences, corporation meetings, funerals and weddings are among the most important. There are also special occasions such as the Stick Dance or *Heeyo,* a Koyukon feast for the dead held at Nulato, which attracts people from communities all over the Interior. Gatherings like these strengthen the old ties between villagers and create new ones, linking the Athabaskans into a network of communities that is closer today than ever in the past.

*Ones Who Walk Ahead.* Life in rural Alaska has grown increasingly complex in recent years, as the villages do more and more business with the outside world. People face many important decisions about various native corporation issues, government programs, land use questions, school policies and community projects or enterprises. Equally important are the daily affairs of organizing and maintaining a relatively isolated, inaccessible small community. All of this would be difficult enough under the most ordinary circumstances, and for people whose lives have changed so dramatically during the past century, the challenges are daunting.

The most important institution for managing an Athabaskan village today is the council, whose members are chosen by regular elections. Certain interior people like the Kutchin, Han and Tanaina already had councils back in the nomadic days, and this kind of organization spread to other groups as the early settlements developed. Then, in 1934, the Indian Reorganization Act (IRA) was passed, with special provisions applying to Alaskan Natives. The act established formal means of organizing village governments with their own constitutions, bylaws and charters of incorporation. Some modern villages govern themselves under provisions of the IRA, others have incorporated as municipalities and a few have reservation status. In all cases the community has an elected council with a presiding officer called the mayor, chief or council president.

Village councils are the main governing bodies in Athabaskan communities, but there are other kinds of local leadership too. These include members of the school board, directors of the village corporation, church officials and individuals such as the health aide or lay minister. People chosen for these positions today are often young adults with high school diplomas, and sometimes college backgrounds as well. Their familiarity with the outside world is an important asset for dealing with distant bureaucracies and handling the blizzard of paperwork that comes from them.

But serving along with educated younger leaders are older persons whose experience and wisdom bring an important balance to village decision making. Some of these elders are members of the formal councils and committees; others lead in more traditional ways by giving advice when asked or by speaking at town gatherings. An outsider might completely overlook the power and influence of these older people because they do not always hold some kind of title or position. But the words of village elders are weighty indeed, and younger people in the elected offices listen for their guidance.

In former times, young people had fewer chances to lead because the ways of achieving power were different. Each clan or band had one or more leader, who took the initiative in making decisions for the group. Usually the leader was a man known for his success as a provider, who shared food and other resources generously and who reliably made correct decisions. He might also be a shaman, a medicine man, who could help or harm people through his manipulations of supernatural power. Women apparently had little visible leadership in the traditional bands but they almost certainly had considerable influence on group decisions. Today women are often chosen or elected for important village positions.

Some traditional chiefs became quite powerful, even to the point where people feared them. A chief who was also a shaman was someone to be especially reckoned with, since he was aided by his spiritual powers. But usually the chief was known for his willingness to help others, an important quality where survival itself could rest on generosity in difficult times. Among some groups like the Ahtna, chiefs attained their status by accumulating food and wealth, then giving it away at large potlatch gatherings. Although the man became poor, at least temporarily, he became powerful in exchange.

A chief might look and act much like everyone else, but on certain occasions his leadership was clearly visible:

> Old Chief Healy, I heard story. He was living yet in the country when I was growing up. When his family eats, he does not eat. He eats all by himself. . . . his wife cooks for him, special way. Poor looking clothes, hard working. He goes out hunting, moose, everything. All hard works. He hunts fish, ducks, all kinds; he kills rabbits, cut spruce tree, puts them in cache. When poor people, he gives away to them. . . . Only certain day, one day, he dresses good; maybe, once a year. Puts on all rich clothes, walks around. . . . That's the only time he would dress. Also when potlatch, three days . . . walks around, does nothing, visits friends.
>
> —Anonymous,
> village of Tanacross

*Spirits of the Two Worlds.* Leaders and political organizations attend to certain needs in the Athabaskan community, but other equally important needs are served in different ways. Village churches are active in varying degrees; some have full-time clergy and others are maintained by itinerant pastors or lay persons from the community. The major denominations include Episcopalian throughout much of the central and eastern Interior, Catholic along the lower Yukon Valley and Russian Orthodox in the Cook Inlet region.

Church services and activities vary from one community or region to another. Often the church is a fairly plain but beautifully made log building, warmed by a stove set amid handmade wooden pews. The altar may be draped with a bleached moosehide, exquisitely decorated in beadwork designs by women of the congregation. The Sunday service includes brief readings, lessons and

*Many Athabaskan villages grew up around Christian missions, trading posts and government schools. This Episcopal church was the focal point for Kutchin people who settled here at Arctic Village. The church was built early in this century under direction of Albert Tritt, a Native minister and leader of the Chandalar people. (Courtesy of Richard Nelson)*

prayers led by someone from the community. Favorite songs are accompanied by a piano or guitar. A visitor will find that the service is much like those held elsewhere, though it has an elegant simplicity and might include special things like a prayer of thanks for success in hunting and fishing, talk of some problems facing the village or a request for help on behalf of a troubled congregation member.

> Every Sunday people used to go up to Nulato to go to Mass and they all go up in poling boat. Some of them walk up, too. Everyone. Old people and all because they like to hear Father Jetté talk in Indian. Preach to them. He used to be a really good preacher in Indian. . . .
>
> In church first they're all singing and praying. In the middle of the Mass he preaches and after that he gives out communion. Then everybody sings again and pray and the last blessing of the Mass. Everybody goes out.
>
> After church everybody goes around and visits. They believed in not working on Sundays. Father told them not to work on Sundays and it was just like holiday for them. . . .
>
> —Madeline Solomon,
> village of Nulato

Father Julius Jetté, a Jesuit priest, worked among the Koyukon people for almost 30 years and made extensive studies of their traditions. His writings are unparalleled in all of Alaskan ethnography, and some of his works are only now being published from handwritten manuscripts he left behind half-a-century ago. Other clergymen who spent long periods among Athabaskan people also made important records of their cultures.

Despite the interest and understanding that some missionaries showed toward native lifeways, most of them worked strenuously against traditional religious practices. They were especially opposed to shamanism and, not surprisingly, the shamans also resisted Christian teachings. In many areas the open practice of shamanism disappeared so long ago that only the elders have seen it. But in others, aging shamans continued to practice healing and other powers until their deaths in recent years. Many adults now living in interior villages tell of being cured themselves by medicine people, and some still follow special restrictions set as a condition of the healing. The shamans' knowledge and skills died with them, although people who listened or watched carefully can describe their activities in detail.

Shamans did not have power of their own — they knew how to invoke and manipulate the spirits of animals, plants or other parts of the natural world. For example, there are stories of a Kutchin shaman who used the spirit of the bumblebee as his helper; and a Koyukon shaman who died in the 1950s called for spirits of the frog, birch tree, raven, northern lights and others when he made medicine. Shamans could exert power even from long distances, to bring in game, cause harm to their enemies or help others to escape dangers and illness.

> About fourth summer I work in Hog River I get sick. I don't know how. It's just from the ground I guess. . . . I got sweat and fever. I thought maybe tomorrow I go to hospital. Now I couldn't do it. Got to sleep.
>
> I go to sleep and dream. Fred say while I sleep crow [raven] come. Crow sit on post in front of house all day, just say *"Kuk, kuk, kuk, kuk."* Crow just stay there. Don't leave. My father used to know crow. Some medicine man know crow. That's his helper. When I dream it's about my father. Maybe he's helping me.
>
> That night, I woke up. I wasn't sweat, nothing. Gee, I woke up good! I eat and went back to work. . . .
>
> —Edwin Simon,
> village of Huslia

Although Athabaskans in some areas still follow many beliefs related to natural spirits, they have almost completely adopted modern medicine for protecting their health. A few old herbal medicines are still used today. For example, people smear softened spruce pitch on wounds as an antiseptic and drink certain kinds of herbal tea for various ailments. But villagers usually turn to their trained health aide and community clinic when they have problems with sickness or injury.

The clinic is generally quite small but has a good supply of medications and basic medical equipment. It is run by a local person who is given fairly extensive training by the U.S. Indian Health Service. The health aide also has a telephone or radio for immediate contact with physicians at a hospital such as the one in Fairbanks. In case of emergency, patients are taken by chartered plane to the nearest hospital.

Despite the many changes in their religious beliefs and health practices, many Athabaskan villagers still maintain traditional ideas about how the world is ordered. Western medicine might cure someone's sickness, but it does not explain why sickness struck that person. Perhaps, then, it is because a traditional belief was violated — someone brought a fresh wolverine hide too near a child, spoke disrespectful words about a spiritually powerful animal or mistreated a young animal that was brought home for a pet. Athabaskan people have always willingly adopted new ideas that serve them well, but they also recognize that older ones may have a place in the modern community. This blending of traditions lies at the essence of interior village life today.

## "Only My Mind Does Work Now"

Grandchild, even though they were out
   there traveling around, the babies
   would be born.
Sometimes even when she was in labor
   he would be riding on the toboggan,
   so they say.
That didn't happen during my lifetime.
Then
while they were moving around
she would have the baby but
she would stay alone behind the rest for one day.
Meanwhile, the others would leave.
That's just what they did.
For only one day, then
she put the little infant
like that inside her fur parka
and the baby
stayed inside her clothing.
She would even have a sled of her own and pull
   it herself.

Ah, grandchild,
those people were really hardy that lived
   at that time.

—Belle Herbert,
village of Chalkyitsik

Although many decades have passed since Athabaskan children were born along the trail this way, a number of people living today were born in outlying camps or in village homes. In recent years, women ready for childbirth have usually taken the regularly scheduled mail plane to the nearest city with an Indian Health Service hospital. This greatly reduces the risk to both mother and child, and since hospitalization has become routine the infant mortality rate has declined throughout rural Alaska.

But each village has its own traditional midwives and health aide should a woman — by choice or necessity — give birth at home. Indeed, some of the elder women are critical of hospitals, because they say childbirth is much easier when the mother kneels or squats. And they prefer the warm, supportive atmosphere of midwives clustered near the woman in labor. One village midwife who is still active today estimates that she has delivered more than 100 babies.

In traditional times, both father and mother were bound by many special restrictions before and after their child was born. They avoided eating certain animals, for example, because doing so would have made the birth difficult or affected the child in some way. Among the Ingalik, the father avoided work for 20 days following his child's birth, and ate no fresh meat or fish during that time.

*Little Faces.* Athabaskan people welcome children as a great blessing and surround them with a large, supportive family group. As Madeline Solomon of Koyukuk village put it, "You know a house just don't seem right with no young people in it to make noise." From an early age, children are encouraged to watch their elders at work and to learn by imitation. There are always jobs to do at home or in camp, such as carrying firewood, helping to prepare meals and running endless errands.

As they grow older, the kids can begin more serious work checking fishnets and cutting fish for the drying racks in summer camps. At the same time, they learn customs such as the right way to behave toward certain kinds of relatives, and in some communities they are still taught to follow taboos. Children and adolescents can suffer from the contagious influences of certain plants and animals. For example, Koyukon children are told not to eat meat from heavy-bodied birds like loons or grebes lest they become clumsy and slow themselves. In the past, Ingalik children learned to drink as little water as possible so they would not perspire too much later in life.

> Soon as we were about ten years old we start to go with our folks, hunt, trap. Four or five men go hunt and haul us kids in canoe. And in evening when people talk they tell story. They tell how to live. How the animal act. That way we learn. . . . They wouldn't let us say a word. We have to listen. . . . That's our education, how to live in the woods. How to take care of myself.
>
> I teach my boy Franklin like that. When he was six years old take him to trapline. Let him play around. Set trap. When he was twelve years old I make a little sleigh for him. I give him two dogs. His mother give him teapot. We say, "You go down that way. You're going to trap. . . . You make fire and put spruce bough down the way I do. Don't let your moccasin get wet." He caught twelve mink and seven beaver that winter.
>
> —Edwin Simon,
> village of Huslia

Today's village children spend as much time in school as children in Anchorage or Fairbanks. This gives them less chance to learn traditional knowledge from their elders and has created some difficulty for the younger generations, who are torn between old and new ways. Until recently, the schools' educational programs were specifically intended to bring native children into mainstream

American culture. But now school officials are trying to incorporate elements of Athabaskan culture into the curriculum; new texts are being developed specifically for village children, community elders are given chances to work with the students, and native languages are taught by bilingual instructors.

The Yukon-Koyukuk School District, for example, has developed a series of biographies about notable villagers from the region, written in their own words. Many quotations that appear in this chapter are from that series, and from other first-person narratives published by the Alaska Native Language Center in Fairbanks and the National Bilingual Materials Development Center in Anchorage. These written sources give Athabaskan children new ways of learning about their heritage in this time of rapid change.

In traditional Athabaskan cultures, puberty was considered the most important life transition, especially for girls. When a girl first began menstruating she was secluded — sometimes for as long as a year — and had to follow many strict taboos. These would prevent the spiritual power of her menses from alienating the game, would assure the health of her future children and would help her to become skilled in women's tasks. Some villagers still follow certain of these puberty restrictions, and adult women may also observe special taboos each month.

A boy's puberty is less important, but he is also expected to begin serious learning and hard work at this age. Once again, there is a conflict between school work and activities like trapping or hunting. Nowadays many young Athabaskan men are unable to learn traditional skills and become active providers until they have finished high school. Other things have changed too, such as learning language. Village parents may speak Athabaskan among themselves but they usually speak English to their children. Because of this, most Athabaskan languages are now spoken only by adults and elders.

Athabaskan languages are difficult for English speakers to learn because of their unfamiliar grammatical structure and sound system. The number of meaningful sounds in these languages is large, averaging 40 consonants and 7 vowels (English has 24 consonants and 9 vowels), and English speakers find some of them extremely hard to pronounce. They also have large specialized vocabularies relating to subjects of particular importance to their life, such as the environment. For example, Athabaskan languages have many words for landscape features, types of ice and snow, and animal anatomy. The 11 Athabaskan languages in Alaska differ in varying degrees; some are as similar as widely separated dialects of English and others are as distinct as English and Norwegian.

Unless there is a drastic change from present trends, Athabaskan languages may vanish during the next century. Some of the languages, like Han and Holikachuk, have only a few dozen speakers today. Kutchin and Koyukon have the largest number of speakers, about 700 each. Apparently, language is one of the most fragile aspects of native Alaskan culture. More and more, adults are speaking only English to their children, feeling they must know it to get along in the modern world yet regretting the loss of their own language.

> This generation now is changing. Just like water in [an] eddy. They
> just go around like that. It's too much changing too fast. . . .
> Maybe after while the next generation will know what to do. I

think they'll make it. There's lot of young people that want to learn our culture. They don't know how to start. But they'll help each other out. Nobody's going to make white people out of us. We're Athabaskans. Nothing can change nationality.

—Edwin Simon,
village of Huslia

*Women and Men.* In the old days, adulthood quickly followed adolescence. Boys were expected to begin taking full responsibility for supporting themselves and others at an age when today they are in high school. Girls could expect marriage soon after their puberty seclusion ended, and the choice of a husband was typically out of their hands. A girl's parents usually negotiated her marriage with a boy's family, or directly with a man if he was older, and she might have little to say about it. There were exceptions among certain groups, and sometimes strong-willed individuals could defy tradition or skillfully manipulate people to get the mates of their own choice.

Belle Herbert of Chalkyitsik, who was well over 100 when she died in 1982, told of her own arranged marriage. Just after she reached puberty her grandfather came and told her "We have a man for you; don't think anything about it." Recalling the experience in her old age, she said, "Ah! it was just like somebody hit me across the face." She had never seen the man in her life, but sometime later he visited the camp and spoke to her:

"They say I'm going to get married to you;
    when do you think we'll do it?" he said to me.
"My mother is very poor and if somebody
    takes care of her for me,
if somebody takes good care of her it will
    be good for me," I said.
So then I didn't say anything more,
but it was about time for us to get married.

Grandchild, really
I didn't like it, but they kept asking me,
    so finally I did it.

—Belle Herbert,
village of Chalkyitsik

A new husband was expected to work for his wife's family for a year or two, proving his ability as a provider. Afterward the couple could choose to live where they wanted to. This custom (called matrilocal residence) is often followed today, so if the man is from another community he generally moves to his wife's village. As elsewhere in American society, many village couples live together before marriage; no stigma whatsoever is attached to a child born during this time.

Today, as in the past, tasks of living are fairly well divided between men and women. A man usually hunts, traps, helps with jobs related to fishing and fish camp, makes and repairs equipment like sleds or boats, builds the house and outbuildings, cuts and hauls firewood and works at seasonal jobs. A woman focuses her work more around home and camp; she cooks and does other household jobs, tends the children, takes main responsibility for fishing activities

*Men and women have distinct roles in Athabaskan society, but many tasks are shared or performed by either sex. Women are often prominent in village life today and are regarded as important tradition bearers alongside the men. Here Steve and Emma Northway of Tok stretch moosehide over a drum frame. (Courtesy of Richard Nelson)*

and hunts or snares small game near the village. But an Athabaskan woman might also hunt larger animals, trap, cut wood and do other jobs either with her husband or on her own. The division of labor is not a strict one by any means, especially today when women are less inhibited by taboos.

Even in the days of arranged marriages, many couples got along well and developed a strong bond. Life was hard and the cooperative relationship between a man and a woman was an essential part of survival. Although a husband and wife rarely show affection openly, they will sometimes talk warmly about each other and describe the happiness they have known together.

> We trapped together, Lorraine and me. We both worked together
> every way and agreed with everything we've done, so that way along
> on life, it was very easy for us.
>
> —John Honea,
> village of Ruby

The Athabaskan tradition teaches certain ideal goals of character and personality that adults should strive toward. Some of these ideals help to create harmony in social life, encourage productivity and maintain a good relationship with nature. Others are simply a part of the Athabaskan character and perhaps cannot be explained in practical terms.

The closeness of a small village or band can easily lead to conflicts between people, especially since they have almost daily interaction throughout their entire lives. Living among Athabaskans, an outsider may notice personality traits that help to reduce the chances of open conflict. For example, people carefully avoid telling anyone what to do, respecting each other's privacy and independence. Many writers have commented on the Athabaskan people's strong individualism, their willingness to let a person do things his or her own way. For example, a man is likely to follow certain traditional taboos and ignore others, according to his own belief and preference. Speaking of someone else's beliefs or ideas about doing things, a villager might say, "That's just his way." People are not much inclined to judge others — as long as they cause no one harm or discomfort — and the resulting freedom helps to keep peace in the community.

> One time when I was young, one guy from this village broke his sleigh. Every time I start to drive dogs I tell that story over and over. Then that same thing happen to me. That's why our stories always tell us not to laugh at different person if something happen to them. Don't talk about it.
>
> —Moses Henzie,
> village of Allakaket

Perhaps because they were so often isolated in the past, people living in the villages today seem to take great pleasure in socializing. Visits are a constant part of daily life, and social occasions like potlatches, dances and meetings are well attended. Incidentally, some villagers complain that since the advent of television, visiting among neighbors and relatives has declined. Although many kinds of hunting and trapping are done alone, people enjoy going out together or meeting at some prearranged place to camp. Henry Beatus of Hughes expressed this feeling:

> I like to hunt with one or two guys. That's when I enjoy my hunting best. You can walk and when you stop you got somebody to talk with. When I go with just myself I'm always moving. I got nobody to talk with. . . . I enjoy hunting with people. . . . And if we catch something we share.

According to Athabaskan tradition, life depends on maintaining a harmonious relationship with nature as well as people. For example, bragging of any kind should be avoided, especially when animals are involved. If a man kills a moose or bear, or if he catches a lot of fur, he should keep quiet about it. He might even belittle his success, and in this way he humbles himself to the greater powers of nature. Humility is the key to living successfully.

> A person never make fun of an animal. Animals remember and it can backfire someday. If animals get a chance to harm the person it can really backfire. [My father] said to just hunt the animal like you got nothing against animals.
>
> —Henry Beatus,
> village of Hughes

Other important qualities that help people to live successfully in the northern wildlands include toughness, perseverance and willingness to work. Traditionally, Athabaskan children were taught from an early age to work long and hard. Elders remember their parents rousing them from bed in the predawn darkness and sending them out into subzero cold to begin a full day's work. Among many groups, children were toughened by a morning jump into freezing water or a naked roll in the snow. They were also taught to speak softly so they would not frighten game away, and this soft-spoken demeanor carried over into adulthood.

Like all people, the Athabaskans have a personality and character of their own. A perceptive outsider will begin noticing aspects of this character fairly quickly, just as the villager will observe things in return. (The late Edwin Simon of Huslia once wryly told me that he understood my interest because he had been studying white people all his life.) As in all other aspects of their cultures, however, different Athabaskan groups have their own distinct collective personalities. Within each group, individuals express this personality differently or deviate from it in varying degrees.

*The Old Voices.* The outsider visiting an Athabaskan community is likely to notice that as people grow older they achieve a special kind of status and recognition. In most areas of the Interior, elders are very much a part of village life, and they are respected for their depth of knowledge and experience. Athabaskan traditions have always been recorded in people's minds, not written down, and elders are the ones who know the most. For this practical reason alone they are valued by the community, especially in these times when many older ways can be learned only through memories of the aged.

Couples beyond childbearing age often adopt children or raise grandchildren, and this also keeps them closely involved with village social life. Adopted children help to care for them in return. Other family members also tend to the elders' daily needs, bringing meat to their homes, supplying their firewood and doing errands for them. The amount of attention given to old people varies among different groups, but in some areas the wisest elders are practically revered. The late Chief Henry of Huslia was such a man, greatly respected for his experience and knowledge. At times, though, even he saw a certain pathos in old age:

> Now I just lie down
> even though out by the door
> the firewood is running out.
>
> Only my mind
> does work now.
>
> What a tough situation to get into.
> I didn't know I was going to become like the old people
>     I used to listen to when they said "I am this way now."
>     I thought, what are they talking about?

> —Chief Henry,
> village of Huslia

Nevertheless, there are certain advantages to growing older in an Athabaskan village. Women beyond menopause, for example, are freed from the female taboos and restrictions that bound them during all their previous life. They no longer carry the spiritual potency of the menses and there is no further need to avoid things that could affect game, hunters or future children. Men are also unburdened when they no longer hunt and trap, because they need not protect their luck by following male taboos. In fact, they can pass some of their luck to younger men just by willing it or giving it along with their knowledge when they teach things like trapping methods.

Athabaskans tend to see luck as a vital part of all success — a powerful and almost tangible thing that a person keeps largely by showing proper respect toward nature. An elder who has lived long and well obviously possesses luck and can bequeath some of it to others. Among certain groups, such as the Upper Tanana, old people are also considered a bit shamanistic and may be feared, especially for the power to take someone with them when they die.

But above all else, the older villagers are seen as a source of learning for everyone. People who visit them are often treated to a rich feast of stories — tales of their personal experiences, remembrances about the group's history or perhaps traditional stories that explain how the earth and all living things began. These explanatory stories are often called folklore or myths, but many Athabaskans interpret them literally, just as orthodox Christians accept and follow the teachings of Biblical stories. They contain a way of viewing and behaving toward the world, a code of morality and belief that has guided Athabaskan people since ancient time.

Hundreds of traditional stories are known among interior people, some widely shared and others unique to particular groups. Most of them describe a time when animals and humans lived together and often changed form, as in the world of dreams. For example, an Upper Kuskokwim story tells of a girl who went to live with the salmon, then returned to her people and taught them what she had learned:

> It became fall, winter, and it got to be summer again. Time for the fish to go back to the stream. She kept swimming with the fish. Finally, the fish had a meeting to see which way they would go. And at the meeting the fish talked about how the people along the stream treated them. Some said they were treated badly. The people did not take care of them when they caught them, like they did not even clean the poles where they dried their fish. These were the things they did not like. But there were other fish that said there were some villages to which they go that treat them really good like cleaning the poles from last year's catch. . . .
>
> The meeting kept going on among the fish. Some agree that they will go to all the villages but some say they will only go where they are treated good. . . . "I will go with you back up the stream," [the girl] told the other fish. "Back to where my home used to be, and to my parents." [When they arrived] she became herself again, and walked back up the bank. . . .

—Miska Deaphon,
village of Nikolai

The elders' teachings are a vital way for modern villagers to keep in close touch with their cultural traditions. In recent years, younger Athabaskans have become more concerned with maintaining these traditions; at the same time many elders have spoken out strongly about the importance of people learning their own heritage. When native groups hold meetings or conferences, speakers seldom fail to acknowledge the respect they owe to the old and wise ones. And when the elders themselves rise to speak, the applause that follows reflects not only what they have said but what they represent in this changing and often ambiguous world.

*The Trail Upriver.* In Athabaskan cultures, death is an event of great social and spiritual consequence for the whole community. If someone dies young, people see it as a profound tragedy, far beyond the death of one who has led a long, full life. Sometimes there are signs of an impending death — an owl may speak ominous words in the night; a dog may woof nervously, revealing that someone's spirit has begun to wander; or there may be a strange event such as a bat entering someone's house. If a person is dying, mothers may tie protective amulets to their children to prevent the lurking spirit from taking them along. Nevertheless, people may gather at a house where death is approaching, to give support to the family that will soon grieve.

After a person dies, people come in from nearby communities for the funeral and potlatch ceremonies. Among most interior villagers, there is a Christian funeral followed by a large communal feast. Some Athabaskans believe that they feed not only themselves but also the departed person's spirit; this placates the spirit and encourages it to leave harmlessly. Koyukon people may burn some favorite foods for the deceased while they ask the spirit to harm no one and bring good luck to those left behind.

Today each village has a graveyard, usually located well away from the community. In some areas, each grave is covered by a little house with a few personal items, flowers or bits of food inside; or there may only be a picket fence, perhaps also a tall flagpole and a carved wood marker. Traditionally, some Athabaskan people cremated their dead or placed them on elevated platforms, and belongings of the deceased were sometimes left with the body. When an Ingalik person was dying, he might say whether he wanted his property burned, buried or given away among those who remained alive.

The potlatch held just after someone's death is fairly small, but within a year or so a much larger one is held. Relatives of the deceased — and fellow clan members in some areas — accumulate large amounts of food and goods in preparation. When the time comes, people converge from the surrounding villages and everyone joins for several days of feasts, songs and dances, speeches, small ceremonies and socializing. An important part of most memorial potlatches is the gift distribution, which can include everything from ash trays and blankets to wolverine hides and handmade parkas.

In part, these gifts are to repay people and clan members who helped with the funeral, but they are also a way of gaining status. Those who make lavish presents in the potlatch can achieve higher social position for themselves and their relatives or fellow clan members. In the old days, potlatches were important ways for chiefs to gain power and rank among the bands. They might be destitute afterward; but hard work, along with return gifts from future potlatches, could eventually make up the losses. A Tanacross man explained in modern terms: "Potlatch is just like bank. When you give away, them people they got to give you back next time. What I put down, they got to remember."

The spirits of the dead remain, in a sense, part of the community that has sustained them during life. Some interior villagers occasionally burn food for the spirits, which may hover invisibly near the grave or even wander for a time among houses in the community. They are asked, once again, to bring luck for the living and to cause no danger. As time passes, however, something spiritual from the dead may also leave the company of people and go to distant parts of the land. Some people from Tanacross and Upper Tanana groups believe that spirits of the dead live in prominent mountains. Koyukon people say that the spirits go somewhere upriver or downriver; those who have lived badly struggle along a difficult trail, but those who have lived well follow the easy trail. All of the dead will finally reach the same good place, nonetheless.

I know that my time is near, though I cannot tell exactly when
it will come. But I have had a good life. I have camped many times
beneath spruce trees, roasting grouse over my campfire. So there
is no reason to pray that I might live on much longer.

—paraphrased from Chief
Henry, village of Huslia


## The Trapline and the Pipeline

Whatever they have to learn in school you just let them go the way
they're learning. Of course you'd tell your kids to learn as much
as they can in school. Then when you take them out [hunting or
trapping] you just teach them what your father taught you when you
were a kid. Show them the same thing. There's not much difference
between going to school and learning this outdoor life. It's pretty
much the same. They learn to make a living.

—Roger Dayton,
village of Koyukuk

Reading about a modern Athabaskan village is probably a little confusing — every aspect of life seems to be a different combination of traditional and modern elements. This is because people do not simply change from one culture to another; they gradually combine aspects of both in varying and unpredictable proportions. What results is a unique and dynamic culture that differs from both of its origins.

But the mixture of old and new is actually far more complicated than it might appear in a general discussion like this one. Some Athabaskan groups are relatively conservative or have been isolated from strong white influences. Others, for one reason or another, have changed much more rapidly. There are also important differences in the amount and pattern of change even among the villages of a given region. And within any village some families are oriented toward traditional ways and others favor newer ways of doing things. In fact, differences like these go clear down to the individual level.

The new village is not a simple thing to characterize, except that it is a bewildering mix of the contemporary and the customary. A casual visitor walking among village houses might wonder at this comment. Things visible on the surface may appear somewhat different or quaint, but they are also surprisingly modern. The visitor's eye is immediately caught by the imported things that are prominent in many village homes — like snow machines, electric lights, thermopane windows, store-bought clothing, propane cookstoves and even television sets. The material evidence of change can be seen easily and everywhere; but continuity and tradition are largely out of the newcomer's sight.

Aside from furs hung outside to cure and caches laden with drying meat or fish, a walk through the village reveals little of the ongoing Athabaskan heritage. This can only emerge slowly, as a visitor travels with villagers to their fishing camps, traplines and hunting areas — places where people and land are closely intertwined. And it comes forth in the way Athabaskans understand the world around them, organize their social and family lives, train their children, observe ceremonial occasions and act according to their innermost values. Material goods and technology are not the full measure of a lifeway, nor do they reveal more than a shadow of the way people think.

But Athabaskan life is certainly taking many important new directions and experiencing profound changes. Anyone who wants to understand the modern village must give careful consideration to recent major developments. There is only space to briefly discuss a few important topics here — such as economy and politics — but we can at least take a small step into the vast subject of change in native Alaska.

*The New Cache.* Since the days of early traders, interior villagers have had ready access to an ever-widening selection of "white man stuff." Furs were the main source of cash until the 1930s or 1940s, and the trappers used them to purchase many kinds of imported food and other goods from local traders. Village elders love to talk about those early days...the times when calico material sold for 25 cents a yard, 50-pound sacks of flour were only $5 and some old-timers still refused to eat sugar.

> He make big open cache for stuff. . . . That's where his store is. A few people from Cutoff would go with dogs and buy stuff.
>
> When somebody come to store we always watch. My sister and brother were by the cache. I was standing by the door. Mamma was up there in the cache so she sell everything. Towels, everything.
>
> Pretty soon Little Sammy take out a box. Cold. About thirty below in daytime. Sun is up. He say in Indian, "Gee, my kids would like this." It's mouth organ. Metal. He put it in his mouth and it stuck from cold! It stuck both side of his lips. Froze on his mouth. He say, *"Haa! Sodaa', gonaaa'."* He say, "Ahh, Sister help me!" So my mamma tell him, "Leave it in your mouth for a while so it get warm." Then, easy she tear it off his mouth.
>
> —Edwin Simon,
> village of Huslia

Those days of unaffected simplicity are gone now. Most villages operate their own stores, often established with money provided through the Alaska Native Claims Settlement Act. Under this legislation, each community was granted funds for the establishment of a village corporation which could undertake any kind of business it wished. Of course, some villages already had their own private or cooperative stores. In these communities, corporate enterprises have ranged from fuel and hardware sales to small-scale hotels and even bush flying services.

One group of interior villages from the Koyukuk region has merged to form a single corporation called K'oyitl'otsina, Limited. Guided by a board of directors and a general manager — all of them from villages — the corporation has progressed well by specializing in investments and operating small retail businesses in the communities. Like many village corporations, K'oyitl'otsina directly benefits its shareholders by providing them with jobs and general stores in their own rural settlements.

The village corporations also manage surrounding acreage deeded to the community under the land claims act. Development on village lands has been minimal, partly because people rank subsistence uses as their highest priority. Some communities have bought small mills and cut limited amounts of timber from their land to make lumber for local use. Interest in small-scale agriculture has grown during recent years, stimulated mainly by government agencies and the University of Alaska; but so far there has been little commercial development.

Although cash-oriented agriculture has not taken hold in rural areas, programs to encourage family-level subsistence gardening have been a great success. Many cultivated plants grow extremely well in the warm, sunny Interior, and garden patches with everything from turnips to tomatoes are now a common sight alongside village cabins.

Local part-time jobs, cutting timber for village homes and buildings, and subsistence gardening exemplify the ways that Athabaskan communities are integrating their traditional life pattern with the cash economy. Rural people are searching for ways to maintain their subsistence economic base while adding local sources of cash income. At the same time, younger Athabaskans are putting their education to work in village schools, businesses and government-funded service jobs. Aside from this employment, they also feel a growing commitment to acquiring traditional skills and knowledge — not just to learn heritage but to support themselves in a dual economy.

> You have to know lots of things in order to live in a village like this. If you don't know how to hunt. If you don't know how to trap. If you don't know how to make a sleigh or snowshoes or sew or tan skins, fish, what? You can't buy everything. . . . If you're going to live in Fairbanks, okay. Lots try it out there, but very few stay. Our young people come back here. It's for their future they learn how to survive.
>
> —Edwin Simon,
> village of Huslia

The village people are also trying to fit their own way of doing things into the conduct of business, including corporate affairs. For example, annual shareholder meetings of the K'oyitl'otsina corporation are held in member villages, with communal feasts and social activities similar to traditional potlatches. The old ideals of sharing and equality that pervade village life also influence approaches to running a business; an enterprise should be for the benefit of all, not just profit for a few. Specific issues like work schedules may be decided with consideration for other priorities such as hunting seasons. And perhaps most important, some village corporations have taken strong positions

*John Luke and John Sam look on as the Yukon River tug* Tanana *unloads at Beaver. Many villages in the Interior depend on barges to supply bulk freight and fuel, but today a large portion of goods arrives by airplane. (Courtesy of Richard Nelson)*

on balancing development or change against the need to maintain a healthy environment and sustain traditional values.

*The Village and the City.* Interior Alaska's villages are grouped into a series of clusters or areas. Each of these includes about three to seven communities — often members of the same or closely related cultural groups — with a single larger community as its hub. For example, Fort Yukon is the center of supply, transportation and government services for the Kutchin villages of Beaver, Birch Creek, Chalkyitsik, Arctic Village and Venetie. People from all of these communities travel to Fort Yukon to find employment, attend regional meetings, receive health care, visit large stores and join social gatherings.

Places like Fort Yukon are also converging points for transportation, because airplanes from Fairbanks stop there to connect with bush flights to outlying communities. All villages from the northern and central Interior depend on Fairbanks for services unavailable in the smaller regional centers. Communities in the southern Interior are linked in the same way to Anchorage. Both cities have major hospitals, the full assortment of government agencies, headquarters for native organizations and retail stores of every kind. Fairbanks is probably the most important center for Alaska's Athabaskan people, because it is close to the largest number of villages and shares a similar overall environment.

It is hard to find an interior villager nowadays who has not visited Fairbanks, and most have also been to Anchorage at least once. In these cities, rural Athabaskans learn what urban life is like. Some village people also have a chance to visit the larger cities of the Lower 48. On her first trip to Seattle, Madeline Solomon of Koyukuk remarked:

> When I look down [from the Space Needle] all I see is just confused like scrap heap. And you know, at home we have lot of mosquitoes summertime but at least they have space to fly between one another. Here it's like there are more people than our mosquitoes!

Some village people enjoy a short visit to the city now and then, others would rather stay at home and still others choose to live in the city . . . at least for a while. Increasingly today, young villagers are deciding to attend the University of Alaska after high school graduation. The university has special programs designed to help rural students adjust to the new environment, and their success rate in college is improving. A native studies program at the Fairbanks campus allows students to do course work on native affairs and cultures, but emphasizes the need to major in a practical field such as business administration or elementary education. A large and rapidly growing number of young Athabaskan leaders have followed the trail between their village and Alaska's college campuses.

Many other organizations located in the cities are significant to rural Alaskans. One of the most important is the Tanana Chiefs Council, headquartered in Fairbanks. The council had its informal beginnings in 1915, when traditional leaders from the central Interior gathered at Tanana village to discuss common concerns such as reservation status (which most interior people rejected). It was formally reestablished in 1961 and eventually became a nonprofit arm of the Doyon regional corporation. Today, the Tanana Chiefs Council provides many services for Athabaskan communities, including political advocacy on land use issues, liaison with government agencies and assistance with health care.

Under terms of the 1971 Alaska Native Claims Settlement Act (ANCSA), 13 regional corporations were established in addition to the smaller village corporations. The largest of these — in fact, the largest private landowner in Alaska — is Doyon, Limited, which represents Athabaskan communities throughout most of the Interior. Doyon (from the Koyukon word meaning "rich man") controls about 8.5 million acres of land. Representing other Athabaskan villages are Ahtna Corporation and Cook Inlet Region, Incorporated, which control a combined area of about 3 million acres.

These corporations were established with portions of the $900 million cash settlement included in ANCSA's reimbursement for native lands taken over by the state and federal governments. Like their smaller village counterparts, the regional corporations are charged with establishing their own businesses and sustaining themselves on profits earned. Lands managed by these corporations will remain tax-free until 1991, and before that time no corporate shares can be sold. Native organizations throughout Alaska are already working to assure that villages and regions will maintain ownership and control of their lands after 1991. A key to this is finding ways to defer taxation on the large acreage until a later date, to avoid involuntary forfeiture or sale to pay taxes.

Each Athabaskan villager holds shares in both the village and regional corporation and earns an annual stock dividend if there has been a profit. To date, these dividends have been small, so individuals have made little money directly from the land claims settlement. Perhaps the greatest importance of regional corporations like Doyon has been social and political, although they also contribute in many ways to the local and statewide economy. The corporation has become a major symbol of native identity and a unifying point for people from different cultural groups within the region.

Business and politics are closely linked in the American governmental system so it is no surprise that regional corporations have become an important arena for expression of native political power and leadership. This, plus the rapid emergence of other native organizations within the past two decades, has brought Athabaskans and other native people into mid-current on the Alaskan political scene. The opportunity has never been better for a young villager to rise quickly to statewide prominence.

For most Athabaskans, however, the connection between village and city relates to something more personal and basic — jobs. Although more jobs are becoming available in rural communities, many villagers leave each year for temporary or long-term work in places like Fairbanks and Anchorage. Their employment runs the full gamut from common laborer to carpenter, night watchman to nurse. One important source of jobs has been the Alaska oil pipeline, especially during its construction but also since completion.

As native people become increasingly educated, new opportunities are opening for them in many fields. One of these is teaching in village schools, where knowledge of the local culture and way of life is an invaluable asset. Other jobs favoring a village background are found in agencies like the National Park Service or Alaska Department of Fish and Game, in businesses such as Yukon River barge lines or in home industries like native arts, clothing and handicrafts.

But for all the new directions and opportunities the city offers, even urban Athabaskans hold strongly to their village ties. However important corporations, native organizations and jobs may have become, people still have a basic need for contact with the familiarity of tradition and the nurturing of an extended family. Some choose the city life and stay with it, others eventually go back; but whatever they do, the village is always home.

*This Time of Trial and Promise.* As elsewhere in the world, the white man's coming has been a mixed blessing for the Athabaskan people. Usually the elders, who lived in nomadic times and remember the pinch of starvation, have the most generous attitude toward changes brought by the outsiders. They speak often of having lived like the animals, without a permanent home or a dependable source of food. Asked if people might have been better off without the white man's coming, a Koyukon elder said only, "Did you ever have to survive by eating ptarmigan droppings?"

Belle Herbert of Chalkyitsik, perhaps the oldest person in Alaska when she died, spoke of the work and hardship she had experienced during her youth:

Ah! grandchild, times were very hard and people
worked hard.
Grandchild, we survived on the food they
hunted and shot.
If we stayed in one place, there wouldn't
be any food.

That's all;
and women
did things by themselves
and men by themselves. . . .
I feel like crying, that's how much the women worked. . . .

Later generations, relieved of this dominating concern with travail and survival, have become more and more aware of the problems brought by whites. Until recent times, the white newcomers looked down on native cultures. They showed little respect for the indigenous traditions and knowledge that had carried Athabaskans through thousands of years in the North Country. Schools and missions labored in near-complete disregard for the achievements of Athabaskan tradition, on the notion that Euro-American culture was inherently superior. It is worth noting that while these ideas are now being left behind, they certainly have not vanished.

As the number of whites gradually increased, they began using Athabaskan lands to harvest fur and game animals, mine various minerals and establish their own communities. Certainly there were compensations, as the emerging trade brought more and more western goods and food supplies; but the white man's coming was also an intrusion in the strictest sense of the word:

Back in the teens the Kennicott people came up and took the mines away from them Indians and they made quite a hole in Kennicott and took several million dollars out of there. And the Copper River people didn't even get one copper cent out of the whole millions of dollars that came out of there. Then not too long ago we have a black gold that came in, came past through our land. . . . The oil is running through our property, and now oil companies say, "You don't own the land. You don't own anything. We own the pipeline."

—Walter Charley,
Glennallen

With the further growth of Alaska's non-native population in recent years, competition for subsistence resources has also intensified. One of the most important political issues affecting rural Alaska today is the allocation of fish and game, and there is a special concern about hunting near villages by residents of other areas. Citing their long ancestral use of surrounding lands and their economic ties to the local resources, Athabaskans have worked to protect these resources for use by local people.

Related to these problems are issues of land management and ownership. The native claims settlement act divided Alaska into a patchwork of federal, state and private lands, so villagers often cross from one management area to another during their subsistence activities. Devising ways to regulate subsistence and other land uses in rural Alaska is a major problem facing Athabaskan people today. Villagers are also concerned about developments — ranging from mines to tourist facilities — that might take place on nearby lands over which they have no control. In former times, people could take the land's changelessness for granted; but now the number and complexity of land-related issues seems to increase with each passing day.

Village people face other problems that are growing within the communities

*Athabaskan villagers work to achieve a healthy balance between traditional ways of living and adoption of new elements from western culture. Margarite Tritt uses modern tools — snow machine and chain saw — to satisfy the need for wood to heat her log home in Arctic Village on the southern slope of the Brooks Range. (Courtesy of Richard Nelson)*

themselves. In this era of rapid change, deep conflicts have emerged between old and new ways of living. Traditional customs and values have come into question, as the teachings of elders are weighed against the influences of community schools, television and other outside contacts. Parents and children struggle not only with the ordinary differences between generations, but with a widening disparity in their cultural learning, in their language, and in their ways of seeing the world around them. Throughout village Alaska, the generation gap extends to depths far beyond most outsiders' experience or understanding.

Athabaskan villagers struggle to deal with social problems that are intensified by these cultural conflicts. Native organizations and health care agencies have responded by developing special programs in mental health, alcohol abuse and services for families and children. While none of these problem areas is unique to native Alaskans, programs specifically designed for rural communities can be far more effective than ones intended for other social and cultural contexts.

During the past decade, interest in traditional culture and lifeways has grown tremendously among younger Athabaskans. This native awareness has helped them to deal with the growing problems of change. At the same time, other Alaskans have recognized more clearly the value and significance of native cultures, and in many ways the distance between Natives and whites has narrowed. For the Natives, emerging pride in traditional ways of living has led toward more assertiveness, dedication to self-determination and growth of an idea that native people should maintain their own identity while adapting to change. As a young Ingalik woman said:

> Being an Alaskan Native today is living in two cultures without much trouble. We should not think in terms of what we are, by race, but who we are. . . . Personally, I think that the Natives are the most flexible people in Alaska. They are adapted to two different cultures. . . .

Native elders stress the importance of maintaining tradition as the basis for this adaptation. Athabaskans survived for countless generations by following the old ways, and they see an uncertain future if those ways are completely abandoned. Shem Pete, a Tanaina elder, tells of a prophecy made long ago by a Susitna shaman. This man — who correctly predicted the great epidemics that followed the white man's coming — warned his people to prepare themselves for a return to traditional ways:

> "There gonna be white man gonna be just like this sand," he pick it up in his hand, the sand. "You fellows gonna be not living one place. Few here, few there, all over just scattered along like little berries between them white people. . . . So I think, what the white man gonna eat out of? They can't live on the berries. They don't know how to hunt. It's gonna be tough for the white man. Listen to me. And all the white men they gonna see something happen. *Grgrgrgrgr* airplane gonna be just like mosquitoes. So they all gonna get into the airplane. Then they gonna pick it up and take them all back to the States.
>
> "And listen, put up lots of fish. And put the matches away. Put the ammunition away. Put up a file and an axe. Pretty soon no more white man in this Alaska. . . . Go up to Rainy Pass country," he told them. ". . . soon as the white man gone, you just take off and take a little fish. When you get there, lots of caribou, lots of game, lots of sheep. And you people so far you can go. And after I go away, you people gonna live quite a long time. . . . "
>
> —Shem Pete, Tanaina

*The New Leaders.* The Athabaskans make a clear distinction between being smart and being wise. Young people may be clever, quick thinking and well-educated — important qualities in this complex world — but they lack the experience and sagacity of their elders; they have not become wise. Wisdom builds slowly through a lifetime of watching carefully, reaping the rewards of good decisions and picking up the pieces after the inevitable mistakes.

With this in mind, Athabaskan people recognize the need for two kinds of modern leaders: the educated and the wise. Educated younger leaders are growing rapidly in numbers, moving through schools and universities, entering positions in business and politics. They are recognized by the public at large, and perhaps sometimes they have power beyond their capacity to manage it. As the late Chief Henry said:

> Now really at that time
> I was at the stage where I thought I could just
> get anything

even though maybe I couldn't.
I was grown up by then
and I was really
confident
but perhaps without reason.

On the other hand, many young Athabaskan leaders have accumulated experience beyond their years by having position thrust on them so early. They have also learned from their predecessors, Natives who overcame the resistance and hardships of previous times to reach positions of importance in the wider world of politics and social affairs. Athabaskan leadership actually began to emerge as far back as the first Tanana Chiefs Conference in 1915, when men like Chief Thomas of Nenana spoke:

All us Alaska Natives, and other Indians will agree with us, that we don't want to be put in reservations. You people of the government . . . don't go around enough to learn the way the Indians are living, so we want to talk to you, explain our living to you. . . .

Some early leaders distinguished themselves at a local or regional level. One of these was John Fredson, the remarkable Kutchin man who was also mentioned in the previous chapter. Fredson was born in 1896 at the headwaters of the Sheenjek River and spent his early boyhood in nomadic camps. While attending a mission school he assisted Archdeacon Hudson Stuck in the first successful climb of Mount McKinley. He was eventually sent to schools outside, and in 1930 he became the first Athabaskan Indian from Alaska to graduate from a four-year college. During his time away, he also worked with the noted linguist Edward Sapir in studies of Kutchin language and culture. A few segments of the narratives he recorded with Sapir are quoted in this chapter.

John Fredson went home to his own people, became a school teacher and was key leader in regional affairs until his death in 1945. Perhaps more important was his leadership by example, successfully integrating his own traditional experience with what he acquired through formal western education. In a 1938 school report, he wrote: "Everything points to harder times ahead. With education there is a chance; little hope without it."

In the generation after John Fredson, more Athabaskans attended village schools and went on to reach prominence. Among these was Emil Notti, from the Koyukon village of Ruby, who became president of the Cook Inlet Native Association, was later the first president of the Alaska Federation of Natives and then was appointed Commissioner of the state's Department of Community and Regional Affairs. Another leader from this generation is Morris Thompson, from the village of Tanana, who served as commissioner of the U.S. Bureau of Indian Affairs during the Nixon administration. Thompson later became an executive with the Doyon corporation.

Other Athabaskans who have achieved political stature include John Sackett, originally from the Koyukon village of Huslia. A University of Alaska graduate, Sackett became the youngest elected member of the state legislature and has served with distinction since 1967. With 16 years on the legislature's finance committee, including six as its chairman, he ranks as one of Alaska's most influential political figures. Sackett has also held various leadership positions with the Doyon corporation since its beginning and has managed several other businesses. Like many native leaders, John Sackett maintains close contact with his village roots, including summers in fish camp along the Yukon River. He combines adeptness in the world of business and politics with fluent knowledge of traditional Athabaskan lifeways.

The pool of Athabaskan leaders has grown large during the past two decades, as new opportunities have opened for those seeking ways to express their talents. More and more today Athabaskans fill management positions in their own corporations and organizations. Notable among them are Doyon's acting president and board chairman Sam Demientieff, and president of the Tanana Chiefs Council, Spud Williams. Native Alaskans serve at all levels in these and other organizations — not just at the top.

But equally significant are the Athabaskan leaders who choose to live in their own villages. These people have the best chance to follow a traditional lifestyle while working with modern challenges, and by doing so they set important examples for village children to follow. Many of these men and women also serve on the boards and committees of regional or statewide organizations, so their efforts also benefit people beyond the home village.

*Elders: The Timeless Wisdom.* Working at all levels alongside younger leaders are the elders. Their power and influence is exerted in a much different way, not through bureaucratic structures or political organizations, but through their words and council. Some are widely known, like Andrew Isaac, traditional chief in the Upper Tanana region. Chief Isaac was born in 1898 at the village

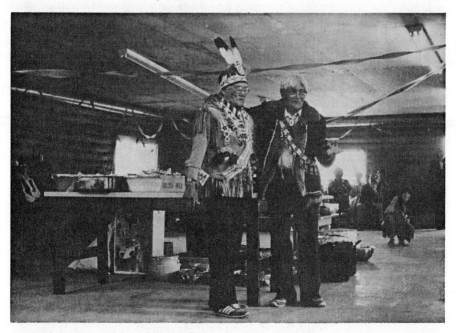

*Athabaskan elders are highly respected for their wisdom, experience and knowledge of tradition. Shown here is Andrew Isaac (left), traditional chief of the Doyon Region, with Walter Northway, traditional chief of Northway village. Chief Isaac is speaking to villagers gathered for a feast in honor of Chief Northway's birthday. (Courtesy of Richard Nelson)*

of Kechumstuk and later settled at Dot Lake. Through the years he traveled widely in Alaska and the Lower 48, working especially with native land claims, formation of the Doyon corporation and establishment of the Tanana Chiefs Council. He also addressed countless meetings of Alaska native organizations and has became a symbol for the importance of incorporating heritage into modern life.

Through the years, Athabaskan elders have spoken at every major political gathering and social occasion, sharing their wisdom and reminding everyone that traditional knowledge is a great treasure. But only a few have had their recollections and thoughts recorded in detail, despite the fact that their numbers diminish every year. In a culture where memory is the storehouse for human experience, each elder's passing is an immeasurable loss. Although it is too late for many who have passed away in recent years, there is a growing effort to record the words of living Athabaskan elders.

Some people are fortunate enough to have the gift of knowledge along with the energy and inspiration to record it themselves. Katherine Peter (Kutchin), Poldine Carlo (Koyukon), Peter Kalifornsky (Tanaina) and Ruth Ridley (Han) have all written important works in recent years. The writings of Eliza Jones, a linguist and native Koyukon speaker, set a high standard for excellence and insight. She has worked extensively to record traditional knowledge of elders like Chief Henry and Catherine Attla. And she is reshaping Father Jette's voluminous handwritten Koyukon dictionary for eventual publication by the Alaska Native Language Center.

During the past few decades, many knowledgeable villagers have instructed anthropologists and others engaged in making permanent records of Athabaskan traditions. The long list of these individuals goes back to Billy Williams, who in the 1930s worked with anthropologist Cornelius Osgood, resulting in a series of remarkable Ingalik ethnographies. In recent years, people like Catherine and Steven Attla of Huslia have given their extensive knowledge with tireless devotion, in the hope that it will be preserved for coming generations. Of all Alaska's resources, probably none is so valuable yet vanishing so rapidly as the native tradition bearers.

*An Elder Speaks.* Edwin Simon was a leader among his Koyukon people for many decades, and he dictated a brief biography shortly before his death in 1979. He was a truly outstanding man, born at Rampart on the Yukon River in 1898, gifted with a lively mind and a way with words. Edwin had great knowledge of Koyukon tradition and he loved to teach. He was also intensely political, a skeptic about the white man and an uncompromising advocate of native rights. The following selections from his published biography reveal more about his character and demonstrate that a formal education is not the only path to understanding.

> You look at how old I am and I can tell you I lived three different lives. Like my life now is with electricity, sno-go, airplanes, refrigerators, freezer, radio, even running water. . . .
>
> Second life, before all that stuff, say 1930 to 1960, we have inboard motor and gas boat. That really changed life around here. Start to have gasoline, oil lamp.

My first life is the way my folks used to live. We lived different kind of life altogether. You see, we had no kind of power. Only candle for light. We use birchbark canoe for all that travel. Make poling boat and let dogs tow the boat for us in summer while we pole or paddle upriver. Take our time.

\* \* \*

There was a lot of people in 1902. I remember part of it. People died that summer. I was four years old. Sternwheeler steamboat came up with the measles. Sternwheeler carrying all those white people. Prospectors, gold mining people. Went all around Yukon and way up to Bettles. All the way up and all the way down people died.

They had a name for it. *K'inaalnonh di saanh,* they say. That's the name of "People Die That Summer." That's the only name I hear.

\* \* \*

I go to school till was I thirteen years old, 1911. Then my father say, "You're thirteen, you're big boy now. You have to go out and trap with us. You got to learn how to hunt, trap, learn how to make what kind of boat we use, snowshoes and sleigh." He says, "That's for your life. . . . You're old enough to learn now."

\* \* \*

My mother used to say, "You have to kill something and make good living like other people. If you don't and got bad name, we women cry for you. . . . " My mother used to say that to us five boys. Andrew; Johnny, me, Frank, and Lee. *Yuhts'a kk'a ahoonoditol.* That means, if you do some bad things to people. Hurt people. It's going to look back at you the last end. You'll get the worst part of it. That's just like going to school when my mother used to talk. . . .

\* \* \*

I never say I used to go head of John River. All over. I kill brown bears and things like that. I did every summer, but I never tell. I never talk about it. . . . That's our way. That's Indian way. . . . Just like me when I trap, I never tell people how much fur I catch. If somebody ask I say, "Oh, I got few skins."

\* \* \*

Potlatches are the same now as when I was young. . . . We have to do the same thing. Just like long time ago. Like when you tie the knot. You got to tie it the same way every time. . . . But if you put a little change in there it'll be nothing left pretty soon. So you have to do it just the way it start long ago. Just like you tie knot same way. That's what our people do.

\* \* \*

You see that picture of Tanana Chief long ago, 1915? I was there. I was seventeen years old at that meeting. All the chief from far as Nenana, far as Steven's Village, far as Nulato all got together in Tanana. . . .

. . . that fall they get a letter back and have another meeting in Tanana. No reservation for Indians! And we could get homesteads on our places. That was good news. If we had reservation we couldn't do what we wanted to do. We would be corralled in.

\* \* \*

After we moved down here to Huslia from Cutoff, BIA [Bureau of Indian Affairs] people used to come around. They wanted people to stake their ground. Put a piece of iron in the ground, survey it. . . . Say we own the ground and make us pay so much. This was way before land claims. I got up at the meeting. "Who I'm going to pay?" I told these people . . . I got house already here. This is our old place in here, from way back history. My father and mother lived around here. Who am I going to pay?

\* \* \*

Now when we come to [be a] state we're equal. We got same price as white people if we work. Same price. Long ago about 1920 when we work white man get five dollars a day, we get two-and-a-half. . . . I work for two-and-a-half a day for I don't know how many years. Now, right now after the State we get equal rights. Now if anyone work alongside white man he get the same price.

\* \* \*

All of my life I speak out. . . . I don't say, "Okay. Okay. You're right." I don't say that. If they say something I don't like, I talk back to them. I always think I'm here where my father used to be, where Athabaskan people used to be thousands of years. Nobody can't take that thing out of my mind that I think Alaska is mine. . . .

My father knew that when I was young man. *"Snaaa,"* he say, "don't talk to white man like that. White people is great people. We never talk back to white people."

"Well," I say, "why?" I'm Indian and I'm proud of it. *"Tl'eeyagga hut'aan aslaanh.* Every nationality is supposed to talk for themselves. Otherwise somebody will just run over us."

\* \* \*

# The Living Tradition

The Athabaskan villages of interior Alaska are experiencing an unparalleled time of change. Even young children have seen major developments within their lifetimes, brought by the increasing momentum of western culture as it spreads into the northern reaches of our continent. Older people who grew up in remote trapline cabins, when the best communication was mail carried by dog sled and steamboat, can now watch presidential news conferences on live television in their village homes.

It is easy to conclude that Athabaskan culture has reached its final moment and that village life in interior Alaska will soon be no different from life anywhere else in small-town America. But this would greatly underestimate the depth of tradition and the meaning it holds for people in these small, isolated communities. Deceived by the superficial appearance of things, outsiders have confidently predicted the demise of native cultures in North America for generations, yet they continue to exist. Cultures mingle and transform, but they do not switch suddenly from one to another. People like the Navajo have maintained an evolving tradition of their own despite continuous contact with Western cultures since the Spaniards rode into their lands on horseback 400 years ago. And it is worth remembering that the Navajo are Athabaskans, late offshoots from their kinsmen in the Far North.

We cannot expect the Athabaskan traditions of interior Alaska to vanish, any more than we can expect them to remain unaltered. They will most certainly continue on the long course of adaptation begun not when the first white men trekked into the northern forests, but when the first ancestral Athabaskans came here. These ancient people changed their lifeways and cultures as their environment evolved, as they met with strangers like the coastal Eskimos and as they invented their own new ways of doing things. The process continues today, only the circumstances and intensity are different. Change is an inherent part of human life, at all times and everywhere on earth.

People living in the far-flung villages of Alaska's Interior follow daily routines still vastly different from those typical elsewhere on this continent. Hunters riding snow machines or dog teams thread their way into the forest, reading the game signs and searching for food, following much the same pattern their ancestors did before the Europeans knew Alaska existed. Mothers teach their children the acceptable ways of behaving, of respecting kin, of treating the wild nature around them — and in this way the customs are passed along.

But even more important and pervasive are the ways that Athabaskan and western traditions are mixed. The minutest fragments of village life are filled with these minglings; English spoken with a uniquely Athabaskan accent and vocabulary, winter boots made from canvas and moosehide sewn with dental floss, people gathering at a graveside to burn caribou meat and cigarettes for spirits of the dead, young boys walking out to set traps for mink and weasel after school, girls in sneakers being warned never to look at a black bear, village corporation meetings ending with potlatches, elders in modern log cabins telling their grandchildren how Raven created the world. . . .

What exists in the Athabaskan villages of interior Alaska is an entirely unique 20th century lifeway, still full of vigor and energy, guided by people who are increasingly aware of the choices to be made between tradition and change. The unquestioning enthusiasm with which they greeted new ideas in times past has been replaced by a growing skepticism, or at least a more cautious weighing of alternatives as they become available. There is a growing sense of dedication to Athabaskan ideals and identity, and above all else a commitment to the future of village life.

Athabaskan people cannot be understood apart from their villages, and it is these communities that will carry them into a future they will design for themselves. In the village they can find enough insulation from the outside to set their own course of change and to preserve a lifeway filled with their own traditions. The village is like an island, and the forest is like a surrounding sea that sustains it, gives it life and sets it apart from everywhere else on earth.

As long as the village can remain alive and the forest is not torn away, the Athabaskan tradition will continue. It will change, but it will not vanish.

So now clay — this time [Raven] shaped clay into a
   human form. . . .
He made it into a human shape.
And this one had a mind, it could think.
It could also reproduce
continuously,
over and over. . . .

Now he had made a man.
Meanwhile, all the animals were in pairs.
And they were quickly multiplying.
So now he started making a woman.
He had made a woman now, it's said.
And now there began to be a lot of people,
both women and men.
They started having children,
one after the other.
. . . I guess they would die and then come back to life
   again,
that was how he had made them, but (then he changed
   his mind) . . .
So he fixed it so that they would live only once.

              —Catherine Attla,
              village of Huslia

# *Appendix*

## The Ceaseless Contest

If you are interested in reading further about the geology of interior Alaska, these sources will give you more detail about the concepts, events and locations described in this chapter.

Hopkins, D.M. "Aspects of the Paleogeography of Beringia During the Late Pleistocene." In *The Paleoecology of Beringia,* edited by D. Hopkins, J. Matthews, Jr., C. Schweger and S. Young, pp. 3-28. New York: Academic Press, 1982.

Jones, D.L., Allan Cox, Peter Coney and Myrl Beck. "The Growth of Western North America." *Scientific American,* November 1982: pp. 70-84.

Pewe, T.L. *Quaternary Geology of Alaska.* U.S. Geological Survey, Professional Paper 482, Washington, D.C.: U.S. Government Printing Office, 1975.

Press, Frank and Raymond Sieve. *Earth.* Second Edition, San Francisco: W.H. Freeman and Company, 1983.

Wahrhaftig, Clyde. *Physiographic Divisions of Alaska.* U.S. Geological Survey, Professional Paper 382, Washington, D.C.: U.S. Government Printing Office, 1965.

## Pleistocene Rhymes and Seasonal Reasons

Armstrong, R. *Guide to the Birds of Alaska.* Anchorage: Alaska Northwest Publishing Company, 1980.

Freeland, W.J. and D.H. Janzen. "Strategies in herbivory by mammals: The role of plant secondary compounds." *American Naturalist* 108 (1974): pp. 269-289.

Guthrie, R.D. "Re-creating a Vanished World." *National Geographic* 141(3) (1972): pp. 294-301.

Hodge, R.P. *Amphibians and Reptiles in Alaska, The Yukon and Northwest Territories.* Anchorage: Alaska Northwest Publishing Company, 1976.

Hopkins, D., J. Matthews, C. Schweger and S. Young, eds. *Paleoecology of Beringia.* New York: Academic Press, 1982.

Kurten, B. *The Ice Age.* New York: G.P. Putnam's Sons, 1972.

Kurten, B. and E. Anderson. *Pleistocene Mammals of North America.* New York: Columbia University Press, 1980.

## Animals Mentioned in "Pleistocene Rhymes and Seasonal Reasons"

AMPHIBIANS:
  Wood frog......................................................*Rana sylvatica*

BIRDS:
  Black-capped Chickadee.............................................*Parus atricapillus*
  Northern Goshawk.................................................*Accipiter gentilis*
  Great horned owl...................................................*Bubo virginianus*
  Ptarmigan.......................................................*Lagopus* spp.
  Common Raven....................................................*Corvus corax*
  Common Redpoll.................................................*Acanthis flammea*
  Spruce grouse..............................................*Dendragapus canadensis*
  Swainson's hawk..................................................*Buteo swainsoni*

**FISH:**

Chum salmon.................................................*Oncorhynchus keta*
King salmon..............................................*Oncorhynchus tschawytscha*
Silver salmon.............................................*Oncorhynchus kisutch*

**MAMMALS:**

Badger.......................................................*Taxidea taxus*
Bear
   Brown (grizzly) bear.................................................*Ursus arctos*
   Short-faced bear..................................................*Arctodus simus*
Beaver.......................................................*Castor canadensis*
Brown bat...................................................*Myotis lucifugus*
Camel
   modern Bactrian camel......................................*Camelus bactrianus*
   Pleistocene camel..........................................*Camelops hesternus*
Caribou......................................................*Rangifer tarandus*
Cheetah.....................................................*Acinonyx jubatus*
Elephant
   African elephant.................................................*Loxodonta africana*
   Asian elephant....................................................*Elephas maximus*
Elk..........................................................*Cervus elaphus*
Ferret
   Alaskan Pleistocene ferret.........................................*Mustela* sp.
   black-footed ferret..............................................*Mustela nigripes*
Fox
   Arctic fox.........................................................*Alopex lagopus*
   Red fox............................................................*Vulpes vulpes*
Ground sloth...............................................*Megalonyx* sp.
Horse
   Alaskan Pleistocene horse....................................*Equus* spp.
Lemming
   brown lemming...................................................*Lemmus sibiricus*
   collared lemming........................................*Dicrostonyx torquatus*
Lion.........................................................*Panthera leo*
Lynx.........................................................*Felis canadensis*
Mammoth...................................................*Mammuthus primigenius*
Marten.......................................................*Martes americana*
Mink.........................................................*Mustela vison*
Moose.......................................................*Alces alces*
   stag moose.......................................................*Cervalces* sp.
Musk-ox.....................................................*Ovibos moschatus*
   bonnet-horned musk-ox.......................................*Symbos cavifrons*
Muskrat......................................................*Ondatra zibethicus*
Pika.........................................................*Ochotona collaris*
Porcupine...................................................*Erethizon dorsatum*
Prairie dog..................................................*Cynomys* sps.
Sabertooth cat..............................................*Homotherium serum*
Saiga antelope..............................................*Saiga tatarica*
Sheep
   bighorn sheep.....................................................*Ovis canadensis*
   Dall sheep........................................................*Ovis dalli*
Shrew........................................................*Sorex* spp.
   water shrew.......................................................*Sorex palustris*
Snowshoe hare.............................................*Lepus americanus*
Squirrel
   Arctic ground squirrel.......................................*Spermophilus parryii*
   red squirrel...............................................*Tamiasciurus hudsonicus*
Steppe bison................................................*Bison priscus*
Tiger........................................................*Panthera tigris*
Vole.........................................................*Microtus* spp.
Weasel
   black-tailed weasel...............................................*Mustela erminea*
   snow weasel......................................................*Mustela nivalis*

Wolf..........................................................................*Canis lupus*
Wolverine....................................................................*Gulo gulo*
Yak.......................................................................*Bos grunniens*

## Footprints on the Land

Bandi, H. *Eskimo Prehistory.* College: University of Alaska Press. 1969.

Campbell, J. "The Tuktu Complex of Anaktuvuk Pass." *Anthropological Papers of the University of Alaska,* 9.2: pp. 61-80, 1961.

Clark, D. "Prehistory of the Western Subarctic: Alaska, the Cordillera, and the Mackenzie Valley." In *Handbook of North American Indians,* Vol. 6, *The Subarctic,* edited by June Helm. Washington, D.C.: Smithsonian Institution, 1982.

Clark, G. and S. Yi. "The Upper Paleolithic of Northeast Asia and the Relevance of the Dyuktai Culture to New World Origins." *Current Anthropology,* 26.2 (February 1985).

Helmer, J., S. Van Dyke and F. Kense, eds. "Problems in the Prehistory of the North American Subarctic: The Athapaskan Question." Calgary: Chacmool, the Archaeological Association of the University of Calgary, 1977.

Hopkins, D., J. Matthews, C. Schweger and S. Young, eds. *Paleoecology of Beringia.* New York: Academic Press, 1982.

Mochanov, Y. "Early migrations to America in light of a study of the Dyuktai Paleolithic Culture in Northeast Asia." In *Early Native Americans,* edited by D. Brownman, pp 119-131. The Hague: Mouton, 1980.

VanStone, J. *Athapaskan Adaptations: Hunters and Fishermen of the Subarctic Forests.* Chicago: Aldine Publishing Company, 1974.

## On The Back Slough

*Direct quotes and oral accounts have been referenced. Brackets refer to pages in this text where the original source has been used. Readers requesting more tightly referenced copy are asked to contact the author.*

Adams, Edward. *Journal Kept Ashore In and Near St. Michael's Alaska, 12 October 1850 - 3 July 1851; Collinson's Franklin Search Expedition, 1850-55.* Cambridge: Scott Polar Research Institute, manuscript –1115, journal entry for 24 February, 1851. [Page 156.]

Alaska Department of Fish and Game. "Profile: Sidney Huntington." *Alaska Fish Tales and Game Trails,* May/June, 1979, p. 22. [Page 185.]

Berry, Mary Clay. *The Alaska Pipeline, the Politics of Oil and Native Land Claims.* Bloomington: Indiana University Press, pp. 34-35, 1975. [Page 187.]

Carter, Jimmy. Letter to the members of the House of Representatives, from Jimmy Carter, President of the United States, titled "Alaska Public Lands Legislation" and reported in *Administration of Jimmy Carter,* p. 855, 1980. [Page 192.]

Castner, J.C. (Lieutenant). "A Story of Hardship and Suffering in Alaska." In *Compilation of Narratives of Explorations in Alaska.* Washington, D.C.: U.S. Government Printing Office, pp. 691-693, 1900. [Pages 165]

Cruikshank, Moses. From tape recorded interview May 31, 1983. On file at the Archives, Alaska and Polar Regions Department, Elmer Rasmuson Library, University of Alaska, Fairbanks. [Pages 163, 173.]

Cruikshank, Moses. From tape recorded interview November 3, 1983. On file at the Archives, Alaska and Polar Regions Department, Elmer Rasmuson Library, University of Alaska, Fairbanks. [Page 153]

Dall, William H. *Alaska and Its Resources.* Boston: Lee and Shepard, pp. 48-52 and 274-277, 1870. [Page 156.]

Dayton, Roger. Yukon-Koyukuk School District. *Biography of Roger Dayton.* Vancouver and Blaine, Wash.: Hancock House Publishers, p. 16, 1981. [Pages 149-150, 174.]

*Fairbanks Daily News-Miner.* "Yukon Flats Villagers Form Group on Rampart Dam Problems." February 3, 1964. [Pages 186-187].

Frank, Sara. From tape recorded interviews with Sara Frank, April 28 to May 2, 1980. On file with Michael Holloway and William Schneider. [Page 125.]

Goodrich, Harold. "History and Conditions of Yukon Gold District to 1897." In *Geology of the*

*Yukon Gold District, Alaska, Part III-Economic Geology.* Eighteenth Annual Report of the United States Secretary of the Interior, 1896-97. Washington: U.S. Government Printing Office, pp. 120-121, 1898. [Pages 161-162.]

Greiner, James. From tape recording made March 11, 1977. On file at the Archives, Alaska and Polar Regions Department, Elmer Rasmuson Library, University of Alaska, Fairbanks, tape number H-83-28. [Page 178.]

Herbert, Belle. *Shandaa, In My Lifetime.* Recorded and edited by Bill Pfisterer. Fairbanks: Alaska Native Language Center, University of Alaska, Fairbanks, p. 184, 1982. [Page 178.]

Honea, John. Yukon-Koyukuk School District. *Biography of John Honea.* Vancouver and Blaine, Wash.: Hancock House Publishers, pp. 26-27 and 29-30, 1981. [Pages 160, 163.]

Hrdlicka, Ales. *Alaska Diary 1926-1931.* Lancaster: Jaques Cattell Press, p. 169, 1943. [Page 177.]

Huntington, James and Lawrence Elliott. *On the Edge of Nowhere.* New York: Crown Publishers, p. 17, 1970. [Page 150.]

Kangas, Hana (Yasuda). From tape recorded interview February 16, 1984. On file at the Archives, Alaska and Polar Regions Department, Elmer Rasmuson Library, University of Alaska, Fairbanks. [Pages 180, 181.]

LeFebre, Charlene. Unpublished field notes, "Telida Notes," p. 3. July 7, 1949. [Page 167.]

MacKenzie, Clara. *Wolf Smeller (Zhoh Gwatsan), A Biography of John Fredson, Native Alaskan.* Manuscript prepared for the Alaska Historical Commission, pp. 11 and 79, 1983. [Pages 172, 174.]

McClellan, Catherine. "Indian Stories about the First Whites in Northwestern America." In *Ethnohistory in Southwestern Alaska and the Southern Yukon,* edited by Margaret Lantis. Lexington: The University Press of Kentucky, pp. 110-111, 1970. [Pages 154.]

McKennan, Robert. *The Upper Tanana Indians.* New Haven: Yale University Publications in Anthropology, p. 3, no. 55, 1959. [Pages 181-182.]

Michael, Henry, ed. *Lieutenant Zagoskin's Travels in Russian America, 1842-1844.* Toronto: University of Toronto Press for the Arctic Institute of North America (AINA). AINA Anthropology of the North: Translations from Russian Sources, n. 7, p.137, 1967. [Page 150.]

Murie, Margaret. *Two in the Far North.* Anchorage: Alaska Northwest Publishing Company, 1978.

Murray, Alexander. *Journal of the Yukon,* edited by L.J. Burpee. Ottawa: Government Printing Bureau (Canada), p. 56, 1910. [Pages 152, 156.]

Nerland, Les. From tape recorded interview August 21, 1981, tape number H82-43. On file at the Archives, Alaska and Polar Regions Department, Elmer Rasmuson Library, University of Alaska, Fairbanks. [Page 185.]

Patty, Stanton. "A Conference with the Tanana Chiefs." *The Alaska Journal,* Volume 1, No. 2., p. 7, 1971. [Pages 168-170.]

Pete, Shem. *Diqelas Tukda,* edited by James Kari. Fairbanks: Alaska Native Language Center, University of Alaska, pp. 25-26, 1977. [Pages 151-152.]

Peterson, Knut. From interview conducted by Terry Haynes, 1981. [Page 182.]

Potter, Jean. *The Flying North.* New York: Bantam Books, pages 33-34, 1983.

Ray, P.H. (letter) from Circle City to Adjutant-General, United States Army in Washington, D.C., October 7, 1897. Reported in *Compilation of Narratives of Explorations in Alaska.* Washington: U.S. Government Printing Office, pp. 533-534, 1900. [Page 163.]

Recollections of Leroy N. McQuesten of life in the Yukon, 1871-1885. Copied from the original in possession of Yukon Order of Pioneers, June 1952, Dawson, Canada. [Page 160.]

Records of the Russian-American Company, 1802-1867. Correspondence of the Governors General, Communications sent. Volume 42, f. 135-136, (no. 46, 5 August, 1860. I.V. Furuhjelm). To the manager of Mikhailovsk Redoubt, Vokhrameev, on Dispatching an Expedition. This translation was done by Katherine Arndt. [Page 157.]

Renner, Louis (S.J.). "Farming at the Holy Cross Mission on the Yukon." *The Alaska Journal,* Volume 9, No. 1, p. 33, 1979. [Page 173.]

Renner, Louis (S.J.). "The Memory of a Brave Man: The Grave of Lieut. John J. Barnard at Nulato." *The Alaska Journal,* Volume 15, No. 1, p. 16, 1985. [Page 156.]

Salmon, David. Reported in *Tundra Times.* "Meeting Held at Fort Yukon Hits at Rampart Dam Project." October 1963. Clippings file of the Alaska Conservation Society Collection at the Archives, Alaska and Polar Regions Department, Elmer Rasmuson Library, University of Alaska, Fairbanks. [Page 186.]

Schneider, William. *Beaver, Alaska: The Story of a Multi-Ethnic Community.* Ph.D. dissertation, Bryn Mawr College, pp. 325-326, 1976. [Page 155.]

Simon, Edwin. Yukon-Koyukuk School District. *Biography of Edwin Simon,* pp. 39 and 43. Vancouver and Blaine, Wash.: Hancock House Publishers, 1981. [Pages 159, 179.]

Stuart, Alice. Letter to Governor Ernest Gruening, April 24, 1942. Reprinted by Ronald Inouye in "The World War II Evacuation of Japanese-Americans from the Territory of Alaska," a compilation submitted to the National Endowment for the Humanities. Summer, 1973, pp. 106-107. [Pages 180-181.]

Stuck, Hudson. *Ten Thousand Miles with a Dog Sled.* New York: Charles Scribner's Sons, p. 356, 1914. [Page 174.]

Stuck, Hudson. *The Alaskan Missions of the Episcopal Church.* New York: Domestic and Foreign Missionary Society, p. 61, 1920. [Page 172.]

Stuck, Hudson. *Voyages on the Yukon and Its Tributaries.* New York: Charles Scribner's Sons, p. 238, 1917. [Page 171.]

Tikhmenev, Petr Aleksandrovich. *A History of the Russian-American Company.* Translated and edited by Richard A. Pierce and Alton S. Donnelly. Seattle: University of Washington Press, p. 351, 1978. [Page 156.]

Tobuk, Frank. Yukon-Koyukuk School District. *Biography of Frank Tobuk.* Vancouver and Blaine, Wash.: Hancock House Publishers, p. 39, 1980. [Page 159.]

Ulen, Tishu. Story told to Shirley English, who published it in *Up the Koyukuk,* Volume 10, No. 4 of *The Alaska Geographic.* Anchorage: Alaska Northwest Publishing Company, page 92, 1983. [Page 167.]

Wien, Ada. From tape recorded interview August 6, 1981, tape number H-82-41. On file at the Archives, Alaska and Polar Regions Department, Elmer Rasmuson Library, University of Alaska, Fairbanks. [Page 185.]

# Raven's People

The following books were used as sources of information in writing this chapter. Each is an excellent reference for learning about certain aspects of Athabaskan life and culture, and readers who wish to learn more should find this list a useful guide.

Arnold, Robert D. *Alaska Native Land Claims.* Anchorage: Alaska Native Foundation, 1976.

Attla, Catherine. *As My Grandfather Told It.* Edited by Eliza Jones. Fairbanks: Yukon-Koyukuk School District and Alaska Native Language Center, 1983.

Beatus, Henry, Sr. Yukon-Koyukuk School District. *Henry Beatus, Sr.: A Biography.* Vancouver and Blaine, Wash.: Hancock House, 1980.

Beetus, Joe. Yukon-Koyukuk School District. *Joe Beetus: A Biography.* Vancouver and Blaine, Wash.: Hancock House, 1980.

Carlo, Poldine. *Nulato: An Indian Life on the Yukon.* Fairbanks: Poldine Carlo, 211 Southern Street, 1978.

Chapman, John W. *Ten'a Texts and Tales: From Anvik, Alaska.* New York: American Ethnological Society, 1914.

Chapman, John W. and James Kari. *Athabaskan Stories from Anvik.* Fairbanks: Alaska Native Language Center, 1981.

Dayton, Roger. Yukon-Koyukuk School District. *Roger Dayton: A Biography.* Vancouver and Blaine, Wash.: Hancock House, 1981.

Deaphon, Miska. *Nikolai: Hwch'ihwzoya.* Edited by Betty Petruska. Anchorage: National Bilingual Materials Development Center, n.d.

Fredson, John, et al. *Stories Told By John Fredson to Edward Sapir.* Fairbanks: Alaska Native Language Center, 1982.

Guedon, Marie-Francoise. *People of Tetlin: Why Are You Singing?* Ottawa: National Museum of Man, 1974.

Helm, June. *Handbook of North American Indians: Subarctic.* Washington, D.C.: Smithsonian Institution, 1981.

Henry, Chief. *The Stories Chief Henry Told.* Edited by Eliza Jones. Fairbanks: Alaska Native Language Center, 1979.

Henzie, Moses. Yukon-Koyukuk School District. *Moses Henzie: A Biography.* Vancouver: Hancock House, 1979.

Herbert, Belle. *Shandaa: In My Lifetime.* Edited by Bill Pfisterer. Fairbanks: Alaska Native Language Center, 1982.

Honea, John. Yukon-Koyukuk School District. *John Honea: A Biography.* Vancouver and Blaine, Wash.: Hancock House, 1981.

Kari, James, ed. *Q'udi Heyi Nilch'diluyi Sukdu'a: This Year's Collected Stories.* Anchorage: National Bilingual Materials Development Center, n.d.

Kari, James and Prisilla Kari. *Dena'ina Elnena: Tanaina Country.* Fairbanks: Alaska Native Language Center, 1982.

Krauss, Michael E. *Native Peoples and Languages of Alaska* (map). Fairbanks: Alaska Native Language Center, 1974. *Alaska Native Languages: Past and Present*. Fairbanks: Alaska Native Language Center, 1980.

Nelson, Richard K. *Hunters of the Northern Forest: Designs for Survival Among the Alaskan Kutchin*. Chicago: University of Chicago Press, 1973. *Make Prayers to the Raven: A Koyukon View of the Northern Forest*. Chicago: University of Chicago Press, 1983.

Paul, Gaither. *Stories for My Grandchildren*. Edited by Ronald Scollon. Fairbanks: Alaska Native Language Center, 1980.

Peter, Katherine. *Neets'aii Gwiindaii: Living in the Chandalar Country*. Fairbanks: Alaska Native Language Center, 1981.

Ridley, Ruth. *Stories in Eagle Han Huch'in*. Fairbanks: Alaska Native Language Center, 1983.

Shalkop, Antoinette, ed. *Exploration in Alaska: Captain Cook Commemorative Lecture Series*. Anchorage: Cook Inlet Historical Society, 1980.

Simeone, William E. *A History of Alaska Athapaskans*. Alaska Historical Commission, n.d.

Simon, Edwin. Yukon-Koyukuk School District. *Edwin Simon: A Biography*. Vancouver and Blaine, Wash.: Hancock House, 1981.

Solomon, Madeline. Yukon-Koyukuk School District. *Madeline Solomon: A Biography*. Vancouver and Blaine, Wash.: Hancock House, 1981.

*Theata '81*. Fairbanks: Cross Cultural Communications Department, University of Alaska, 1981.

VanStone, James W. *Athapaskan Adaptations*. Chicago: Aldine Publishing Company, 1974.

Wiggins, Linda E., ed. *Dena—The People*. Fairbanks: *Theata* Magazine, University of Alaska, 1978.